Introduction to Brazilian Law

Introduction to International Law

Introduction to Belgian Law (2001)
Introduction to Brazilian Law (2011)
Introduction to French Law (2008)
Introduction to German Law (second edition 2005)
Introduction to Greek Law (third edition 2008)
Introduction to Hungarian Law (1998)
Introduction to the Law of Israel (1995)
Introduction to Italian Law (2002)
Introduction to Polish Law (2005)
Introduction to the Law of South Africa (2004)
Introduction to Swiss Law (third edition 2004)
Introduction to Turkish Law (sixth edition 2011)
Introduction to the Law of the United States (second edition 2002)

Introduction to Brazilian Law

Edited by

Fabiano Deffenti

Welber Barral

Wolters Kluwer
Law & Business

Published by:
Kluwer Law International
PO Box 316
2400 AH Alphen aan den Rijn
The Netherlands
Website: www.kluwerlaw.com

Sold and distributed in North, Central and South America by:
Aspen Publishers, Inc.
7201 McKinney Circle
Frederick, MD 21704
United States of America
Email: customer.service@aspenpublishers.com

Sold and distributed in all other countries by:
Turpin Distribution Services Ltd.
Stratton Business Park
Pegasus Drive, Biggleswade
Bedfordshire SG18 8TQ
United Kingdom
Email: kluwerlaw@turpin-distribution.com

Printed on acid-free paper.

ISBN 978-90-411-2506-4

Printed in Great Britain.

To Juliana, my wife, love, life companion.

Welber Barral

To my wife, Cass, for the selfless assistance and endless support, for which I will be forever thankful.

Fabiano Deffenti

List of Authors

Welber Barral	Lawyer in Brazil. Former Secretary of International Trade (Brazil). LLD (USP) LLM (UFSC) LLB (UNIMONTES). Visiting Scholar (Georgetown)
Luís Roberto Barroso	Professor of Constitutional Law, Rio de Janeiro State University (UERJ). Visiting Professor, University of Brasilia (UnB) and University of Poitiers, France. SJD (UERJ). LLM (Yale Law School).
Manoel Eduardo Alves Camargo e Gomes	Professor of Public Law at the Federal University of Paraná. LLD, LLM, LLB (UFSC).
Luciano Benetti Timm	Professor of Contract Law at the Pontifical Catholic University of Rio Grande do Sul. Visiting Scholar (UC-Berkeley), LLD, LLM (UFRGS) LLM (Warwick) LLB (PUC/RS)
Celso Campilongo	Professor of Jurisprudence (University of São Paulo and Pontifical Catholic University of São Paulo). Post Doctorate (PUC/SP and Salento) LLD LLM (USP) LLB (USP)
Cristiano Carvalho	Professor of Law at the Brazilian Institute of Tax Studies. President of the Tax Academy of the Americas. Visiting Scholar (UC–Berkeley), LLD LLM (PUC/SP) LLB (UNISINOS)
Fabiano Deffenti	BBus (International), LLB (Hons) (QUT). Attorney-at-Law (New York), Legal Practitioner (Queensland and Australian Capital Territory), Barrister and Solicitor (New Zealand), Lawyer (Brazil).

Antônio Sérgio Altieri de Moraes Pitombo	LLD, LLM, LLB (USP).
Eurico Marcos Diniz de Santi	Professor of Law at FGV School of Law. Coordinator of the Center of Tax Studies (NEF - FGV). LLD LLM (PUC/SP) LLB (FDSBC)
Cláudio Filkenstein	Professor of International Law, Pontifical Catholic University of São Paulo. LLD (PUC/SP), LLM (Miami), LLB (USP).
Lucas Lixinski	PhD Candidate, European University Institute, Italy; LLM Central European University, Hungary; LLB (UFRGS)
Rafael Bicca Machado	MSc (PUC/RS). LLB (PUC/RS).
Estêvão Mallet	Professor of Labour Law at the University of São Paulo School of Law. Post-Doctorate, LLD, LLM, LLB (USP). Advisor to the Brazilian Bar Association, São Paulo Chapter.
Claudia Lima Marques	Professor of International Law Federal University of Rio Grande do Sul, Brazil; LLD (Heidelberg) LLM (Tübingen), LLB (UFRGS)
José Isaac Pilati	Associate Professor of Law (UFSC), LLD, LLM (UFSC) LLB (UFPR).

Summary of Contents

Table of Contents

List of Abbreviations

ADC	Declaratory Action of Constitutionality (*Ação Direta de Constitucionalidade*)
ADI	Direct Action of Unconstitutionality (*Ação Direta de Inconstitucionalidade*)
ADI-O	Direct Action of Unconstitutionality by Omission (*Ação Direta de Inconstitucionalidade por Omissão*)
ADPF	Claim of Non-compliance with a Fundamental Precept (*Arguição de Descumprimento de Preceito Fundamental*)
BDR's	Brazilian Depositary Receipts
BM&F	Mercantile and Futures Exchange (*Bolsa de Mercadorias e Futuros*)
BOVESPA	São Paulo Stock Exchange (*Bolsa de Valores de São Paulo*)
CDC	Consumer Defence Code
CLT	Consolidated Labour Laws (*Consolidação das Leis do Trabalho*)
COFINS	Contribution for Social Security Financing (*Contribuição para o Financiamento da Seguridade Social*)
CPC	Code of Civil procedure (*Código de Processo Civil*)
CPI	Congressional Investigating Committee (*Comissão Parlamentar de Inquérito*)
CSLL	Social Contribution over Net Profits (*Contribuição Social sobre o Lucro Líquido*)
CTPS	Employee's Work and Social Security Card (*Carteira de Trabalho e Previdência Social*)
CTN	Brazilian Tax Code (*Código Tributário Nacional*)
CUT	Workers' Central Union (*Central Única de Trabalhadores*)
FGTS	Unemployment Guarantee Fund (*Fundo de Garantia do Tempo de Serviço*)

ICC	International Chamber of Commerce
ICMS	State Tax on the Sale of Goods and Services (*Imposto sobre a Circulação de Mercadorias e Serviços*)
ILO	International Labour Organization
IOF	Tax on Financial Operations (*Imposto sobre Operações Financeiras*)
IPI	Excise Tax over Industralised Products (*Imposto sobre Produtos Industrializados*)
IPTU	Tax over Buildings and Land (*Imposto Predial e Territorial Urbano*)
IRPJ	Company Income Tax (*Imposto de Renda de Pessoas Jurídicas*)
ISS	Municipal Services Tax (*Imposto sobre Serviços*)
ITBI	Intervivos Real EState Transfer Tax (*Imposto de Transferência de Bens Intervivos*)
ITR	Rural Land Tax (*Imposto Territorial Rural*)
IVA	Value-Added Tax
PIS	Social Integration Program (*Programa de Integração Social*)
PND	National Privatisation Program (*Plano Nacional de Desestatização)*
SESC	Social Service for Commerce
SESI	Social Service Industry
STF	Federal Supreme Court (*Supremo Tribunal Federal)*
STJ	Superior Court of Justice (*Superior Tribunal de Justiça*)
SUS	Integrated System of Health (*Sistema Único de Saúde*)
TEC	Common External Tariff (*Tarifa Externa Comum*)

Preface

Brazil has recently become a major destination for foreign investors. However, when trying to become acquainted with Brazil's legal system foreigners are often perplexed with its complexity and idiosyncrasies.

Perhaps surprisingly, there has been little written about Brazilian law in the English language, with no recent work having ever been compiled to provide the reader with an overview of the main areas of Brazilian law. This book aims to close this gap.

Part of this complexity comes from the fact that Brazilian law draws from a number of sources. While the Portuguese and Roman law tradition is still strongly felt, over the centuries – and, especially, in the last few decades – Brazilian law has borrowed from the German, Italian, Spanish and American rules in a variety of legal fields, yet without a complete legal transplant from any foreign jurisdiction. This is largely due to a sophisticated legal elite, which has assisted courts and legislators in the adaptation of foreign rules to Brazil's realities.

In the late twentieth century, Brazilian law saw major improvements, after the coming into force of the Federal Constitution of 1988. Criticised by many as cumbersome and overly analytical in many parts, no one doubts that it has provided major improvements, especially in relation to individual protections and human rights. The legacy of the military dictatorship has all but vanished from the legal rules although in practice the protection of human rights has some way to go.

Administrative Law also saw a number of positive changes. The passing of the Procurement Law in 1993, the privatisation process, together with the various statutes creating regulatory agencies, and the Fiscal Responsibility Law in 2000, all of which brought about a more solid institutional structure for both local and foreign investors and business people. The Fiscal Responsibility Law, especially, is considered the key piece of legislation that has enabled Brazil to keep up with its international financial obligations and part of the reason for Brazil's recent economic success.

In 2002, the new Brazilian Civil Code was enacted, replacing the 1916 version. The Civil Code Bill sat idly for twenty-seven years in the Congress, until it passed without much scrutiny from Congress. Albeit already an old Code when it was passed, a number of provisions were modernised – especially in the fields of Property Law and Family Law. On the other hand, in a step which is criticised by many, the new Code gave greater State influence over contractual relationships with the introduction of the 'social function of contracts' principle. Courts have used this principle to change contractual terms, severely eroding the almost unanimously accepted *pacta sunt servanda* rule.

In the dispute resolution arena, the last ten years have seen a number of changes to the Code of Civil Procedure aimed to speed up the notoriously slow Brazilian courts. The passing of the Arbitration Law in 1996, essentially implementing the UNCITRAL model with minor modifications, did not immediately have a major impact on Brazilian litigation. This was largely a consequence of the uncertainty relating to whether the Arbitration Law would be considered constitutional. Once the doubts over the validity of the Arbitration Law were put to rest by the Supreme Court's decision in *Appeal 5,206-Spain (MBV v. Resil)*, Brazil has seen a spike in the number of disputes resolved by arbitration. Large investors probably have been the greatest beneficiaries of this, embracing the new law to the extent that Brazil is now one of the key markets for arbitration bodies such as the ICC.

Advances have also been seen in the insolvency field, with the new Business Restructuring and Bankruptcy Law being enacted in 2005. Borrowing heavily from Chapter 11 of Title 11 of the United States Code, the Law shows a change of mindset on the part of legislators. Now it is clear that great efforts must be made to keep companies in trouble in business. Also, the adoption of fiduciary transfers (alienações fiduciárias), in particular, relating to real property (which occurred in 1997) and securitisations, giving further comfort to creditors in business transactions and to financial institutions, thus increasing the availability of credit in the market.

Unfortunately, it is in the key areas of Labour Law and Taxation Law that little has changed. In relation to the former, rules and regulations date back to a time when there was a much clearer employer-employee relationship than today. Created during the Getulio Vargas government in the 1940s, Labour Laws are both complex and very demanding on employers. The detail and complexity of the laws reflects in major bureaucratic costs whose clear beneficiaries are not altogether clear. Taxation Law, on the other hand, became a major source of litigation with the coming into force of the Federal Constitution in 1988. The burdensome procedures for passing tax-related laws and a poor level of procedural compliance on the part of the Congress saw hundreds of thousands of cases litigated before the courts. Tax laws have grown in an unstructured manner, with loopholes being included amidst relevant changes in various statutes not always connected with one another. This myriad of laws and regulations has now made Brazil one of the hardest places in the world to comply with tax norms. Hopefully, the newly elected legislators will make the required changes.

This book aims to provide the reader with sufficient knowledge to navigate through the major areas of Brazilian law. It is hoped that it will allow foreign lawyers and scholars to begin looking into the issues faced by Brazil and consider undertaking closer research and analysis into the laws that govern this very large developing economy that over the years has been much better known for its soccer successes than for its compliance with the rule of law.

Fabiano Deffenti
BBus (International), LLB (Hons) (QUT)
Attorney-at-Law (New York), Legal Practitioner (Queensland and Australian Capital Territory), Barrister and Solicitor (New Zealand), Lawyer (Brazil)

Welber Barral
Lawyer in Brazil. Former Secretary of International Trade (Brazil). LLD (USP) LLM (UFSC) LLB (UNIMONTES). Visiting Scholar (Georgetown)

Chapter 1

History and Sources of Brazilian Law

Celso Campilongo[*]

I. BRAZIL IN COLONIAL TIMES

To introduce Brazilian Law to the foreign reader implies setting out, from the beginning, the important differences between Portuguese America and Spanish America, as well as to point out the other specificities of Brazilian history and geography.

Unlike the European tradition of lengthy processes for the creation of political institutions and the formation of the State, Brazil was, at the time of discovery (i.e., the arrival of the Portuguese in Brazil in the year 1500), a large and scantly inhabited area (it is estimated that there were between 3 and 5 million individuals in Brazil). Unlike other parts of Latin America, Brazil did not have local people with developed cultures and institutions (such as those created by Incas, Aztecs and Mayas, for instance).

Portuguese colonisation was also different from the Spanish and English model. The relationship with the indigenous population, the distribution, occupation and exploration of the land (hereditary captaincies and *sesmarias*, that is, the large landholdings granted by the Portuguese Crown), the ways, speed and difficulties in advancing towards the inner lands, the multi-deity, polygamous and nomadic characteristics of the indigenous people, the collective use of the land and the

* Professor of Jurisprudence (University of São Paulo and Pontifical Catholic University of São Paulo). Post Doctorate (PUC/SP and Salento) LLD LLM (USP) LLB (USP).

Fabiano Deffenti & Welber Barral (eds), *Introduction to Brazilian Law*, pp. 1–14.

non-existence of equivalent concepts or of private property relationships – or even writing (despite the important and old cave paintings) – made the Brazilian circumstances one of a truly new world, primitive and exotic in the eyes of the Portuguese coloniser.

At the time, Portugal had all factors required for maritime expansion. The early establishment of the monarchic State, the inner peace, intense commercial activity, favourable geographic position, a succession of nautical conquests and old navigational technical knowledge, as well as cartography and astronomy, for instance, explain the Portuguese leadership in the process. Portugal created the Imperial colony in 1415 (with the conquest of Ceuta) which lasted until 1999 with the handing over of Macau to China. The Portuguese domains extended through Africa, America, Asia and Oceania.

Colonial life was not easy. The distance from Portugal as well as poverty, isolation, the feeling of abandonment and the shock created by the new world persisted throughout the colonial period. From the beginning, the Portuguese prioritised the exploration of African and Asian colonies and only in the year 1530 the colonisation of Brazil began. At first, the administrative and territorial division was established, aiming to occupy the territory and to control the economic activity. After that, in 1548, in light of the failure of the hereditary captaincies, Portugal created a central body to manage the colony: the general-government (*governo-geral*). The 'Gift Letters' (*Cartas de Doação*) of the hereditary captaincies and the *forais* (Portuguese royal decrees which set land borders and granted administrative powers) are among the first legal documents relevant to the colony. The Gift Letter granted possession of the land to the grantee. Title, however, continued to belong to the King. A *foral* gave wide powers to the grantee, including applying Portuguese Law in the land, imposing taxes and organising the military defence of the area.

There is, thus, from the colonial period, a use of land which is governed by legal norms transplanted to Brazil following the Portuguese tradition and the strong influence of Roman Law. The land gifts known as *sesmarias* date back to 1375 and continue to exist throughout the colonial period up until close to the declaration of Independence of Brazil in 1822. Without a doubt, from the point of view of the origins of the Brazilian legal system, Brazil's tradition is definitely linked to western European continental law: the civil law tradition.

Customs and social, religious, political and legal practices of the local people which inhabited Brazil originally were ignored, disqualified and oppressed by the Portuguese colonisers. Clearly, with the exception of legal practices, these indigenous habits exerted great influence on the making of Brazilian culture. Family, property rights, language, the relationship with nature, food, medicine, agricultural production and various other types of the creation of colonial Brazil were influenced by indigenous practices. Portuguese Law applied during the colonial years was not totally insensitive to the local social situation. However, these were at odds with their social practices prevailing at the time, both from an indigenous and Portuguese point of views – the latter now distant from the motherland and surrounded in an enormous territory, with new people and products, and in an environment which was largely unknown and hostile. All of this contributed to the low effectiveness, difficulty of access and lack of legitimacy of the colonial legal order. It was not the type of environment which foments the establishment of a rule of law culture. The disdain with which customary practices ignored the protests from the *quilombos* (communities of former slaves who had escaped from their masters) and the indigenous segments (*reduções indígenas*, which were communities founded on collective practices).

The Portuguese administrative practices developed slowly, from the time Brazil was discovered until 1815, when Brazil was recognised as a kingdom and, finally, in 1822, when it became a monarchy, separate from Portugal.

Brazilian economic activity went through many cycles. These cycles shaped both Brazilian economic and legal history. Initially, the Portuguese explored the extraction of *pau brasil*, a type of wood which was very useful in Europe. Soon after, the cultivation and exploration of sugar cane became widespread, especially in the north-eastern part of Brazil. It was called the 'sugar cane cycle'. A system of very large rural properties was used. Economic activity was associated with a regime of land grants by the king which also aimed at establishing settlements in the colony. Subsequently, during the eighteenth century, the colony lived the 'gold cycle', in Minas Gerais. After independence, especially in São Paulo, the 'coffee cycle' prevailed (from nineteenth century to the beginning of the twentieth century).

Unlike Spanish America, which after independence of the colonies created various countries, the area controlled by the Portuguese, even though it had administrative divisions (Brazil, on one side, and Grão Pará and Maranhão, on the other), capped its territorial unity even after independence. Despite the significant regional differences – perfectly comprehensible in light of the size of the territory, the different economic activities and climate, and by the various types of settlement, colonisation and migration – Brazil kept its unity and this, today, represents a great advantage in the country as compared to its neighbours. Since colonial times, the bases were set for the construction of an enormous internal market.

Until recently, a great part of the literature on Brazil in colonial times considered that the stratified society, the concentration of rural property in a few hands, the submissive position vis-à-vis the motherland and the dependence on exports and the slavery regime, as social-political model with feudal roots. This model was perceived as having major difficulties for the adaptation and expansion of capitalism, the establishment of an internal market, the construction of a middle class set between the wealthy large landowners and their slaves. The polarisation between the large landholdings and the slave workforce set the standards for colonial exploration. For this reason many believe that the chances for the establishment of a successful representative democracy and of the rule of law in Brazil were remote. Yet, in the last twenty years various studies have been reviewing this previous analysis. They are studies which portray the strength of the small land owners and urban merchants during the colonial years. Clearly, however, it is not a Brazilian reproduction of the utilitarianism which was then commonplace in capitalist Europe. Traits of personal interdependence, trust and mateship made the differentiation between economic system, legal rules, religious practices and family relationships less clear.

But none of this excluded or shunned the beginnings of a slow process of accumulation, financing and investment in the colony itself.

The colonial years received different and contradictory interpretations. This debate is far from being superseded. It involves explanations that identify feudal elements in the creation of the nation. Other authors, on the other hand, tend to support the capitalist expansion and give greater weight to the participation of the colony in the international community and Brazil's role as a mere supplier of raw materials.

Some theories seek to identify and describe a peculiar and local slave-based production method. Finally, in more recent studies, the idea that Portuguese America was poor and explored by the European colonisers is being reviewed. The reasons for Brazil's slow development were more recent and a consequence not of the colonial exploration, but of political and economic decisions made by Brazil's elites.

None of this neglects or dismisses the analysis which identified a patrimonial, bureaucratic and authoritarian tradition that was part of the making of the Brazilian State. The individual power of rural landowners, sprawl around an immense country, combined with the centralising efforts of the Portuguese Crown, allowed for the construction and maintenance of the country as a unit. At the same time, the slave-master mentality and a strong Catholic influence made Portuguese America – and the motherland – insensitive to the cultural advances of European Renaissance.

The legal system in force during colonial times (the period which goes from the arrival of the Portuguese in Brazil up until independence, from 1500 to 1822) is made up by the Royal Ordinances which compiled laws and customs in use in the motherland: Alfonsine Ordinances (*Ordenações Afonsinas*), from 1446 (during the Alfonse V reign); the Philippine Ordinances (*Ordenações Filipinas*), from 1603 (during the reigns of Philip II in Spain and Philip I and Portugal – countries which remained united, under Spanish rule and known as the Iberian Union, from 1580 to 1640). The Alfonsine Ordinances are the most unique of the three compilations and can be considered among the first attempts of compiling norms in a similar manner to the modern codes. The Manueline Ordinances (*Ordenações Manuelinas*), which were an improved version of the Alfonsine Ordinances, are regarded as the first ever printed out code anywhere. The Philippine Ordinances are mere copies of the Manueline Ordinances. The Alfonsine Ordinances drew heavily from Roman Law, which was considered both as a source as well as a complementary set of rules. They include uses, customs, general laws, court rulings, agreements made with the Holy See, in addition to canonical and Visigothic Law. Book V of the Philippine Ordinances, known for the violence of the penalties imposed (generally, natural death), remained in force even after the proclamation of independence, up until the time when the Criminal Code of 1830 became law. Book IV extended its term until 1 January 1917, when the Civil Code drafted by Clovis Bevilacqua came into force.

The colony's court system encompassed a trial court comprised of single judges and special judges, with separate and decentralised territorial jurisdiction.

The Relationship Courts (*Tribunais de Relação*) were the appellate courts of the time. The first, which was established in 1587, never got to hear its first case. It was only established and given proper regulations in 1609, only to be abolished in 1626 (as a consequence of the Dutch invasion) and re-established in 1652. In 1751, a second Relationship Court was created in Rio de Janeiro, with territorial jurisdiction over the south of Brazil. Subsequently, the Relationship Courts of Maranhão (in 1812) and Pernambuco (1821) were set up. Appeals against the decisions of the Relationship Court went to the Supplication House (*Casa da Suplicação*), based in Portugal. Judges and court staff had formal qualifications and had been trained in Portugal. They were expected to be loyal to the Crown and to distance themselves from local life.

Judges were drawn from the middle class. A small number of members of the aristocracy and of the bureaucracy, with law degrees obtained from Coimbra University, saw a career as a judge as a means to gain greater social standing. In accordance with a few studies available, colonial justice was a mixture between, on the one hand, a standard of efficiency, professionalism and technical organisation (all joined by bureaucratic relationships and rational procedures) and, on the other hand, the marked presence of personal relationships based on friendship, blood relations, mutual trust, undue influences and corruption. If we take: (a) the separation between what is public and private; (b) the differentiation of functional systems (law, economics, politics, family and religion, for instance); and (c) the 'disenchanted' application of formal rules as pre-requisites developed and consolidated during modern times, the legal system in Brazil during colonial times shows important signs of resistance and rejection of these elements. Personal gains, exchanges of favours, abuses of power, deviation from the rules and work outside of the court system, as well as many other types of distortion and deviation from the professional standards, were tolerated by the Crown in light of the political loyalty of these employees. From this we may identify the roots of our peripheral modernity and of the reduction of the legal system set by decisively political, economic and social factors, and not necessarily legally technical.

It is worth mentioning that the Inquisition, which was so strong in the Iberian Peninsula, also left its marks in Brazil. There were many Visitations of the Holy Office to Brazil. There were no Inquisition courts in the colony, but in more important cases, the Brazilian accused were taken to the Lisbon Inquisitorial Court.

During the eighteenth century, in addition to a new economic cycle which moved the key economic centre from the sugarcane-driven north-east to the mining exploration in Minas Gerais, a feeling of rebelliousness against the abuse of taxes imposed by the Crown began to appear. This feeling expanded, gradually and slowly, in the second half of the eighteenth century when the liberal ideas led to the *Inconfidência Mineira* Movement which fought for Brazilian independence between 1788 and 1789. The discovery of gold mines in 1693 and diamond mines in 1729 were immediately followed by legal provisions which regarded those assets as Crown property, subjecting the explorers to compulsory Crown exploration licences and the payment of one-fifth of the gains to the Crown.

II. LAW AND ORDER DURING THE MONARCHY

In 1808, running from the threats of invasion from Napoleonic Portugal, the Royal family and the headquarters of the Portuguese empire were moved to Brazil. The government settled in Rio de Janeiro. The judicial bodies, including the House of Supplications and the *Desembargo do Paço* (the Crown's legal advisory body), were also transferred to Brazil. In the same year, a regal letter opened the Brazilian ports to trade with friendly nations. In 1815, a decree letter elevated Brazil to a kingdom: the United Kingdom of Portugal, Brazil and Algarves. King John VI articulated the independence process thinking of his son's future. He returned to Portugal but left his son Peter I well informed that Brazil's independence would not take long and that he himself should abdicate from the throne and create the new monarchy. New bases were established for the preservation of Brazil's political, territorial, linguistic, religious and legislative unity.

Formal independence from Portugal came on 7 September 1822. Soon afterwards, the first Constitutional Letter was issued (in 1824), together with the creation of law schools in São Paulo and Olinda (in 1827), the coming into force of the Criminal Code (in 1830) and the Commercial Code (in 1850), both followed by their respective legal procedure laws. No Civil Code was introduced during the 1822–1889 period. There was fear that the strife for independence would bring about slave revolts or anger the regional elites. Emperor Peter I and the statesman that assisted him were capable of getting around these obstacles and guaranteeing national unity.

The first Brazilian Constitution established a romantic and centralised government. The constitutional assembly was set up in 1823 and dissolved soon after. The Constitutional Letter was decreed by King Peter I and came into force in 1824. A parliamentary monarchy was established with the setting up of a fourth power – the Moderating Power – which gave wide powers to the emperor. Important issues in the beginning of the nineteenth century, such as the Republican regime, federalism, a secular State, the civil freedoms and representative democratic ideals, for instance, were brushed aside by the Monarchic Constitution of 1824. The centralisation of the monarchy was seen as fundamental to the maintenance of the new national identity. Catholicism was declared as the religion of the empire. The clergy lived under the sponsorship of the Crown, almost as a public servant. Finally, the Constitution absolutely neglected the shameful slave-based structure in the country.

The Moderating Power placed the emperor in the position of arbitrator over disputes among the branches of government. The emperor was put above electoral demands and time limitations. Among other powers, the emperor could dissolve the Chamber of Representatives, suspend judges and reduce penalties. The powers of the emperor were sacred and unbreachable. It was a liberal-conservative arrangement, inspired by Benjamin Constant's writings and the French political practices of the beginning of the nineteenth century. The Constitution also incorporated a set of civil liberty rights (a Bill of Rights) and other English concepts, such as trial by jury and writs of habeas corpus. However, these liberal characteristics were always in contrast to the slave-based regime. The abolishment of slavery was gradual and took many decades to be fully implemented. Only in 1888 was the process concluded, on the eve of the Republic being established. The electoral process was not direct: the people elected the voters and these elected deputies and senators.

The main objective of the new law schools established in 1827 in Olinda and São Paulo was to form the new managing elite of the country. The main bureaucratic posts – both during the Empire as well as after, during the Republic years – were from these law faculties. Only in 1900 new courses were created. The dominant legal theory between 1827 and 1870 was a conservative version of jus naturalism. From 1870, philosophers such as Auguste Comte and Herbert Spencer began to have a greater influence on the law schools.

The views over Brazil's liberalism in the nineteenth century is controversial. There are those who consider it anti-democratic, aristocratic, moderate and reformist. Nevertheless, its role in the political-legal Brazilian history is more related to the arrangement needed for the overcoming of the colonial situation, the formation of the National State and the maintenance of the country's unity than, as it happened in Europe, the rupture of an absolutist order. It has greater institutional than revolutionary character. That is why some call it 'lip service liberalism' or 'idea out of place' – that is, a forced adaptation wrongly and improperly applying European ideas. A liberalism strangely attached to the wide powers of owners of large land holdings, agricultural production based on slavery, the elitist and oligarchic character of the political model, the favouring, bias and selective protections based on personal relationships, a dual relationship between the rural elite and their slave masters which supposedly crushed any possibility of the flourishing of other economic sectors. In sum: it was a conservative liberalism that facilitated the cohabitation and conciliation of hegemonic sectors.

The monarchic legal order faced the challenge of restructuring the State. The intention of changing society and the State through laws, even constrained by the problems involved in the independence process, allowed for the expansion of a legalistic and elitist legal culture. The legalistic idealism has a determining role in the construction of the national political order. The number of laws issued during the Empire years – the Constitution, various codes, procedural legislation, real property ownership, organisation of the public administration – and the strategic importance of the law schools are clear examples of the role developed by the legal system in creating an independent Brazil.

During the nineteenth century (especially during its second half), in addition to independence, other important factors contributed to the changes in Brazilian Law. From an economic viewpoint, the expansion of the coffee cycle moved the production axis to the south-eastern region, especially to São Paulo. From a political viewpoint, Brazil received enormous contingents of migrants and made its first steps towards a significant process of urbanisation and industrialisation, which was consolidated late in the twentieth century. This process had two important legal landmarks: the abolishment of slavery in 1888 and the proclamation of the Republic in the following year. Still during the monarchic period, important reforms inspired by liberal ideals expanded the autonomy of judges vis-à-vis the public power and gradually prepared for the transition of slave labour to a free workforce. Yet, these reforms are also associated with the increase of powers to oppress workers and police control over free and poor men and women, as well as the recently freed slaves and migrants. These were also not sufficient to destroy the bureaucratic and wealth-based heritage from Iberian origins.

III. THE BEGINNINGS OF THE REPUBLIC

The Republic was declared on 15 November 1889. The establishment of a Republican way of government, the presidential system and of the federal State had a strong American and Argentine influence. A constitutional assembly was set up and in 1891 the first Republican Constitution was approved. This Constitution had a liberal profile and abolished the Moderating Power. The first years of the Republic included disputes between political groups with different visions about the Republican ideal. Once the Republic was established, from 1898 to 1930, a system that united and conciliated the coffee-producing São Paulo oligarchy with the Minas Gerais elite was established. The system became known as the 'Coffee with Milk Republic' ('*República Café com Leite*') or the 'Old Republic' (*República Velha*). The political arrangement of the Republican Constitution broke out from the monarchic structure, but kept liberal, conservative and contrary-to-a-democratic-structure ideals of the past.

The Republican liberalism, on the same bases as the monarchic liberalism – but, now, adhering to the new demands from the more dynamic sectors of the Brazilian economy – was more a consequence of arbitrary constructions by legislators than the result of concrete constitutional practices. If, at the constitutional and public law sphere, the dual nature between the idealism of jurists and the national reality was always considered as a characteristic of Brazilian Law, a similar debate took place at the private law level. At first, at the forefront was the debate over the overlapping, unification or separation between civil and commercial law. Later, complacency by legislators with the slave-based structure was in the spotlight. At the end, as a consequence of these problems, the continued attempts for the drafting of the Civil Code failed during the Empire and the beginning of the Republic.

The Consolidation of the Civil Laws, drafted by Teixeira de Freitas in 1857, followed by the Draft Civil Code (drafted by the same author in 1860 and with great reputation over the process of civil litigation throughout Latin America), set the stage for the approval of the Brazilian Civil Code in 1916. This Code was greatly influenced by the German Civil Code of 1896 and came into force in 1917. Only then the Portuguese Ordinances relating to civil matters were revoked. Civil litigation, one of the first achievements of a legal nature of the young Republic, was still very much attached to the patriarchal and rural mentality of the nineteenth century. It combined the individual aspirations of merchants and urban intellectual sectors with the consolidated positions of the landholding aristocracy.

The Civil Code of 1916 received its greatest influence from the pandectist civil law tradition. The structure of the Code and its main principles descended from this influence, with the French Civil Code having a lower impact. Property laws were complex and formal, clearly derived from the Roman-Germanic formulation in force in the nineteenth century.

From 1891 Brazil adopted constitutional judicial review. The Federal Supreme Court gained powers to control the Executive and the constitutionality of laws approved by Congress. In many occasions the Court protected the rights of minorities, the opposition and trade union leader, through the use of writs of habeas corpus. Especially from 1988, in addition to the decentralised control over constitutionality, a system of direct judicial review was implemented, similar to those which exist in Italy, Germany, Portugal and Spain. As such, Brazilian constitutional law, in terms of judicial review, combines influences from the United States together with the doctrines and principles from a continental European origin.

IV. THE VARGAS ERA

During the Getúlio Vargas government (from 1930 to 1945), Brazil saw a strong industrialisation and urbanisation process. Brazilian law was significantly changed during this period due to new social conflicts, the strengthening of trade unions, the influences of some thinkers demanding greater State intervention in the economy – from the American New Deal to Italian Fascism, from Weimar's Fundamental Law to the echoes of the Russian Revolution of 1917 – as well as the efforts of adapting national production to the limits imposed by the Second World War to international commerce.

During the Vargas era, Brazil faced a civil war in 1932 which sought the restoration of constitutional order. In 1934, a new constitution was passed that introduced, for the first time, social and economic rights that went beyond the individualistic tradition of the previous constitutions. The Constitution of 1934 set up professional representation in the Chamber of Deputies, as well as the establishment of the Electoral Courts (which were responsible for ensuring a fair electoral process) and of the Employment Courts (responsible for the growing labour conflicts). Soon after, in 1937, a new constitution inspired by fascist principles established a corporatist authoritarianism and a dictatorship with powers centralised in the Republic's President. Brazil would only return to democracy after the Second World War with the passing of the Constitution of 1946.

The Vargas period may be described as a reaction to the liberal and oligarchic ideologies of the preceding periods. During the Vargas years, the most important developments were seen in the criminal, procedural and employment-related laws. In the employment law field, for instance, until 1930 there were very few statutes concerned with the rights of employees as well as trade union rights. The Vargas government sought to fill this space, but also used the labour legislation as a tool for obtaining the backing of those groups that supported him and to discriminate against those trade unions or employees' groups that opposed him. From 1935, when the National Security Law (*Lei de Segurança Nacional*) was passed making various political and social activities as crimes, the abrasive character of the Vargas period was even more evident. The National Security Law was followed by various repressive measures and, finally, by the establishment of the New State (*Estado Novo*). The Constitution of 1937 was imposed without preliminary debates and signed into law by Vargas. It was the first time that this occurred.

V. THE BRIEF AND TROUBLED DEMOCRATIC PERIOD: 1946 TO 1964

In 1946 the fourth republican (and fifth Brazilian) constitution came into force. The Liberal Republic (*República Liberal*) period (from 1946 to 1964) began. The Dutra government (from 1946 to 1950) was known for wasting monetary reserves which had been accumulated during the Second World War period. He reduced import taxes and wasted the country's savings.

Vargas returned to power, by popular vote, in 1950. As he had done in his previous time in power with the steel sector, this time he launched nationalistic policies into another field: oil. It is during this time that Petrobras (which today is Brazil's largest company) was set up. Vargas mapped out the fragile spots of the Brazilian economy, set up the National Economic Development Bank (*Banco Nacional de Deselvolvimento Econômico*) and tried to implement policies to get the country out of poverty. Without obtaining economic success, targeted by opposition campaigns and politically isolated, Vargas committed suicide in 1954.

Elected in 1955, Jucelino Kubitschek came to power in 1956. The constant presence of the State in the economic domain, which had been a characteristic of Brazilian history since colonial times, always found its way in legal measures. Kubitschek's government is exemplary in this. His political platform promised '50 years in five'; that is, develop the country exponentially within his five-year term. The government set up the Target Plan (*Plano de Metas*). In fact, Brazil lived a period of enthusiasm and strong industrial growth. Kubitschek moved the capital from Rio de Janeiro to Brasília and launched the automotive industry in the country. This quick jump in growth took a toll: inflation and foreign debt grew substantially. Actually, these two hurdles continued, for different reasons, at least until 1994.

In 1961, also elected by popular vote, Jânio Quadros was inaugurated as president. His government lasted only seven months. With political difficulties at the Congress level which, in his view, prevented him from exercising his powers, Quadros resigned. Congress had already vetoed the anti-trust and international profit remittance laws proposed by Quadros. After his resignation, there was a major institutional crisis. Vice-President João Goulart, the constitutional successor, suffered from strong resentment from the military and the more conservative political sectors. Goulart's taking over of power was only accepted with a change from a presidential to a parliamentary system.

Goulart tried to implement the Triennial Plan (*Plano Trienal*) drafted by Celso Furtado, and a number of basic reforms in the financial, tax and rural sectors. Inflation and foreign debt remained as major hurdles. The socialising tendencies of Goulart deepened the political crisis and the parliamentary system limited his powers and capacity to control inflation and regain economic growth. Finally, in 1964, a military coup took over power and ended the liberal period, establishing a military dictatorship which lasted until 1984.

The Brazilian dictatorship was followed by similar coups in various parts of Latin America: Argentina (in 1966) and Chile (in 1973), for example. The period which preceded these dictatorships was characterised by a removal of parliamentary powers and by strong resistance of the media, business elite, part of the judiciary, the military and the United States government.

VI. THE MILITARY DICTATORSHIP: 1964 TO 1984

The military coup of 1964 established a dictatorship. The old parties were banned, elections were suspended and the repression of social movements increased. The military promised to control inflation, fight corruption, keep the country away from socialism and retake economic growth. The military sought to organise and modernise the power and bureaucratic structure. Changes were made to social security, the financial and tax systems, housing and education. Adult alphabetisation, pro-indigenous policies and infrastructure investments also were prevalent in this period.

From 1968, when the Institutional Act Number 5 was signed by the military, authoritarianism and oppression grew substantially. The dictatorship imposed a new Constitution in 1967 and a constitutional amendment in 1969, basically augmenting the powers of the president and restricting individual rights. The goal was to pull apart the liberal moral in force which had been in place between 1946 and 1964. During the dictatorship, the legal system was used merely as an arm of the Executive. A bureaucratic-authoritarian State was established in Brazil (as well as in various countries in Latin America), strong enough to oppress society, but weak to implement public policies capable of overcoming chronic problems of the country. From an administrative viewpoint, the Executive and the bureaucracy of the ministries and the administration began to have a fundamental role. The ministries' regulations became supreme, over and above laws passed by the parliament.

In the early 1970s, Brazil saw an important surge in economic development. The period became known as the 'Economic Miracle' (*Milagre Econômico*). Boastful nationalism and overconfidence became common among the authorities and the middle class. Important laws were passed during this period, such as the Code of Civil Procedure (in 1973) and the Corporations Law (in 1976). However, the petroleum crises of the 1970s, in a context in which Brazilian production still depended very much on oil imports, together with international recession around the world, interrupted the brief growth cycle.

President Geisel (who was in power from 1974 to 1978) began a slow, safe and gradual release of the military's grip on power. President Figueiredo (from 1978 to 1985) continued this slow and difficult process. The virtues of the economic growth model faced headwinds and the re-democratisation movement gained strength. Foreign debt and inflation continued to hinder students, intellectuals, the Brazilian Law Society (*Ordem dos Advogados do Brasil*), certain sectors of the Brazilian business sector and a new trade union movement organised the fight against the dictatorship. In 1978, for instance, the Metallurgic Trade Union of São Bernardo do Campo, in São Paulo, organised the first strike in the sector since 1964. The Trade Union's leader, Luis Inácio da Silva, known as 'Lula', in addition to having a major role in the re-democratisation process, later became president (from 2003 to 2010).

Between 1970 and 1980, Brazil saw an enormous rural exodus, followed by rapid growth of the urban population and the expansion of the slums. If in the 1940s Brazil only had 20% of its population living in the urban areas, in the beginning of the 1980s this ratio had reversed: 80% of the population was already living in the cities. From a rural country, Brazil became an industrial country. Slums, urban violence and grave public safety problems became major sources of concern, together with the traditional difficulties relating to economic growth and control over inflation.

VII. THE NEW REPUBLIC: FROM 1985 ONWARDS

From 1985, a new political and legal stage commenced in Brazil. All efforts and hopes were concentrated on the National Constitutional Assembly which, in 1988, passed the new constitution over intense popular political participation. During this period, the high rate of inflation forced the government of José Sarney (who was in power from 1985 to 1989) to make plans for improving public accounts, controlling prices and creating new currencies – all in an attempt to contain inflation. The various economic plans brought with them legal changes which deepened political influence on the economy.

While constitutional debates were taking place, the new Congress became heavily involved in passing very important laws such as the Class Action Law of 1985 (*Lei da Ação Civil Pública*), which recognises the right to file proceedings on behalf of various parties which make up a class, and the Consumer Protection Code of 1990. The period after the passing of the Constitution sees tough battles for passing laws relating to the many provisions in the Constitution requiring statutory implementation.

The Constitution of 1988 is considered a modern and very detailed document. This perhaps may be a consequence of the fact that the new Constitution sought to avoid the problems imposed during the military dictatorship. The Constitution of 1988 follows the European 'welfare state' model. It recognises, in addition to laws and individual guarantees, important economic, social and collective rights. However, it was not able to solve the profound social and economic inequalities in Brazil.

Soon after the approval of the Constitution of 1988, to finalise the transition to democracy, Brazil saw in 1989 the first direct election for president of this new Democratic period. The last direct election had taken place in 1960. By a small margin, Fernando Collor de Melo was elected, with Lula coming second. Collor took over power in 1990, and passed a set of laws confiscating bank accounts and financial investments. The 'Collor Plan' was primarily implemented with a view to fighting inflation. Collor also opened the country to international trade. He gained the presidency while as a member of a largely unknown and brand new party. Collor was charged with corruption, impeached in 1992, and left the government. Vice-President Itamar Franco took power and implemented greater protections to the local industry. Franco appointed Fernando Henrique Cardoso as Treasurer, giving him the task of putting together a plan for controlling inflation and stabilising the economy. After the successive failures of the prior presidents – Sarney and Collor – finally, the 'Real Plan' (*Plano Real*), which was conceived for gradual implementation divided in various stages, was able to control inflation. This paved the way for Cardoso's election as president in 1994.

The Constitution of 1988 respects and establishes the independence of the Judiciary. The Attorney General's Department (*Ministério Público*) is given a career which is separate from the courts. It also has very important powers. This gives greater hope for the population in having access to a judicial system which is more egalitarian and democratic. Judges and members of the Attorney General's Department gain greater political importance.

Cardoso finished two terms (from 1995 to 1998 and from 1999 to 2002), having always been elected by direct vote. His economic plan gave him great prestige. The Brazilian legal system goes through changes (many of them via constitutional amendments) which allow for privatisations, the creation of regulatory agencies in various sectors (especially those which were the subject of privatisations), improvements to the anti-trust legislation, approval of the Fiscal Responsibility Law (*Lei da Responsabilidade Fiscal*) and, in 2002, the approval of the new Civil Code. The reduction of inflation and the adjustments of the public accounts were the key legacies left to his successor, Lula. However, the economic development of the period was modest.

Lula, who also finished two terms (from 2003 to 2006 and from 2007 to 2010), continued Cardoso's policies of fiscal austerity and control over inflation. He added social policies which were more aggressive than those implemented by Cardoso. In the beginning of 2008, Brazil paid off all of its debts to the International Monetary Fund. Brazil had reasonably good economic growth from 2006 to 2010. Despite the economic crisis of 2008, the strength of internal policies and the size of the Brazilian internal market allowed Brazil to suffer little from the major problems faced by other nations.

It is estimated that, during the two Lula terms, a fantastic contingent of more than 20 million Brazilians overcame poverty and, gradually, joined the formal workforce and the consumer market. From the beginning, Lula stimulated measures of macroeconomic and fiscal sustainability. Many microeconomic reforms were introduced to the credit market and the financial system. Policies of social inclusion also expanded the availability of housing to the underprivileged. Brazil's Civil Procedure rules were also improved with a view to reducing the costs and time required for resolving disputes. A new insolvency law, which drew heavily from Chapter 11 of the American Bankruptcy Code, was enacted. Greater protection to business rights and a closer relationship between the public and private sector marked Lula's time in office.

Despite the gradual advances in the effectiveness of the legal system and the creation of a pro-business environment, Brazilians still face serious challenges. The main challenge is to eliminate the unequal access to basic rights and allow for the eradication of poverty. The good economic forecasts for Brazil's future will not take place unless the country can promote economic, social, education and digital inclusion. Law and economics will, in future years, have important tasks to fulfil: keep control over inflation, maintain democracy, promote national development and reduce social inequality.

Selected Bibliography

In English

P.H. Glenn, *Legal Traditions of the World* (3rd edn, Oxford University Press, 2007).

S.L. Graham, 'Slavery's Impasse: Slave Prostitutes, Small-Time Mistresses, and the Brazilian Law of 1871' (1991) 33 *Comparative Studies in Society and History* 669.

J. Holston, 'The Misrule of Law: Land and Usurpation in Brazil' (1991) 33 *Comparative Studies in Society and History* 695–725.

J.R.L. Lopes, 'Brazilian Courts and Social Rights: A Case Study Revisited', in R. Gargarella; P. Domingo and T. Roux (eds), *Courts and Social Transformation in New Democracies: An Institutional Voice for the Poor?* (1st edn, Aldershot, Ashgate, 2006), 185.

J.R.L. Lopes, 'Portuguese Colonial Law (South America)', in S. Katzand and W. Menski (eds) *Oxford International Encyclopedia of Legal History* (Oxford University Press, London and New York, 2009).

In Portuguese

J. Caldeira, *História do Brasil com empreendedores* (Ediora Mameluco, São Paulo, 2010).

A.C. Costa, *Consolidação da Leis do Trabalho* (34th edn, LTR, São Paulo, 2007).

S.P. Martins, *Direito do Trabalho* (23rd edn, Atlas, São Paulo, 2007).

A.M. Nascimento, *Iniciação do Direito do Trabalho* (33rd edn, LTR, São Paulo, 2007).

M.D. Segurado, *História Resumida do Direito Brasileiro* (Editora Rio, Rio de Janeiro, 1982).

A.C. Wolkmer, *História do Direito no Brasil* (Forense, Rio de Janeiro, 2007).

Chapter 2
Constitutional Law

Luís Roberto Barroso[*]

I. THE BRAZILIAN CONSTITUTIONAL EXPERIENCE

When Dom João VI returned to Lisbon, his eldest son, crown prince Dom Pedro, remained in Brazil. A series of disputes with the Portuguese Court culminated in Brazil's Declaration of Independence on 7 September 1822, and Dom Pedro was the first man to be crowned Emperor of Brazil. He called for the convening of a Constitutional and Legislative Assembly to draft a Constitution for the newly created country. However, as heir to an absolutist tradition, Pedro I soon stifled the liberal aspirations of those who were drafting the new Constitution and dissolved the Assembly. Without any popular support, an Imperial Constitution was drafted by the Council of State, whose members were appointed by the Emperor, and approved on 25 March 1824. It lasted until 1889, when the Republic was established and Brazil's second and last Emperor was deposed.

The second Brazilian Constitution, dated 24 February 1891, led to a triple revolution in Brazil: (i) the form of government went from a monarchy to a republic; (ii) the system of government, which had been parliamentary throughout almost the entire second empire, was converted to the presidential system; and (iii) the

* Professor of Constitutional Law, Rio de Janeiro State University (UERJ). Visiting Professor, University of Brasilia (UnB) and University of Poitiers, France. SJD (UERJ). LLM (Yale Law School).

Fabiano Deffenti & Welber Barral (eds), *Introduction to Brazilian Law*, pp. 15–30.

country, which had been governed as a single unit, was transformed into a federation of states. Formally, this Constitution lasted until the Revolution of 1930, a movement that symbolically marked Brazil's transformation from an agrarian and rural country to an urban newly industrialising nation. The new regime was institutionalised under the third Brazilian Constitution, of 1934, which was an attempt to organise the country according to the pattern of liberal democracies. Ironically, this model arrived in Brazil precisely at the same time authoritarianism was spreading throughout Europe, under dictators such as Hitler, Salazar, Franco and Mussolini. An attempted communist takeover in 1935 hastened Brazil's adoption of a dictatorship implemented by Getúlio Vargas, which led to a new Constitution in 1937.

Brazil's return to democracy occurred shortly after the end of World War II, with the Constitution of 1946 (the fifth of a long series). The nation subsequently experienced years of turbulence and instability until the military takeover of 1964. That military movement became institutionalised in the Constitution of 1967, which was soon replaced by another more authoritarian Constitution in 1969. Brazil had its seventh Constitution implemented while mired in a deep military dictatorship marked by the abolition of free elections, the lack of free speech and recurring episodes of torture of political prisoners. A process of gradual and peaceful re-democratisation began in 1974, culminating in the election of a civilian President in 1985.

In 1986, a National Constitutional Assembly convened to draft the Brazilian Constitution of 1988, which is still in effect to this day.

II. THE BRAZILIAN CONSTITUTION OF 1988: CONVENING OF THE ASSEMBLY, DRAFTING AND STRUCTURING OF THE TEXT

The Constitution of 1988 was the result of a peaceful political transition, although its drafting was driven by the grievances of organised civil society and popular mass demonstrations during the first half of the 1980s. Although the Constitutional Assembly was convened in a formal way, via a previous Constitutional Amendment, the typical elements of true constituent power were there: civic mobilisation, popular demand for a new institutional order and the assembly's sovereignty. The theory that the Constitutional Assembly should be dedicated exclusively to the task of drafting a constitution and subsequently be dissolved did not prevail. On the contrary, constituent power was assigned to the members of National Congress, which prevented the desirable cleavage between the power of the Constitutional Assembly and the legislative branch. This political decision favoured the inclusion of numerous topics in the Constitution that would have been more appropriately addressed in statutes.

After months of public hearings and debates, the final text was approved on 5 October 1988. Acclaimed as the 'Citizen's Constitution', the Constitutional Charter was promulgated with 245 articles in the main body and 70 Transitory

Provisions. Its general structure was distributed throughout nine Titles, set out as follows: Title I – Fundamental Principles; Title II – Fundamental Rights and Guarantees; Title III – Organisation of the State; Title IV – Organisation of the Branches of Government; Title V – Defence of the State and Democratic Institutions; Title VI – Taxes and Budgets; Title VII – Economic and Financial System; Title VIII – Social Order; and Title IX – General Constitutional Provisions.

III. MAIN FEATURES AND GENERAL EVALUATION

A. The Institutional Success

After twenty years, in 2008, the Brazilian Constitution was widely celebrated as a symbol of a success: the transition from an authoritarian, intolerant and often violent state to a rule-of-law democracy. In just two decades, freedom of speech and political party affiliation was possible with broad participation. Under this Constitution, five presidential elections were held with universal suffrage and broad public debate, resulting in change of power among different political parties. Furthermore, the Constitution has guaranteed a long period of institutional stability for Brazil, providing the country with proper conditions to absorb numerous political crises without compromising its democratic structure. One of the most important events of the period was the impeachment of the first president elected by popular vote after the end of the military dictatorship.

The Constitution of 1988 was, therefore, the rite of passage for Brazil's political-institutional maturity, overcoming the worst Latin American tradition of successive coups d' état, counter coups d' état, military revolts and authoritarian uprisings. Under this Constitution, the country was able to consolidate democracy: periodic elections were now held and presidents were now serving their office terms or being replaced in the manner prescribed by the Constitution. Additionally, the National Congress was now functioning without interruptions, the Judiciary was operating independently and the Armed Forces were now no longer involved in politics. This has continued until today.

B. The Structural and Institutional Difficulties

Numerous political circumstances associated with the end of the dictatorship led to the creation of a Constitution with two atypical and potentially negative features: (a) the large number of topics addressed in the text; and (b) the excessive degree of analysis. In other words, the Constitution covers many subjects that would be addressed more adequately by ordinary statutes. And the topics that should in fact be in the Constitution were regulated with an excessive amount of detail.

Some remarkable consequences derived from this scenario. The first is the fact that excessive constitutionalism hinders the exercise of political power, thereby limiting the role of statutes. Three-fifths majority is required to amend the

Constitution rather than the simple majority required for the approval of statutes. The practical result is that, in Brazil, ordinary politics (i.e., implementation of the will of the majorities formed at each occasion) is accomplished through multiple constitutional amendments.

The second consequence of an excessively detailed Constitution is the vast number of amendments that have been passed since it was first promulgated. After twenty years, there were fifty-six amendments to the Brazilian Constitution, concerning a wide array of issues: limiting the salaries of members of Congress; restricting the creation of new municipalities; introducing economic, administrative, social-security and judicial reforms; renewing temporary taxes; reducing the president's office term and allowing the president's re-election, to name a few. Although, so much change could have compromised the Constitution's role as a symbol of the prevalence of long lasting values over political contingencies, the reality is that, for the first time in its history, Brazil developed a shared perception of its potential to set limits on the political power and entrench fundamental rights.

IV. FUNDAMENTAL RIGHTS

The Constitution of 1988 presents an extensive bill of rights as its first major Title, before the provisions concerning the 'Organisation of the State and the Branches of Government'. This change in the traditional structure, which is typical of post-war constitutions, performs the symbolic role of emphasising the importance of those rights in the new system. Article 1(III) of the Constitution raised the principle of Human Dignity to the level of a Foundation of the Republic and made it the axiological centre of the Brazilian constitutional system. The text within this section primarily focuses on the trilogy of individual, political and social rights along with an additional category referred to as collective or diffused rights. Despite serious deficiencies and violations in several areas, the Constitution of 1988 enabled a greater focus and prioritising of fundamental rights.

In fact, individual rights are now flourishing in Brazil. Freedom of speech and freedom of the press have toppled years of censure and blatant interference by the State. The topics of due process of law and respect for the rights of defendants in criminal proceedings are still subject to heated discussions, but have made notable progress. Additionally, political rights are fully exercised through regular elections, mandatory voting and the right of illiterates to vote (approximately 12% of the population). These rights have made Brazil a democracy of the masses with one of the highest percentages of voter turnout in the world. There have also been gains in social rights, in areas such as education, health and social security. This great expansion includes complex and ambitious models of social inclusion. One of which is an Integrated System of Health (*Sistema Único de Saúde*, 'SUS'), which makes free access to the public health network available to all citizens. Finally, in the so-called diffused rights, issues like environmental protection and consumer rights now occupy a prominent place on Brazil's public agenda and in case law.

One important point to highlight is the rise of comprehensive case law relating to the protection of fundamental rights at all judicial levels, especially at the Federal Supreme Court (*Supremo Tribunal Federal*, Brazil's highest court). This court has ruled that it is possible to identify fundamental rights beyond those that are expressly listed in Article 5 of the Constitution. As an example, the Supreme Court treated as a fundamental right the constitutional provision that protects taxpayers from paying a new tax at the same year of its enactment.[1] In another historic decision, the Supreme Court repudiated anti-Semitism.[2] It also deemed unconstitutional a law that prohibited the gradual adoption of more flexible penitentiary regimes for criminals sentenced for heinous crimes.[3] Additionally, the Court considered embryonic stem cell research compatible with the Constitution, rejecting the pro-life argument and has also allowed direct application of fundamental rights to private relations, for example, holding that a foreign company established in Brazil cannot treat Brazilian and foreign employees differently, since it would be considered a violation of the principle of equality.

V. THE BRAZILIAN FEDERATION

During the Empire (1822 to 1889), Brazil was politically organised like a unitary State. Federation was introduced in 1891 by the first Republican Constitution and since then has been maintained in all subsequent Constitutions. The Brazilian Federation has always been characterised by a high concentration of authority in the central government, which reached its apex during the dictatorships: from 1937 to 1945 and during the military regime between 1964 and 1985. The Constitution of 1988 expanded the autonomy of local government, including a more balanced distribution of tax revenue. In practice, however, central government has conserved its more relevant powers, both in the legislative and political-administrative scopes. Below are three additional remarks for a better understanding of the Brazilian model.

The first one has to do with the entities that make up the Brazilian Federation. In addition to the central authority (the Union) and the twenty-six States, the Federal Republic of Brazil also has a local level of government, represented by the Municipalities, today amounting to more than 5,000. The autonomy of the Municipalities is even more limited, since they are subordinated to the Federal Constitution and to the constitution of the State where they are located. Additionally, the great majority of the Municipalities face financial difficulties and depend on funds from the Federal government and the States. Finally, there is also the Federal District, where is located the city of Brasília, Brazil's capital. It is a *sui*

1. The Federal Supreme Court (STF) held that not even a constitutional amendment can determine that a tax must be collected in the same year in which it is created. STF, DJU 18 Mar. 1994, ADIn 939-DF, Reported by Justice Sydney Sanches.
2. STF, DJU, 19 Mar. 2004, HC 82,424, Reported by Justice Maurício Corrêa.
3. STF, DJU 1 Sep. 2006, HC 82,959-SP.

generic federal entity, half way between State and Municipality, holding prerogatives of both.

The second remark concerns the contents of the autonomy granted to the federate entities, which is shaped by the Federal Constitution, also responsible for organising the central authority framework. The entities are given the power to organise themselves, which can be effected via State Constitutions, in the case of States, and by Organic Laws, in the case of Municipalities and the Federal District. In effect, however, the Federal Constitution is quite restrictive, as the States, the Federal District and the Municipalities do not have much leeway in changing their political structures. That centralisation is reinforced by Federal Supreme Court decisions, according to which all local entities are subject to most of the Federal Constitution's rules that regulate the activities of the central government. This includes all the provisions related to Separation of Powers (e.g., the States and Municipalities cannot create new mechanisms of checks and balances), as well as the provisions for the legislative process (e.g., the States and Municipalities cannot institute procedural rules that differ from those established for the Federal government).

Each of the entities has its own legislative and executive branches, whose members are elected by direct vote, within each jurisdiction. The central government, the States and the Federal District also have a judicial branch, whose core is made up of judges selected through public examination. In most courts, one-fifth of the judges are appointed by the Chief of the Executive Branch of the respective entity; whereas, in the higher federal courts, judges appointed by the President must be confirmed by the Senate. The entities also have the right of self-administration, by which they are entitled to organise their own bureaucratic structure, perform acts and enter into contracts that are in their own interest.

Finally, the third remark has to do with the sharing of authority among the entities. The Constitution of 1988 has adopted the so-called 'cooperative federalism', based on the German model. This means that, in addition to each federate entity's own exclusive authority, the Constitution establishes a certain amount of discretion for joint jurisdiction, both in relation to legislative as well as political-administrative matters. In the case of concurrent legislative powers, the Federal government is to enact provisions of general content and States are to deal with more specific aspects. The Municipalities, in turn, legislate on issues of local interest. Also, Federal, State and Municipal governments must act according to the predominant interest (national, regional or local, respectively). The Constitution also provides for the tax jurisdiction of the three federal spheres. Here, there is no joint action, but part of the revenue collected by the central government shall be delivered to States, Municipalities and the Federal District, according to criteria established in the Federal Constitution.

VI. SEPARATION OF POWERS

The Constitution of 1988 reduced the imbalance between the branches, enabling the Legislative and Judicial Branches to perform an independent and more effective role. The hegemony of the Executive Branch is a characteristic that has been present through Brazil's history, and which was still more obvious during the military regime (1964 to 1985). Although, Congress remained formally open during the majority of the period, political opposition was kept under strict control via arrests and removal from office of certain political leaders, several of whom sought exile abroad. The Judiciary also suffered persecution with the compulsory removal of the more independent judges, including three Federal Supreme Court justices, who were forced to retire. Judges and courts were seen as having no major influence and lacking any real ability to enforce constitutional guarantees. The Constitution of 1988 eventually established effective constitutional supremacy in Brazil, giving each branch of government the opportunity to exercise its institutional role. The balance between them is still a work in progress, in which the influence of the Executive Branch continues to prevail.

A. The Executive Branch

Brazil established the presidential system of government in the Republic's first Constitution. Since then, the adoption of a parliamentarian system has always been defended by influent scholars and political leaders, but the presidential system has always prevailed. As a compromise, a plebiscite was scheduled in 1993 to establish a definitive form of government. This plebiscite was held and a majority of votes upheld the presidential system and the republic. The President is now elected by direct vote for a four-year term of office and can run for a second term in office.[4] The President has a broad set of powers, including active participation in the legislative process, through his or her own exclusive initiative on certain matters or via veto right.[5]

Two powers that are frequently misused by the Executive Branch are worth mentioning, since they accentuate that branch's predominance in politics. The first is the misuse of 'provisional measures' (*medidas provisórias*, 'MPs'), which were conceived as a mechanism for the President to exercise legislative authority in cases of 'relevance and urgency' (Article 62 of the Federal Constitution). Provisional measures are subject to control of the legislator, in which they can be rejected and even have their effects undone. Despite these seemingly strict constitutional requirements, undue tolerance of the Legislative and Judicial Branches resulted in approximately 6,000 provisional measures between 1988 and 2002. As a matter of fact, provisional measures became a routine mechanism for the Executive Branch to legislate, thus minimising the role of the National

4. The possibility of re-election was introduced by Constitutional Amendment 16/1997. The two presidents elected since then, Fernando Henrique Cardoso and Luís Inácio Lula da Silva, succeeded in being re-elected with relative ease.
5. As a rule, the laws approved by the National Congress depend on presidential signing in order to go into effect. Signing is not required in the matters of exclusive responsibility of the Houses of Congress, which are not numerous. The veto can be total or partial and is always submitted to Congress, which can vote it down by an absolute majority vote of its members.

Congress and often compromising transparency and public debate over legislation. This flaw was partially mitigated with the passage of Constitutional Amendment 32/2001, which stipulated that provisional measures could not remain in effect for more than sixty days, and could only be renewed once for an equal period, with the suspension of other votes in the Houses of Congress until they reach a decision on the subject.

The second power misused by the Executive Branch involves budget control. In fact, budget preparation, receipt of tax revenues and spending constitute an arena of democracy that is still neglected in Brazil. The Executive Branch's authority is nearly omnipotent, beginning with the preparation of the draft budget. Lawmakers have reduced power to amend the budget and, once it is approved, the President may, at his or her own discretion, impound the funds without being checked by Congress. Although this pattern of budgetary system is common in various countries, Brazil's history has been marked by excessive dominance of the Executive Branch on such matters.

Finally, one prominent characteristic of the Executive Branch in Brazil introduced in the 1990s is the presence of independent regulatory agencies in charge of strategic economic sectors or over the management of essential services. These include but are not limited to telecommunications, electrical power, the petroleum industry, health and hydrological resources. In adapting the American model, which is also followed in the European Union, these agencies aim to minimise political influence and aggregate technical expertise on the management of the regulated sectors. The agencies were provided with normative powers and guarantees of independence, particularly through the appointment of its directors for fixed terms.[6]

B. The Legislative Branch

The legislative powers in Brazil are exercised by the National Congress, which consists of two Houses: the Chamber of Deputies – a body of popular representation – and the Federal Senate, in which the States and the Federal District have equal representation (State voters elect three senators for the Senate, each for an eight-year term). Both houses participate in the lawmaking process. As a rule, discussions take place separately in each house of Congress. Joint deliberation occurs only in some issues specifically stipulated in the Constitution, such as deliberation over a presidential veto. A Bill approved by the House where it originated goes then to the other House for further examination, where it may be

6. Regulatory agencies and its powers have been considered compatible with the Constitution. In effect, the STF expressly recognised the validity of a law that called for the creation of a regulatory agency with the appointment of a director for a specific term of office, without the possibility of being removed at any time by a political decision of the chief of the Executive Branch: STF, DJU 25 Nov. 2005, ADInMC 1979/RS, Reported by Justice Sepúlveda Pertence. Likewise, the Court also has allowed laws that delegate regulatory powers to different levels of the Public Administration, provided they contain minimum standards.

rejected (a situation that leads to the Bill's rejection), fully approved or approved with changes. In the latter case, the Bill returns to the originating House for the changes to be discussed. That House will have the final word on the Bill, so that a certain prevalence of the originating House can be identified. Deliberations always begin in the Chamber of Deputies, unless the Bill is proposed by a senator or Senate Committee.

Additionally, both the Chamber of Deputies and the Senate have some exclusive powers. They are generally related to the internal management of each House, but there are exceptions to this. The Senate has the authority to control public finances by imposing debt limits for all entities of the Federation and authorising credit operations, especially when it comes to foreign loans. The members of both Houses enjoy full material immunity and are not subject to civil, criminal or administrative liability for their votes and opinions related to public office. They also enjoy partial immunity from arrest and criminal prosecution, which can be suspended by vote of the House of Congress they belong to.[7]

It is worth noting some structural and functional flaws in the Brazilian political system that have compromised the legitimacy of the political system. Throughout the military regime, the Legislative was the Branch that suffered the most serious consequences of authoritarianism. From 1964 to 1977, many of its members were removed from office and striped of their political rights. In this period, the National Congress was shut down several times and the President seized all legislative powers including constitutional reform. Additionally, under the Constitutions of 1967 and 1969, the legislative powers of the President increased sharply via 'Decree-Laws', acts issued by the President which were as binding as laws. Finally, most of the bills voted on Congress were proposed by the President, who has always been able to impose his own agenda. Under the Constitution of 1988, the threats to congressmen independence and the possibility of shutting down Congress disappeared. However, the role of the Legislative Branch in lawmaking remained endangered due to the excessive amount of provisional measures and the major influence exercised by the Executive Branch over the Congress' agenda.

In view of the Executive Branch's growing pre-eminence in lawmaking (which is actually a worldwide phenomenon), the role of the Legislative Branch has shifted to overseeing government acts and public administration. Under the Constitution of 1988, one of the main instruments of the Legislative Branch is the 'Congressional Investigating Committee' (*Comissão Parlamentar de Inquérito*, 'CPI'). CPI's have attracted a high level of public attention, awakening the interest of the media. The powers of these committees are gradually being defined by case law in the Federal Supreme Court. It has already recognised that CPI's may hear witnesses and lift telephone, banking and data secrecy protection, but denied them

7. On the topic of procedural parliamentary immunity, Constitutional Amendment 35/2001 introduced a substantive change, no longer requiring permission from the Chamber or Senate before criminal charges are filed against a member of Congress. Under the new regimen, the STF can receive the charges directly. However, the House of Congress may, by majority, suspend the action during the member's term of office.

the power to determine the use of wiretapping and to issue arrest warrants. The STF has also ruled that when constitutional requirements are met, minorities have the right to convene a CPI and that it cannot be frustrated by the majority.[8]

C. The Judiciary

The Constitution lists various principles that govern the functions of the Judiciary including the obligation to justify and give full publicity to its decisions. The Constitution also sets forth the partition of judicial duties among the Federal and State Courts.[9] The Federal Judiciary is divided in: (i) Federal Courts, which have jurisdiction over disputes involving the central government; (ii) Labour Courts, which are responsible for individual and class action lawsuits derived from employment relation disputes; (iii) Military Courts, responsible for judging military crimes; and (iv) Electoral Courts, in charge of organising the elections and judging conflicts that arise in this context. State Courts, in turn, are responsible for judging all civil, criminal or administrative cases that do not fall under the competence of the other aforementioned structures. Each of these court divisions is organised in trial courts (first instance) and appeal courts. Federal specialised branches – Labour, Military and Electoral – have also higher courts at their summits, designed to harmonise case law and decide on issues of greater relevance. In addition to that, the Constitution has also created two superior courts with national general jurisdiction (the STF and the Superior Court of Justice, STJ), respectively in charge of rendering the final word on constitutional interpretation and on interpretation of federal law.

In recent years, the Judiciary has performed a more important role in Brazil, due to many factors. Some of them are directly associated with redemocratisation. Once democratic liberties and judges' guarantees were restored, courts became capable of assuming and independent posture in relation to the other branches. At the same time, the Constitution protects new rights and expands the possibilities of legal protection, inclusively via class actions and other forms of collective litigation.

This growing demand for justice, combined with the raise of constitutionalism in Brazil, has given way to a visible phenomenon: the judicialisation of political and social relationships. Numerous important political decisions, including the most significant constitutional reforms, have ultimately been decided or confirmed by the STF. As an example, the creation of the National Council of Justice – a Board designed to control the efficiency of judicial administration – has been challenged under the claim that it violated several constitutional provisions that

8. STF, DJU, 4 Aug. 2006, MS 24,831/DF, Reported by Justice Celso de Mello.
9. Regardless of this fact, the STF has already decided that the Judicial Branch is a national structure, uniformly subject to principles instituted by the Constitution. See, for instance, STF, DJU 17 Mar. 2006, ADI 3367/DF, reported by Justice Cezar Peluso and STF, DJU, 29 Jun. 2007, ADInMC 3,854/DF, Reported by Justice Cezar Peluso.

were rejected by STF. The same thing happened in relation to social security reform programmes,[10] especially when a constitutional amendment imposed on retirees the obligation of keep contributing to the maintenance of the system. In disputes involving the rules of political campaigning and elections, STF has decided issues related to party coalitions,[11] political parties with low electoral performance,[12] the reduction in the number of city councillors in the Municipal Chambers[13] and party loyalty.[14]

The shifting of such issues to the courts is made easier due to the large number of subject that were addressed in the Constitution and the open texture of several of its provisions. Though, it is the legal system itself that encourages individuals and political actors to seek for a court-based solution for these matters, a situation that has important parallels in comparative Law. A similar phenomenon is judicial activism, which is a posture deliberately assumed by segments of the Judiciary consisting of a more proactive interpretation of open-ended constitutional provisions, extending its vague principles to situations that are not expressly or clearly set out in the text. Judicial activism in Brazil has eventually functioned as a means to meet social demands that have not succeeded in getting beyond the bottleneck of the political system for various reasons.

There are three recent decisions of the STF that serve as examples of judicial activism. The first one was handed down in a constitutional action in which it was sought confirmation of the validity of a resolution of the National Council of Justice against nepotism, prohibiting the hiring of spouses and close relatives for positions and functions in the Judiciary.[15] This practice was traditional in Brazil and, in spite of the growing dissatisfaction of the general public, its prohibition was opposed by private interests within the courts themselves. STF dismissed the argument that an act of Congress was necessary to prohibit such practice. The court avoided the easy argument of violation of the principle of legality (i.e., the Constitution reserves to the law the role of regulating requirements for public employment) and adopted a more sophisticated theory: the act was considered to be directly enforcing the constitutional provisions that prescribe equality and morality in public service. The court went ahead and extended the prohibition to administrative functions in the Executive and in the Legislative.

The second example involved an injunction writ, intended to control omissions of the Legislative or the Executive branches which can prevent the exercise

10. STF, DJU of 16 May 2003, ADIn 1,946/DF, reported by Justice Sydney Sanches. The STF interpreted Art. 14 of Constitutional Amendment 20/2008 to exclude paid pregnancy leave from the maximum limit of the benefits paid by Social Security, in the name of protection of maternity and non-discrimination of women in the labour market. See also STF, DJU of 12 Apr. 2002, ADIn-MC 2,010-DF, reported by Justice Celso de Mello and DJU of 18 Feb. 2005, ADIn 3105-DF, reported by Justice Cezar Peluso (per curiam).
11. STF, ADIn 3,685-DF, Reporting Justice: Ellen Gracie, DJU 10 Aug. 2006.
12. STF, ADIn 1,351-DF, Reporting Justice: Marco Aurélio, DJU 30 Mar. 2007.
13. STF, RE 197,971-SP, Reporting Justice: Maurício Corrêa, DJU 7 May 2004.
14. STF, MS 26,602-DF, Reporting Justice: Eros Grau, DJU 3 Oct. 2007.
15. STF, DJU, 12 Sep. 2008, ADC 12, reported by Justice Carlos Ayres Britto.

of rights granted by the Constitution. According to traditional case law, the decision in this type of action would be limited to declaring the existence of omissions and notifying the agents responsible for it. In other words, the decision would have the purpose of producing a weak method of institutional dialogue and politically embarrass the inert branch (i.e., the legislative power) into acting. Recently, however, the STF altered its position and began to allow the possibility of temporarily suppressing the omission until the body responsible for acting abandoned its inertia. In the case in question, the Court decided that the right of public employees to strike – established in the Constitution and never regulated by law – could be exercised under the law governing the right to strike of private employees.

Finally, in an even more controversial and unorthodox decision, STF established that any member of Congress who changes to another political party without reasonable justification could lose the mandate at the request of the party that had elected him or her. The underlying rationale is based on the assumption that it is necessary to preserve the balance of party representation as derived of the elections. It was also considered that candidates heavily depend on the structure of their parties to successfully run for a public office. In practice, the Court created a new situation in which someone can be removed from elected office, in addition to those directly set out in the Constitution. This decision imposed party loyalty, thus overcoming a long period of inertia of the Congress on this issue. Due to the repercussions on the political system and the detailed analysis set out in the judgment, which listed various situations that could justify party switching – that decision can be considered the high point of judicial activism in Brazil to this day.

It is important to briefly note that the role of the Judiciary, especially of the Supreme Court, must be to safeguard the democratic process and to enforce entrenched constitutional provisions. On the contrary, judges should not use their power to exercise political preferences instead of defending constitutional principles. The delicate balance of this equation is dynamical and each society tends to reach its own formula. In Brazil, STF has been playing a leading role on the subject with the general support of the civil society.

VII. JUDICIAL REVIEW

Brazil has a fairly complex and sophisticated system of judicial review combining features of two models adopted in contemporary democracies. Thus, in the course of litigation, any court may refuse to apply a law that it deems unconstitutional. This is the decentralised, incidental form of judicial review that has been rooted in the American tradition ever since the US Supreme Court handed down *Marbury v. Madison* in 1803. Parallel to this model is the centralised, abstract form of judicial review, by which a direct action may be filed before the STF challenging the constitutionality of a law. It is a proceeding borrowed from the system devised by Hans Kelsen for Austria and now adopted by most countries in Europe.

Incidental judicial review is exercised by the courts – either by a judge who sits alone or by a panel of judges[16] – as part of their ordinary role of applying the law to a case or dispute. In deciding litigation, a court may refuse to apply a Federal, State or Municipal law. The constitutional issue may be raised by any of the parties, by the Public Ministry (the Attorney General)[17] or even by the court itself at its own motion. The effects of an incidental declaration of unconstitutionality are limited to the specific matter and parties involved, not affecting the validity of the law, which may be applied by any other court. According to the Constitution, an extraordinary appeal may be filed at the STF against a final decision that declares a treaty or a federal statute or decree unconstitutional.[18] It has been said that the effects of a decision declaring a law unconstitutional are binding only on the litigants. However, if the matter reaches the STF in an extraordinary appeal and the Court declares the law invalid because it violates the Constitution, the Senate will be notified of that decision. Upon receipt of such notification, the Senate may suspend the application of the law, thus making the decision binding *erga omnes*, that is, on everyone.[19]

Judicial review by direct action or *principalitur* consists of bringing a constitutional issue involving a Federal or State law or regulation to the STF, *in abstract*, that is, without the requirement of a concrete dispute, a *case or controversy*.[20] Under previous Constitutions, only one type of direct action existed, aimed at declaring a law unconstitutional. The Constitution of 1988, however, provides for several types of direct actions. Furthermore, prior to 1988, only the Attorney General was eligible to file such actions. However, Article 103 of the Constitution of 1988 lists a number of public and private agencies and entities that can bring matters directly to the attention of the STF. Decisions rendered in such cases produce *erga omnes* effects, which means they are binding on everyone, including lower courts and the public administration. According to the Constitution, four types of actions are filed directly at the STF:

(a) direct action of unconstitutionality (*ação direta de inconstitucionalidade*, 'ADI'), in which the STF may declare a federal or state law unconstitutional;
(b) direct action of unconstitutionality by omission (*ação direta de inconstitucionalidade por omissão*, 'ADI-O'), in which the STF may declare the Congress or Executive Branch negligent in failing to pass a law or a decree

16. Article 97 of the Federal Constitution of 1988 establishes that an absolute majority of a court is required to declare a law or a decree unconstitutional.
17. See K. Rosenn, 'Judicial Review in Brazil: Developments under the 1988 Constitution' (2000) 7 *Southwest Journal of Law and Trade in the Americas* 291. See also Arts 127–130 of the Federal Constitution.
18. In practice, a decision that declares a law unconstitutional – be it Federal, State or Municipal – usually will be followed by an extraordinary appeal to the STF, since such appeal is possible whenever a decision is contrary to the Constitution (see Art. 102, III).
19. Article 52, X.
20. At State level, it is also to challenge the validity of state or municipal laws and normative acts under state constitutions. See Art. 125, para. 2 of the Federal Constitution of 1988.

required by the Constitution as necessary to make some of the latter's provisions fully effective;

(c) declaratory action of constitutionality (*ação direta de constitucionalidade*, 'ADC'), in which the STF declares that a Federal law is constitutional, when its validity is being questioned in various cases before lower courts, thus generating uncertainty as to whether or not the law should be given full effect;

(d) claim of non-compliance with a fundamental precept (*arguição de descumprimento de preceito fundamental,* 'ADPF'), which is similar to an ADI but with two peculiarities. The first is that its scope is much broader, serving to challenge any act or behaviour on the part of the Government – legal, administrative and even jurisdictional. The second peculiarity is that fact that the qualified party cannot allege a violation of just any constitutional norm but only those deemed to be fundamental precepts. Case law has interpreted this to include provisions dealing with separation of powers, federalism and fundamental rights.

In cases of incidental as well as abstract judicial review, laws incompatible with the Constitution are, as a general rule, considered null and void. Consequently, a typical effect of decisions of this nature is a declaration of unconstitutionality, with retrospective effect (*ex tunc*), resulting in the need to undo all acts carried out pursuant to the voided law. However, the STF recognises the need to attenuate or eliminate retrospective effects in situations where it would produce grave legal uncertainty, particularly in decisions that overrule long-lasting precedents. In these cases, the STF has employed the 'prospective overruling' doctrine, as it is referred to other courts, such as the US Supreme Court and the German Federal Constitutional Court. However, this measure has been characterised by the STF as very exceptional.[21]

VIII. CONCLUSION

A. The Burden of the Past

Not until 1808 – 300 years after Brazil was discovered – when the Portuguese royal family fled to Rio de Janeiro, did Brazil truly begin to exist as a nation. Before then, the ports were closed to trading with all other countries except Portugal. Manufacture of products and road building was prohibited. There were no institutions of middle or higher education and even the access to the most basic schooling was limited. More than 98% of the population was illiterate. Also, one out of every three Brazilians was subjugated to slavery, which would persist for another eighty

21. As an example, the STF gave prospective effects to the decision in which it overturned previous case law regarding a certain rule of jurisdictional authority so that previous court decisions would not be considered null and void.

years like a moral plague and social time bomb. Worst of all, Brazil was under the rule of Portugal, which was the last country in Europe to abolish the inquisition, the slave trade and absolutism. Thus, it is not surprising that at the end of the twentieth century, Brazil was still struggling to modernise its institutions and reduce the inequality among its citizens. Amidst these conditions, the political system remains under a severe crisis of legitimacy. In spite of that, Brazil has made remarkable progress.

B. Perspectives for the Future

Democratic constitutionalism was the victorious ideology of the twentieth century. This institutional arrangement seeks to combine the rule of law (supremacy of the law, Rechtsstaat) with the sovereignty of the people as part of its moral autonomy. This entails limitation of government's power, human dignity, fundamental rights, social justice and tolerance. This model did not arrive in Brazil until the eve of the new millennium. The Brazilian Constitution, which turned twenty years old at the end of 2008, symbolises the efforts of many generations to overcome authoritarianism, patrimonialism and social exclusion. An eternity has passed in the two hundred years that separate the arrival of the royal family from the twentieth birthday of the Constitution of 1988.

Selected Bibliography

In English

L.R. Barroso, 'The Saga of Indigenous Peoples in Brazil: Constitution, Law and Policies' (1994–1995) 7 *St. Thomas Law Review* 645.

C.D. Cole, *Comparative Constitutional Law: Brazil and the United States* (2nd edn, Vandeplas Publishing, 2008).

J. Dolinger, *The Influence of American Constitutional Law on the Brazilian Legal System* (American Society of Comparative Law, 1990).

A.C. Figueiredo and F. Limongi, *Presidential Power, Legislative Organization, and Party Behavior in Brazil* (The City University of New York, New York, 2000).

S. Mainwaring, *Politicians, Parties and Electoral Systems – Brazil in Comparative Perspective, Comparative Politics* (The City University of New York, New York, 1991).

G. Reich, 'Executive Decree Authority in Brazil: How Reactive Legislators Influence Policy' (2002) 27, no.1 *Legislative Studies Quarterly Comparative Legislative Research Center*, 5.

K. Rosenn, 'Judicial Review in Brazil: Developments under the 1988 Constitution' (2000) 7 *Southwest Journal of Law and Trade in the Americas,* 291.

the Federal District),[1] in the executive, legislative and judicial branches when performing an administrative function.

The current structure of the federal public administration was implemented by Decree Law 200/1967. The administrative reforms that brought about this decree did not manage to modify the predominant thinking in Brazilian public administration, in which everything is submitted to strict formalities and procedures. The changes only came with the Constitution of 1988, which upholds the application of important principles such as the principle of impersonality, morality, publicity (Article 37), legitimacy and cost-effectiveness (Article 70), both for the direct and indirect administrations. Only then, influenced by European countries that adopted this type of thinking in the last century, did the Brazilian public administration become receptive to a material rationality (not, obviously, to detract from the formal rationality).

The 1967 reformist thinkers established a division between direct and indirect public administration, which has been the subject of various legislative changes. Further changes were brought about by the administrative reform of 1998, promulgated in Constitutional Amendment 19/1998.

The administrative reform of 1998 brought structural changes in the Brazilian public administration model implemented by Decree Law 200/1967. The reform sets out three segments: (a) State public space (*espaço público estatal*); (b) non-State public space (*espaço público não-estatal*); and (c) the market (*o mercado*).

In the public legal system, public State space became comprised of a strategic centre (comprising the legislative branch, the judicial branch, the Attorney General, the President, the Ministries and the special departments) a regulatory and executive agencies implemented by specific law in the form of special governmental agencies.

It is in this framework that public policies are now formulated (strategic centre) and the exclusive activities of the State performed (such as those dependent on public authorities to be carried out and those pertaining to the legislative, judicial, tax and control functions).

In the private sphere, the non-State public space became comprised of social organisations and public interest organisations, both being private legal entities in the form of associations or foundations regulated by private law rules (*direito civil*).

The non-State public space is covered by non-exclusive or competitive services that could be performed without the use of 'State power'. These services could be performed by private entities. According to the lawmakers who sponsored the changes, public authorities would compete with private initiatives. The participation of the State would only be justified if such services involve fundamental rights or produce goods that cannot be sourced from market forces.

Nowadays, the Brazilian administrative structure can be divided as follows: (a) direct administration (*administração direta*), which comprises the President and Ministries; (b) indirect administration (*administração indireta*), which is

1. The federal nature of the Brazilian State under the terms of Art. 18, preamble, of the Federal Constitution, admits the four legal bodies cited above: Federal, State and Municipal, as well as the Federal District, capital of the Brazilian Federal Republic. The authority of each legal body is defined in the Federal Constitution (mainly Arts 20 and 32).

subdivided into: (i) public legal entities (*pessoas de direito público*): governmental agencies, public foundations, regulatory and executive agencies; (ii) private legal entities (*pessoas de direito privado*): mixed capital companies and public companies; (iii) private or public legal entities (*pessoas de direito público ou privado*): public consortia. Parallel to this structure and operating in a collaborative scheme would be the social organisations, public interest organisations of civil association and autonomous social services.

B. Direct Public Administration

In the Federal sphere, direct administration is regulated by Law 10,683/2003,[2] which adopts a subjective criterion and establishes, in detail, the organisation and competence of the direct administration's bodies. According to this law, the federal administration is made up of the President and the Ministries.

The executive branch of government is comprised of the President, the State Office, the General Office, the Department of Institutional Affairs, the Cabinet, the Cabinet of Institutional Security and the Centre for Strategic Affairs.[3] Various other councils which deal with specific areas (such as the Social Development Council, the National Energy Policy Council and the Attorney General's Department, to name a few)[4] make up the executive branch.

Law 10,683/2003 also sets the number of Ministries. The Federal District, the States and the Municipalities all have similar structures.

C. Indirect Public Administration

Indirect public administration is comprised of public and private legal entities, all instituted by law, focusing on carrying out administrative functions that include services of a public nature and economic activities carried out by the State.

Under the terms of Decree Law 200/1967, the indirect administration is made up of only governmental agencies, mixed capital companies and public companies. Currently, under Laws 7,597/1987, 9,649/1998 and 11,107/2005, respectively, public foundations, agencies and public consortia can also make up the array of legal entities that comprise this area of administration.

1. Governmental Agencies

Decree Law 200/1967 defines 'governmental agency' (*agência governamental*) as 'an autonomous service, created by law, with its own legal personality, assets and

2. With the changes brought by Law 10,869/2004, Law 11,036/2004, Law 11,065/2004, Law 11,098/2005, Law 11,129/2005, Law 11,204/2005, Law 11,284/2006 and Law 11,314/2006.
3. Article 1 of Law 10,683/2003.
4. According to Law 10,683/2003, paras 1, 2 and 3 of Art. 1.

revenue to carry out public administration activities that require decentralised administrative management in order to operate better'.[5] This legal definition has been criticised by scholars because of the omission of the legal personality in public law. The view held by the majority of scholars is that income and assets are considered as having a public nature with a special destination and an independent administration.

Governmental agencies perform decentralised activities and services for the State entity responsible for setting them up, within the limits established by the law that granted them the licence to do so. The same law defines the means of control (especially ministerial supervision), the capacity for self-administration and the institutional connection to the direct administration.

With a more specialised and flexible operating structure than the centralised administration, the governmental agencies have managerial, financial and administrative autonomy. In Brazil, this autonomy has important limits, including: the choice of managers, budgets, spending limitations and the role conferred upon the ministerial level.

Public legal entities operate through administrative acts and, as such, largely have the same rights and duties as the public administration. For this reason, their duty of care is the same one that covers public authorities, with the qualification that governmental agencies are primarily liable for their acts, with only secondary liability falling to the State. The same principle justifies the restraint of mortgage of the agency's assets, the benefit of tax immunity and similar maters. Finally, the public legal system imposes the same control on governmental agencies as placed on bodies in direct administration.

2. Public Foundations

Under the terms of Law 7,596/1987, a public foundation is 'a non-profit entity with legal personality, created by virtue of statutory authorisation, for the development of activities that do not require performance by public bodies or entities, with administrative autonomy, assets managed by the respective management bodies and operations financed by resources from the Brazilian State and other sources'.

The legal personality of a private nature set up in Law 7,596/1987 has not been accepted by Brazilian scholars. However, scholars recognise the legal personality of the foundations which are set up by public authorities. These must follow the same rules applicable to governmental agencies, specifically: (a) the procurement and contractual obligations imposed on public entities; (b) control of their activities by the Audit Court; and (c) adherence to budget rules. These entities' civil servants are also regarded as equivalent to public officials for administrative and criminal law purposes. Public foundations are also immune from taxes.

Whether considered public or private, foundations that are part of the indirect administration generally focus their activities on health, education, culture,

5. According to Art. 5, item I of Decree Law 200/1967.

environmental protection, social welfare and scientific research. These entities are granted the authority to self-manage and are not subordinate to the Ministries in their areas of operation.

Irrespective of the public or private nature of the foundations, they are directly liable for their acts, with the State only being liable if the foundation does not have sufficient assets to meet its liabilities.

3. State Companies and Mixed Capital Companies

Article 5 of Decree Law 200/1967 defines a public company (*empresa pública*) as an 'entity with legal personality of a private nature, with its own assets and with exclusive capital from the Brazilian State, created by law for the carrying out of economic activity that the Government is led to exercise by force of contingency or administrative convenience, and having of any of the types admitted by law'.[6]

Decree Law 200/1967 also defines a mixed capital company (*empresa de capital misto*) as an 'entity with private legal personality, created by law for the carrying out of a commercial activity, in the form of a corporation, whose voting shares belong to the Brazilian State or to the entity of the indirect administration'.[7]

Based on liberal principles, the Federal Constitution limits the direct carrying of commercial activities by the State to matters pertaining to national security or relevant collective interests. It further establishes that the law setting up a public company or mixed capital company must: (a) provide details as to how the State may audit the entity; (b) adhere to the rules applicable to private companies; (c) observe procurement principles applicable to administrative contracts; (d) contain rules relating to setting up and operation of the overseeing boards, with the participation of minority shareholders; (e) set out the mandates, assessment of performance and the liability of officers. The same constitutional provision vetoes the concession of tax privileges that are unavailable to companies from the private sector.

Scholars recognise that these entities can carry out activities that are not limited to commercial activity, such as providing public services or coordinating the construction of public works.[8] This distinction is important because the degree of derogation of the private laws by the rules of public law depends on it.

Hence, according to Meirelles,[9] State companies providing public services have their assets protected due to the impossibility of creditors from enforcing rights against them, while the companies that exercise commercial activities are submitted to the private law enforcement system. A similar implication follows in regards to the regime for the procurement and sale of assets where State companies providing public services are subject to the same bidding procedures of the direct administration (which is set out in Law 8,666/1993), while State companies that

6. Article 5, Clause II.
7. Article 5, Clause III
8. Mello, at 191.
9. Meirelles, at 350.

exercise commercial activities can have their own regulations that generally observe only public procurement principles.

Whether they perform an activity of an economic nature or not, these companies have various things in common (aside from the need for a law to provide for their creation or liquidation and their legal personality to be of a private nature). Some of the common points are: the political choice for the appointment of their managers; the equivalency of their civil servants to public officials for administrative and criminal law purposes, and administrative and financial autonomy under ministerial supervision.

The differences between State companies and those of mixed capital companies are essentially limited to their creation and the nature of their capital. The former are incorporated companies, with the majority of capital being public, while the later may adopt any corporate form permitted by law, yet its capital must fully belong to the State (regardless of the sphere of government).[10]

4. Public Consortia

Public consortia are 'associations made up of political legal entities (the Federation, States, Federal District or Municipalities), with legal personalities of a public or private nature, created through statutory authorisation for the associated management of public services'.[11]

Public consortia are regarded, by Brazilian law, as a mere agreement for the achievement of common purposes, entered into between federal entities of the same sphere.[12] They have legal personification through the express provision contained in Article 6 of Law 11,107/2005 which states that:

> public consortia will acquire legal personality: I – of a public nature, in the case of it being a public association, through the force of ratification of the protocol of intentions; II – of a private nature, if meeting the requirements of civil laws are complied with.

As a legal entity created to develop State activities in general services of administrative nature, consortia of a public or private legal nature are part of the indirect

10. Decree Law 900/1969 establishes that observing the requirement that the majority of the voting capital is owned by the Brazilian State, participation is admitted by other internal Public legal entities or by indirect administration entities in the formation of the public company's capital (Art. 5). It must also be considered as a difference between these entities that legal action in which public companies are plaintiffs, defendants, assistants or opponents will be brought before the Federal Court while actions involving mixed capital companies will be brought before the State Court.
11. Di Pietro, at 468.
12. Brazilian law used to reserve the agreements between States or Municipalities to consortia and the agreement that involved entities from different federal levels (between the Brazilian State and States or Municipalities and between States and Municipalities) to conventions.

administration of the consortia in the Federation.[13] Those of private nature must observe civil laws with the necessary derogations of public laws.

Law 11,107/2005 expressly grants the following authority to consortia:

> I – to enter into conventions, contracts, agreements of any nature, to receive aid, contributions and social or economic grants-in-aid from other government entities and bodies; II – under the terms of the public consortia contract of public nature, to promote expropriation and to establish public easement under the terms of the declaration of public interest or public convenience, or social interest, executed by public authorities; and III – to be contracted by the direct or indirect administration of entities that have consortia with the Federation, excluding procurement obligations.

Further, the consortia may issue invoices and collect levies and other public fees for the rendering of services or for granting the use of public assets administered by them or through the specific authorisation made by the consortia of the Federation. Additionally, they may grant concession, permission or authorisation for public works or services.

Liability of consortia does not have the joint and several nature that lawmakers had intended. With the presidential veto of the main clause of Article 10 of Law 11,107/2005, secondary liability remains for entities that are members of the consortia, and will apply on an equal basis.

Law 11,107/2005 establishes in Article 7 that the statute for public consortia must adhere to the principles and laws of administrative law, observing the provision in the protocol of intentions and in the contract. Further, Article 13 refers to the contracts that regulate the obligations that a federal government entity has with another or with a public consortia in the associated management sphere where there are services being rendered. The law forbids the contracted party to have power over planning, regulation and inspection of the services provided by the contracted party. These powers must remain under the control of the contractor.

III. ADMINISTRATIVE REFORM: FROM 1998 ONWARDS

The constitutional reform alters the structure of the Brazilian public administration, envisaging three segments: (a) the State public sphere; (b) the non-State public sphere; and (c) the market.

The first is made up of the strategic nucleus (comprising the Legislative Power, the Judiciary, the Attorney General's Department, the Presidency, the

---

13. Although this law reserves this possibility exclusively for public consortia (Art. 6, para. 1), scholars are unanimous in concluding that these entities are part of the indirect administration of the consortia members.

Ministries and the Secretaries) and by the Regulatory and Executive Agencies set out by specific laws, as special autarchies, all governed by the public law regime. The non-State sphere is mainly made up of the social organisations and the social organisations of public interest, both set up as associations or foundations, governed by the private law regime.

A. Regulatory and Executive Agencies

Although one of the main objectives of the reform implemented in the 1990s was to develop a market economy, the broad process of transferring public services and goods to the private sector ended up (as it happened in regard to the protection of users of these services) increasing the State's regulatory power.

Thus, regulatory agencies were created in addition to the Administrative Council for Business Defence, the Department of Business Law, the Department of Business Management and the Central Bank, which already had the task of overseeing the market.

In Brazil, these agencies were implemented by Law 9,649/1998 and later regulated by Decrees 2,487/1998 and 2,488/1998. Under these statutes, the executive agencies would be no more than a new type of classification attributed to certain governmental agencies and foundations which were to be subject to a strategic restructure, a development plan and a management contract under the relevant Ministry's supervision.

In pursuit of these institutional goals, some governmental agencies would be given regulatory powers, while others would be involved in the performance of public services where 'State power' would be necessary. The former are called regulatory agencies and the latter executive agencies.

Given that these agencies were implemented in a period of fiscal, credibility and government crises, the agencies received greater autonomy from the government bodies. Motivated by the principle of efficiency and the effort to administer the bureaucracy, the idea was to distance these agencies from political influences which, in theory, would favour a more technical (objective) management, rather than one that is conducive to political pressure.

Hence, regulatory agencies in Brazil are made up of entities of a governmental nature (a government agency or foundation) with regulatory authority and special autonomy over governmental bodies. Lacking regulatory power, executive agencies may be defined as special governmental agencies because of their link with the direct administration (as a management contract). As special governmental agencies, they were granted a differentiated regulatory approach with regards to: (a) the procedure for hiring and firing managers; (b) immunity in the administrative review of their acts by bodies or authorities of the direct administration; (c) financial autonomy, including guaranteed revenues; and (d) the system of private authority transferred from the direct administration (in the case of regulatory agencies, including the authority to issue regulations).

af … ntial order,
tr … cy adminis-
j … lable) court
I … due process
… ar is required
… regulated by

… ermitted. This
… nd ministerial
… thority that is

… tonomy of the
… to contingency
… he possibility of
… inspections they

… et up regulatory
… for the National
… ns Agency,[16] the
… ce Agency[18] and

… nt, single agencies
… created to regulate,
… he respective State
… e the object of con-

… rned solely with the
… of their operation.
… oncession of Public

14. There is no generic law for the institution of the agencies.
15. Implemented by Law 9,427/1996 regulated by Decree Law 2,335/1997.
16. Implemented by Law 9,472/1997 regulated by Decree Law 2,338/1997.
17. Implemented by Law 9,478/1997 regulated by Decree Law 2,455/1998.
18. Implemented by Law 9,782/1999 regulated by Decree Law 3,029/1999.
19. Implemented by Law 11,182/2005.
20. See, for example, the Regulatory Agency for Public Services delegated by the State of Rio de Janeiro (Implemented by Law 2,686/1997) and the State Agency for Regulation of Public Services of Minas Gerais (Implemented by Law 12,999/1998). Examples of sector agencies are the one from São Paulo State – which created the Commission for Public Energy Services (Implemented by Complementary Law 833/97) and the Regulatory Agency for Public Transport Services of the State of São Paulo (Implemented by Complementary Law 914/2002) – and the municipality of Cachoeiro de Itapemirim – which created the Municipal Regulation Agency for Sanitation Services (Implemented by Law 4,798/1999).

Service Law,[21] created a Defence Committee of Users of Telecommunications Services (implemented by Resolution 107/1999) by establishing in detail the users' rights, making the deliberative sessions of the Directors Council public and setting mandatory guarantees and rights on the contract of concession and the obligations of the users. The fourteen-member Committee must have seven representatives of users from various segments of the telecommunications sector.[22]

B. Social Organisations

Social organisations were implemented by Law 9,637/1998. This law did not specifically define what they were but established that 'the executive branch may qualify as social organisations, private, non-profit legal entities whose activities are focused on teaching, scientific research, technological development, protection and preservation of the environment, culture and health, meeting the requirements set in this Law'.[23]

Scholarly writings have defined social organisations as 'private, non-profit legal entities, focused on activities of relevant social value, independent of concessions or permissions from public authorities, created [. . .] according to the model set by law, recognised, inspected and fostered by the State'.[24] It seems more appropriate to think of social organisations as private legal entities, qualified as such by the public authorities, which operate without profit in the areas of education, scientific research, technological development, protection of the environment, culture and health, with a structure set by law.

Created to make up the 'non-State public space', these organisations began to operate after liquidation of public bodies or entities that originally performed these tasks. Under Law 9,637/1998, social organisations can receive funds, public goods, have civil servants and, in some cases, have the same name of the liquidated entity or body.

---

21. Law 9,897/1995.
22. Under the terms of Art. 5 of the Internal Code of the Committee referred to (Annex to Resolution 107, of 26 Feb. 1999), with one representative from the Department of Consumer Protection and Defence at the Ministry of Justice, one representative of users of the commuted fixed line telephone service (STFC of individual use), one representative of users of commuted fixed line telephone service (STFC of collective use), one representative of users of mobile services, one representative of users of mass communications services, one representative of users of other telecommunications services and one representative of telecommunications service providers.
23. Article 1.
24. Paulo Modesto, *Reforma administrativa e marco legal das organizações sociais no Brasil. II Inter-American Congress on Reform of the State and Public Administration* (Venezuela: CLAD, 1977), 2.

Formed in the form of a private association or foundation, these entities are directed by a hybrid council made up of representatives from public authorities[25] and civil society, with their administration regulated by a management contract that monitors public resources to achieve targets set out by the government.

To guarantee the use of these resources, observing the principle of finality, the law provides that the only entities that may be qualified as social organisations are those whose articles of association include: (a) the social nature of their objectives; (b) the mandatory investment of financial surplus resources in the development of their own activities; (c) the prohibition of the distribution of assets (including in case of resignation, withdrawal or death of an associate or member of the entity); and (d) a provision to add all the assets of bequests or donations, in the event of liquidation or disqualification, to the assets of another social organisation.

The wide discretion granted to the executive branch in determining which entities can be qualified as social organisations has been a point of considerable criticism. Regardless of the complete satisfaction of all legal requirements, public officials may still refuse the classification as a social organisation.

There are a number of benefits granted to entities that are qualified as social organisations. These include (a) tax exemptions; (b) permission to use public goods; (c) subsidies and contributions received from public authorities; (d) waiver of compliance with bidding requirements for entering into contracts with public entities; and (e) the right to obtain transfers of civil servants free of payment by the social organisation.

C. Public Interest Organisations of Civil Association

Created to establish partnerships with public authorities to perform activities of social nature, these entities, with the social organisations, also make up the 'non-public State space'. Unlike social organisations, public interest organisations of civil association are not successors to the liquidation of State bodies or entities, but are set up out of the qualification of pre-existing private associations and foundations. They are established by a civil (non-profit) association, and are able to enter into a partnership with the Brazilian State to provide services of a social nature.

Law 9,790/1999, which set up the public interest organisations, also did not define what they were. Article 1 of the Law merely states that 'private, non-profit legal entities may qualify as public interest organisations from civil associations as long as the respective social objectives and articles of association meet the requirements implemented by this law'.

According to the drafters of the bill, the aim was to classify and qualify organisations from the 'third sector' (i.e., non-government institutions and similar organisations) and allow them to enter into partnerships with public authorities in

25. The formation of the administrative board of social organisations is established in Art. 3 of the Law, which expressly requires the presence of '20% to 40% (twenty to forty percent) of members to be representatives of the public authority, defined by the entity's statute'.

the performance of social services. Additionally, it was hoped that the organisations could implement adequate mechanisms of social control and liability to assure that State resources would be administered by the third-sector entities and used for public purposes as established in the terms of the partnership.

With the progressive reduction of State assistance to the public, the intent was to convert more qualified non-governmental organisations into partnerships with the State providing services that were not attractive to the private sector. Such services, under the terms of Article 3 of this law, involved the following areas: social work; culture; defence and conservation of historic and artistic heritage; education; health; food and nutritional safety; environmental protection; economic and social development; poverty fighting; citizenship rights; promotion of ethics, peace, human rights and democracy; research, production and publication of technical and scientific knowledge.

Unlike what happened with the regulation of social organisations, lawmakers allowed the organisational structure of those qualified entities to be more liberal, only requiring 'the constitution of the fiscal council or equivalent body, with the authority to express an opinion on the financial and accounting performance reports; on asset transactions that were carried out and to issue opinions for superior bodies of the entity'.[26]

Lawmakers held a similar position regarding the role of these entities, establishing the necessary controlling measures regarding the destination of public resources. With this aim, Law 9,790/1999 established a duty to maintain formal accounts, carry out independent audits and render accounts to public control bodies, under the terms of Article 70 of the Federal Constitution. The agreement between public authorities and these entities, under the terms of Article 9 of Law 9,790/1999, is the partnership agreement, which has the same nature as the management contract for social organisations.

Unlike the qualification process for social organisations, the administrative act that grants the classification of an entity as a public interest organisation from civil association, is not discretionary in nature. This means that the unjustified denial of a request for qualification is considered to be an abuse of the law and is therefore subject to judicial review.

After some years, the qualification of organisations of civil association was widely accepted by entities in the third sector in Brazil. Currently, thousands of qualified entities are applying for governmental resources for the development of activities that justify their creation, and thus require special attention from public control bodies.

D. Autonomous Social Services

Autonomous social services, like the organisations covered in the previous sections, are private legal entities, which do not perform public service delegated by

26. Article 4(III) of Law 9,790/1,999.

the State, although it does collaborate with it. As Meirelles teaches, there are entities 'implemented by law, with private legal personality, to assist or educate certain social categories or professional groups, not for profit, being maintained by a budget or partial tariff contributions [...] with their own administration and patrimony, covered in the form of conventional private institutions or peculiar to the performance of their institutional roles'.[27]

Known in Brazil as 'system S entities,' the Federal Constitution of 1946 created the autonomous social services based on Decree Laws 9,403/1946 and 9,853/1946 which conferred, respectively, the National Confederation of Industry and the National Confederation of Commerce the role of creating, organising and defining the Social Service Industry (SESI) and the Social Service for Commerce (SESC).

After four decades from the creation of other autonomous social services, the Federal Government created the Autonomous Social Service for Social Pioneers,[28] with structural differences from the other entities mentioned above.

Social services of the first type are entities that focus specifically on social, educational or technical need of a limited field of certain social categories or professional groups. This allows them to ignore the principle of universality of access, unlike the social services included in the second type.

As can be inferred, social services of the second type are essentially maintained by their own resources and government grants (either from public funds or loans taken out externally or internally). These grants are controlled by public bodies under the terms of Article 70 and following in the Federal Constitution. Social services of the first type are legally authorised for partial fee collection, using the resources obtained for the maintenance or performance of their institutional activities.

Regardless of the funding model used, these entities are not subordinated to the State, even though they are still linked to the Ministry in their area of operation. This autonomy, however, does not rule out the liability of their managers' acts or change the equivalent status of their civil servants to public officials for administrative and criminal law purposes.

Autonomous social services do not enjoy administrative, fiscal or procedural privileges.

IV. PUBLIC ADMINISTRATION IN TRANSITION: THE NATIONAL PRIVATISATION PROGRAMME

In considering the administrative structure, the constant transition of State bodies and entities in the market realm cannot be overlooked, as a result of the privatisation process in Brazil.

---

27. Meirelles, cited work, 359.
28. Law 8,246/1991.

The initial step in the process of privatisation was taken in the 1980s, with the issue of Decree Law 86,215/1981, which regulated the transformation, transfer and deactivation of small companies controlled by the Federal Government. It specifically dealt with companies that were taken over by the State as a result of debt default with public entities or those who were going through bankruptcy.

In 1985, with the issue of Decree Law 91,991/1985, partial privatisation of companies under Brazilian State control was included, in addition to the closure of several companies.

The National Privatisation Program (*Plano Nacional de Desestatização*, 'PND') was implemented through Law 8,031/1990. The Programme provided that the following were to be privatised: companies controlled, directly or indirectly, by the Brazilian State and implemented by law or by act from the executive branch, and those created by the private sector which passed into direct or indirect control of the Brazilian State.[29]

With the issuing of Decree Law 1,068/1994, minority shareholdings owned by foundations, governmental agencies, State companies and other entities controlled directly or indirectly by the Brazilian State were included in the privatisation process.

With the issue of Administrative Ruling 970/1995, the terms contained in Article 2 of Law 8,031/1990 were extended, taking over the public services which were the object of concession, permission or authorisation as well as the public and State financial institutions that had their social capital shares dispossessed in the form of Decree Law 2,321/1987.

With the issuing of Law 9,461/1997, the possibility of workers using their Unemployment Guarantee Fund (FGTS)[30] holdings to acquire securities in the scope of the PND was introduced.

According to the latest official report, during the period between 1990 and 2005, the PND (only considering the federal level) turned seventy-one State companies into private companies within the steel, chemical, petrochemical, electrical, railroad, port, finance, fertilizer and mining sectors. This total involved the privatisation of thirty-one companies controlled by the State, twenty-six sales of minority shareholdings, seven concessions and seven leases.

V. PUBLIC ADMINISTRATION IN TRANSFORMATION: EFFICIENCY AND CONSENSUAL CONTRACT

Considering that there is a relationship of mutual involvement between structure and function of government, the Brazilian administrative structure is also subject to transformations arising from changes to its functions. Among these, perhaps the most significant – by virtue of their impact on the legal system and the influence on

29. In this period, there was a profound change in the system of privatisations, with emphasis on increasing the treasury credit through the so-called 'rotten assets', in addition to the elimination of restrictions on foreign capital.
30. Refer to the Labour Law chapter.

the constitution of a new administrative model: (a) the recent constitutional adoption of the principle of efficiency; and (b) the vigorous deepening of constitutional and statutory nature of the principle of popular participation.

Constitutional amendment 19/1998, by triggering these modifications, distanced itself from the administrative reform of 1936, 1967 and 1988, giving rise not only to a new administrative concept, but also to the possibility of profound structural transformations in the Brazilian public administration.

In Brazil, two government projects represent this option for greater efficiency: the Quality and Participation Program and the Restructuring and Quality of Ministries Program. The former is guided by the 'strategic decision to opt for the citizen-client, a decision that serves as a general principle on how to take all decisions and actions to pursue the excellence in Public Administration'.[31] The latter is focused on the most general implementation of this program by the various ministers, particularly regarding the distribution of functions among the federal units and the organisational changes.

Regarding the administrative reasoning, the principle of efficiency leads to improved administrative acts. These acts are regulated by a planning methodology based on private practices, which defines missions, objectives and targets. Additionally, *ex post* control of private practices are established to substitute the traditional procedural controls. Therefore, among the objectives of the State reform, the text states 'substituting the bureaucratic, rigid public administration focused on a priori control of the processes, for managerial public administration, based on a posteriori control of the results and the competition of administration'.

Aside from increasing the contractual administrative relations (management contract, partnership terms, agreement, consortia), the great focus on efficiency has impacted the Brazilian administrative structure. The primary effects of this impact are: (a) the reduction of the administrative and economic direct involvement by the direct administration; (b) the granting of greater autonomy for indirect administration entities that have independent legal capacity, although with public ownership; (c) the growth in the number of regulatory agencies, specifically at State and Municipal levels of government; (d) the reengineering of State companies for new demands from the market; (e) the proliferation of partial State entities, with the enlargement from the non-State public sphere; and (f) the expansion of the concessions of service and public works to the private sector.

Consequently, the expansion of the principle of popular participation, first implemented by the Federal Constitution in 1988 and then by the Constitutional amendment 19/1998, also offers opportunity for profound transformations within the Brazilian administrative structure. Distinct from what has conventionally been called efficiency, the expansion of the principle of popular participation produces more results, affecting the internal structure of the bodies and entities of the public administration. Popular participation in Brazilian law represent affects the structuring of decision-making processes, the division of tasks, and the distribution of authority and the decision-making.

---

31. Pereira, *Reforma do Estado para a Cidadania*, 220.

Based on the understanding that popular participation is part of the principles present in the Federal Constitution, the Congress has consistently and perhaps paradigmatically produced many opportunities for participation in the structure of the public administration. The most common opportunities are reserved for committees made up of representatives from civil society, organised in the form of councils or commissions. To illustrate the quantity of bodies of this nature in the Brazilian administrative structure, it is important to mention those created in the federal scope starting in the 1990s including the Health Council, the National Council for Social Assistance, the Management Council for National Worker Registration, the National Council for Children's and Adolescents Rights, the Social Communication Council, the FGTS Administrative Council, the National Monetary Council, the Information Technology and Automation Council, among many others. Aside from these options of participation, public ombudsmen in the form of administrative units were created in the internal structure of the direct and indirect administration. Brazilian ombudsmen are focused on the defence of citizens' legitimate interests and rights before acts performed by the public administration, and who also control the performance of administrative functions by the State.

Although not directly relevant to the structural aspect of the public administration, it is important to mention the adoption of new instruments of popular participation such as the public hearing (*audiência pública*)[32] and the public query (*consulta pública*).[33]

With the strengthening of the principle of participation in Brazil, the idea of participative budget (*orçamento participativo*) arose. Created in 1989 and today fully disseminated among Brazilian Municipalities and States, this instrument gathers a set of strategies focused on making civil society's participation in the public budgeting process more direct and effective. The Participative Budget Council has special relevance as it consists of representatives of society in general, with independent authority to draft the internal rules for the participative budget preparation process and to define the overall regional and technical criteria of resource distribution in the territory where it acts.

Although not regulated by federal law, the participative budget gained legal standing with the issue of the Fiscal Responsibility Law[34] which, in Article 48, established mandatory transparency in the drafting process of budgetary laws. Also contributing to the strengthening of the institution was the position taken by the Federal Supreme Court in considering the hearings by State powers to gather public investment proposals from citizens as constitutional in order to draft public budgets.

The acceptance of the principle of efficiency and the greater influence of the principle of popular participation brought about by Constitutional Amendment

---

32. Included in various legal documents, among them Law 8,666/1993 (the Procurement Law), Resolution CONAMA 9/1987 (environmental regulation), Law 8,689/1993 (public health), Law 9,427/1996 (electrical power), Law 9,478/1997 (petroleum), among others.
33. Set out, for example, in Law 9,472/1997 (telecommunications) and in Law 9,784 (administrative proceedings).
34. Complementary Law 101/2000.

19/1998, has had consequences both at the structural level and as well as at the administrative law regime level. At the structural level, there are two tendencies moving in opposite directions: (a) a retraction of state influence via the compulsory migration of the bodies and entities of the Public Administration to the private and non-State areas; and (b) the expansion of the state influence via the creation of spaces for participation outside of the existing public and private bodies.

As for the administrative law regime there are, on the one hand, a growing adoption of management models with the predominance of technical criteria for assessment of competencies and, on the other, the greater use of group decision-making processes with the participation of civil society.

As such, the Brazilian experience has shown – although through forward and backward steps – that it is possible to combine these different tendencies: greater administrative efficiency with more effective popular participation (here understood as the means of improving the administrative activities to the public or collective public interest).

Selected Bibliography

In English

C.D. Cole, *Comparative Constitutional Law: Brazil and the United States* (2nd edn, Vandeplas Publishing, 2008).
J. Dolinger, 'The Influence of American Constitutional Law on the Brazilian Legal System' (1990) 38, no. 4 *American Journal of Comparative Law* 803.
C. Souza, *Constitutional Engineering in Brazil: The Politics of Federalism and Decentralization* (St Martin's Press, New York, 1997).
A. Stepan. 'Brazil's Decentralized Federalism: Bringing Government Closer to the Citizens?' (2000) 129, no. 2 *Daedlus* 145.
M.M. Prado, 'The Challenges and Risks of Creating Independent Regulatory Agencies: A Cautionary Tale from Brazil' (2008) 41 *Vanderbilt Journal of Transnational Law* 435.

In Portuguese

A. de Moraes, *Direito Constitucional Administrativo* (Atlas, São Paulo, 2002).
C.A.B. de Mello, *Curso de Direito Administrativo.* (21st edn, Malheiros, São Paulo, 2006).
H. Meirelles et al., *Direito Administrativo Brasileiro* (29th edn, Malheiros, São Paulo, 2004).
L.C.B. Pereira, *Reforma do Estado para a Cidadania: A Reforma Gerencial Brasileira na Perspectiva Internacional* (34th edn, ENAP, Brasília, 2002).
M. Justen Filho, *Curso de Direito Administrativo* (4th edn, Saraiva, São Paulo, 2009).

Chapter 4

Family and Succession Law

Claudia Lima Marques & Lucas Lixinski[*]

I. INTRODUCTION

In the past, family law in Brazil was strongly influenced by the Catholic Church (monogamy, marriage by consensus of the spouses, religious marriage and 'civil' secular marriage, prohibition of marriage among relatives, indissolubility of marriage). Brazil resisted the world's changes to family law until 1977, when the Constitution was changed to allow for divorces.[1]

Brazilian Family and Succession Law is mainly contained in the Civil Code. Indeed, the rules in the Brazilian Civil Code of 1916 (which was replaced by the Civil Code of 2002) had remained relatively undisturbed for decades, but after 1950, the status of women and the status of children born outside of marriage were radically altered, mostly by the courts and by some special legislation. The modernisation of Brazilian law continued with the Brazilian Constitution of 1988 coming into force and ultimately with the much improved Brazilian Civil Code of 2002.

* Claudia Lima Marques, Professor of International Law Federal University of Rio Grande do Sul, Brazil; LLD (Heidelberg) LLM (Tübingen), LLB (UFRGS). Lucas Lixinski, PhD Candidate, European University Institute, Italy; LLM Central European University, Hungary; LLB (UFRGS)

1. Constitutional Amendment 9/1977 and Law 6,515/1977.

Fabiano Deffenti & Welber Barral (eds), *Introduction to Brazilian Law*, pp. 49–69.

Equal rights for men and women have transformed asset division within the family[2] and the rise of rights of children has changed the legal notion of family, assuring the same family rights and equality for all offspring, whether born inside or outside of marriage. The notion of family, no longer linked to legal marriage but rather to the *affection* between the participants, has led to the emergence of new legal rules. It is now recognised that a family can be built with only one parent ('single-parent' family or *família monoparental*), opening the window to joint custody (*guarda conjunta*) of children. The person is the central focus in the legal system, as several rights in family relations are recognised and linked to cultural identity.[3] The influence of international instruments and the constitutional recognition of rights are strongly felt in family relations.

Current Brazilian family law, just as is the case with contemporary private law in general, is filled with positive rules known as general clauses (*cláusulas gerais*), that is, rules that state principles and are of an open nature that require judicial interpretation on a case-by-case basis.

II. FAMILY LAW

A. The Foundations of the Law Concerning Man-Woman Relationships

Perhaps the most basic tenet of Brazilian family law today is equality between man and woman. The principle of equal treatment and non-discrimination by reasons of gender is widely recognised in international human rights instruments,[4] and it is also said to be a norm of *jus cogens* status, that is, a norm of international law to which all of the international community is bound, regardless of treaties, and for the protection of which all of the members of the international community are responsible.[5]

The first steps towards equality between man and woman in family law were given by the Married Woman Statute (*Estatuto da Mulher Casada*),[6] yet the man remained at the head of the family (*chefe de família*) and maintained parental power (*pátrio poder*). Total equality between men and women in all rights and

2. See about the influence of American law, J. Dolinger, 'The influence of American Constitutional Law on the Brazilian Legal System' (1990) *The American Journal of Comparative Law*, 835.
3. See E. Jayme, 'Multicultural Society and Private Law – German Experiences' in Saggi, Conferenze e Seminari (1999) *Centro di Studi e Ricerche di Diritto Comparato e Strangiero* 33.
4. See, for example, as applicable to Brazil: Art. 2 of the Universal Declaration of Human Rights; Art. 2(1) of the International Covenant on Civil and Political Rights; Art. 2(2) of the International Covenant on Social, Economic and Cultural Rights; Art. 1(1) of the Inter-American Convention on Human Rights; Art. 6 of the Inter-American Convention on the Prevention, Punishment and Eradication of Violence against Women (stating that gender-based discrimination is a form of violence against women).
5. See 'Inter-American Court of Human Rights' *Juridical Condition and Rights of the Undocumented Migrants*. Advisory Opinion OC-18/03 of 17 Sep. 2003, para. 101.
6. Law 4,121/1962.

duties in family law was recognised by the Constitution of 1988, and was later inserted into the Civil Code of 2002.

One of the reasons why it took so long for Brazilian law to recognise equality between men and women in family law was due to the influence exerted by canonical law on family law. This shift of focus, that no longer views the family as under control of the man, can be seen as well in the change of the expression 'patriarchal power' (*pátrio poder*) to 'family power' (*poder familiar*).

Another innovation brought about by the Civil Code of 2002 is the systematic separation between personal and property rights in marital relations. The previous Civil Code of 1916 did not address this distinction. This innovation can be seen as a reflection of the idea that private law is no longer concerned only with material interests arising out of legal relations, but is also concerned with protecting the human rights of the parties involved.

Also, current Brazilian law sets out rules for stable unions (*uniões estáveis*) which are de facto relationships between a man and a woman. These rules were brought about in case law in response to a social urge coming from the existence of unions where the parties did not marry, either because they simply chose not to do so, or because they came from previous unions given that in Brazil marriages could not be totally dissolved until 1977 (with the passing of the Divorce Statute).

Another basic concept of Brazilian Family Law is the recognition by law of unions solely comprised of a man and a woman, excluding gay and lesbian unions. This is provided in Article 1,514 of the Civil Code which states: 'Marriage is accomplished in the moment the man and the woman manifest, before the judge, their willingness to establish a marital bond, and the judge declares them married.' Furthermore, the law only recognises, besides marriage, the union between a man and a woman to be a family unit.[7]

Persons of the same sex who wish to 'marry' can informally enter into gay or lesbian cohabitation, but they have no other legal option. They cannot get married because marriage has been defined by both jurists and courts as a voluntary union for life of one man and one woman. Scholars have argued the unconstitutionality of such a provision vis-à-vis the principle of equality. Therefore, as the law currently stands in Brazil, marriage or cohabitation with legal recognition is defined as only involving members of the opposite sex.

B. Marriage: Capacity, Impediments, Qualification, Proof, Effects and Invalidity

To lawfully marry, a man and woman must be at least 16 years old.[8] Brazilian law, however, only considers persons over 18 fully capable (*sui juris*). Therefore, whenever the person is above 16 and below 18, authorisation from both parents

7. Art. 226, para. 3 of the Federal Constitution; Arts 1,723 and 1,727 of the Civil Code. See also Art. 1 of former Cohabitation Law (*Lei da União Estável*), Law 8,971/1994 (repealed).
8. See Arts 1,517 to 1,520 of the Civil Code.

or of the legal representatives of the minor is required. This authorisation can be revoked at any time prior to the marriage celebration. If parents are in disagreement, a court order is necessary. The marriage of a person under 16 can take place in exceptional circumstances, such as in the case of pregnancy or in order to prevent the imposition of criminal liability upon one of the parties (such as in the case of statutory rape).

There are situations that prevent marriage at any time called 'impediments' (*impedimentos*) and situations where a marriage cannot take place until one of the parties fulfils some other obligation, called 'suspending causes' (*causas suspensivas*). *Impedimentos* include: (a) marriages between ascendants and descendants (regardless of whether this bond is natural or legal); (b) marriages between relatives by marriage; (c) marriages between blood relatives by direct line and between siblings; (d) marriages where one or both of the parties is already married to a third person; and (e) marriages where between a person convicted of killing or trying to kill his or her former wife or husband.

Causas suspensivas are usually related to asset disputes involving third parties, such as: (a) the widow or widower who has a child with a deceased de facto spouse, as long as succession proceedings are not finalised; (b) the divorcee, as long as the distribution of marital assets is not concluded; and (c) the legal guardian or attorney or his or her ascendants, descendants, siblings (actual or in-laws) and nephews/nieces, as long as the guardianship (*guarda*) or the attorney and the person with diminished capacity represented by him or her (*curatela*) does not cease and accounts must be rendered. An exception is the prohibition of a widow or woman who had her marriage annulled or declared void to get married within ten months after the death of her husband or the annulment of the marriage. This is because any child born within 300 days after the termination of the marriage is presumed to have originated from that marriage. It is necessary to note that *causas suspensivas* do not prevent the actual celebration of the marriage. However, if the marriage celebration occurs before the relevant existing *causa suspensiva* ceases, the separation of property marriage regime (addressed further below) must be adopted.

A marriage licence application must be signed by both parties and filed at the Registry with proper jurisdiction. The Registry will send the requirement to be analysed by the Attorney General's Department (*Ministério Público*), who will give an opinion before the judge who can make a decision as to whether or not the marriage is possible. Once the marriage licence application procedure is concluded with all of its formalities, a marriage licence valid for ninety days will be issued.[9]

The marriage must be celebrated before a duly registered celebrant, to whom a valid marriage licence must be presented. The celebration will take place at the Registrar's office or another place chosen by the parties and consented to by the granting authority, with all due public attention, witnessed by at least two persons (if the ceremony is in the Registrar's office) or four, otherwise. Four witnesses are also necessary whenever one of the parties cannot write.

---

9. Article 1,532 of the Civil Code and Art. 67 of the Registration of Civil Status Law (*Lei do Registro Civil*), Law 6,015/1973.

A solemn declaration must be made by the celebrant so that the marriage will be deemed to have taken place. This seems to be a residual influence of Roman law, where solemn declarations (formulas) were necessary so that certain acts could produce effects.[10]

Normally, the marriage is concluded by declarations of the bride and groom before the celebrant (before or during the religious ceremony) that they want to enter into a contract of marriage with each other. A marriage concluded without the participation of a celebrant in a religious ceremony can have the same effects, yet Brazilian law requires that the religious marriage ceremony registered in the Civil Status Register within ninety days. The same requirements and impediments of the civil marriage apply to religious marriages.

The marriage is then registered in a public book, containing all data pertaining to the capacity of the husband and wife, the witnesses and the property regime chosen when different from the standard legal regime.[11]

Proof of marriages celebrated within Brazilian territory are made by presentation of the certificate of registration, or, in case of justified loss or absence of this document, by any other admissible means of proof. Marriages of Brazilian citizens celebrated abroad before Brazilian consular authorities must be registered within 180 days from the return of one or both spouses to Brazil. Marriage can also be proven through a court order, in which case the effects will be counted retroactively, since the date the marriage took place, and not from the day the decision was handed down.

The main effect of entering into a marriage is to confer on the man and the woman the condition of spouses, making them both equally responsible for family duties. Various duties are owed by one spouse to the other, namely: reciprocal faithfulness, common cohabitation in the marital domicile, mutual assistance, support, guardianship and education of the children, and mutual respect and consideration. The direction of the marital partnership will be carried out in collaboration by the husband and the wife, reflecting the equality among them. If, however, one of the spouses is in a remote or unknown place, incarcerated for over 180 days, or temporarily unable to express his or her will, the remaining spouse will be deemed to be solely responsible for directing the family, being incumbent upon him or her the administration of all marital property.

Marriages can be deemed void or voidable. Marriages are deemed void when contracted against impediment or by mentally handicapped persons. This declaration of a void marriage can be requested by any interested party, or in case of total incapacity, incest, bigamy and homicide in the family, it can be requested also by the Attorney General's Department (*Ministério Público*).

Marriages will be considered voidable when one of the spouses has not reached the minimum age to marry, when a minor between 16 and 18 does not have the necessary consent from his or her parents, when at least one of the spouses is incapable of consenting, where the celebrant does not have proper powers and in

10. The rule is a copy of Art. 194 of the Civil Code of 1916.
11. See further below and Registration of Civil Status Act (*Lei do Registro Civil*), Law 6,015/1973.

the case of marriage entered into by coercion. Other types of voidable marriages include: (a) where there is an essential mistake in relation to the person of either one of the spouses (an essential mistake is one in relation to the identity, honour or good reputation of the spouse, if subsequent knowledge of these facts makes cohabitation unbearable to the mistaken spouse); (b) lack of knowledge of a crime committed prior to the marriage ceremony that makes cohabitation unbearable; (c) ignorance, prior to the marriage ceremony, of an irreversible physical defect or grave and transmissible disease which is capable of endangering the health of the other spouse or of the offspring; and the ignorance, prior to the marriage ceremony, of serious mental illness that makes cohabitation unbearable to the spouse without prior knowledge. This declaration of void marriage can be requested only by the interested party who acted without prior knowledge or under the threat of violence.

In the cases of both void and voidable marriages, but especially in the latter, the marriage will have effects until the annulment is declared by the court vis-à-vis any offspring and the spouse or spouses who entered the marriage in good faith. Decisions that declare marriages void will have a retrospective effect to the date of celebration of the marriage, but third parties in good faith affected by the marriage will be protected.

C. Matrimonial Property Issues

1. Asset Division and Marital Regimes

Prior to the celebration of the marriage, the fiancés can make stipulations regarding their property. The property regime enters into force from the date of the marriage, and can only be altered after that with court approval, based on a reasoned request from both parties and guarantees the rights of third parties.[12]

A prenuptial contract is made for the choice of a property regime different from that of partial community of property (*comunhão parcial de bens*). This contract must follow certain formalities and be made through public proceedings before a Registrar or else it will be deemed void. The provisions of this contract will only have effects in relation to third parties (*erga omnes* effect) once registered in the Land Titles Registry of the spouses' domicile[13] and it will be rendered unenforceable (*ineficaz*)[14] if the marriage does not take place.

12. Article 1,639 of the Civil Code. The former rule was the impossibility of change of the matrimonial regime, with the exception of Art. 7, para. 5 of the Law of Introduction to the Civil Code (*Lei de Introdução ao Código Civil*, Decree-Law 4,657/1942), where the person becomes a Brazilian citizen.
13. Article 1,657 of the Civil Code. See Art. 167 of the Law of the Public Registrations (*Lei dos Registros Públicos*), Law 6,015/1973.
14. In this, Art. 1,653 of the Civil Code makes a difference between the null and void (*nulo*) prenuptial agreement, due to non-compliance with a formality (Art. 166, IV of the Civil Code) and the unenforceable (*ineficaz*) prenuptial agreement.

There are four main regimes of property provided in the Civil Code:

(1) Separation of property (*separação de bens*): This regime is mandatory in some situations, such as in the marriage of a person over 60 years old, of persons marrying under a *causa suspensiva* and of persons whose right to marry depend on a court order. Under this regime, each spouse is totally free to deal with his or her own property as he or she pleases. Both spouses are required to contribute to the common expenses, proportionately to their income, except if provided otherwise in the prenuptial contract.

(2) Partial community of property (*comunhão parcial de bens*): This regime is the default legal regime, so if no property regime is expressly chosen by the parties, or if the parties' choice is void or ineffective, then the partial community of property regime will apply. All property existing at the time of termination of the marriage is deemed to belong to both spouses. The following property, rights and obligations will be excluded from the scope of marital property: (a) property owned prior to the marriage; (b) property gained by each individual spouse by gift or inheritance; (c) property acquired with funds exclusively belonging to one spouse; (d) obligations existing prior to the marriage; (e) obligations arising from torts, except when the tortious act has provided a benefit for both spouses; (f) personal belongings; (g) fruits of the individual labour of each spouse; and (h) pensions and other similar incomes received by each spouse. The following property will be included in the scope of marital property: (a) property acquired during the marriage, even if registered in the name of only one spouse; (b) property acquired by an unusual event (a lottery award, for example); (c) property gifted over or bequeathed to both spouses; and (d) the fruits of common property or of individual property, gained or pending at the moment cohabitation is terminated by the parties. The administration of marital property in this regime is incumbent upon either spouse and the spouse responsible for the administration is individually liable for acts during the administration that harm third parties. Individual property must be administered by each individual spouse.

(3) Full community of property (*comunhão universal de bens*): Under this regime, all present and future property is deemed to belong to both spouses,[15] except for: (a) property gifted over or inherited with an incommunicability clause (a clause that states that the property belongs solely to its receiver);[16] (b) debts existing prior to the marriage; (c) prenuptial gifts between spouses with an incommunicability clause (except for profits from the property): (d) personal belongings, the fruits of each spouse's work; and (e) pensions and other similar incomes. The same provisions

15. Article 1,667 of the Civil Code. This was the default regular matrimonial regime in Brazil since 1890: Decree 181/1890.
16. This rule does not apply to the fruits from the property.

regarding partial community of property apply in relation to the administration of property.

(4) Participation in goods acquired during the marriage (*participação final nos aquestos*): In this marital regime, each spouse has his or her own property and, when the marriage is terminated, each spouse is entitled to half of all property acquired by the couple during the marriage. The liabilities of one of the spouses, if exceeding that spouse's personal property and half of the matrimonial property do not extend to the remaining property which belongs to the other spouse. If the marriage is terminated, the property excluded from the marital property will be comprised of property prior to the marriage or in replacement of it, property acquired by each spouse through inheritance or gift and debts relating to these. Real estate assets are presumed to belong exclusively to the spouse under whose name it is registered.[17]

Regardless of the chosen matrimonial property regime, both man and wife can freely deal with their own property as they wish[18] and practice all acts necessary to their profession, as well as incur all liabilities necessary for the maintenance of the household, and both spouses are jointly responsible for these liabilities. Except when authorised by the court, one of the spouses cannot, without the other spouse's consent, sell real estate, file court proceedings concerning rights relating to real estate or make gifts over the matrimonial property.

2. Alimony

Alimony (*alimentos*) does not apply exclusively to spouses. The Civil Code provides that alimony must be assessed proportionately to the needs of the person requesting it and the resources of the person paying for it. Alimony should be restricted solely to what is indispensable to a person's subsistence when payment of alimony is caused by fault of the requesting party (e.g., a spouse who gives cause to terminate the marriage due to adultery).[19] Alimony is owed when the person requesting it cannot provide for himself or herself and the person paying alimony can do so without jeopardising the essential needs for his or her own survival. The duty to pay alimony ends if the person receiving it marries or enters into a stable union or concubine relationship (see below). However, the above does not apply if the person receiving the alimony enters into a new relationship.

---

17. Article 1,681 of the Civil Code. This entirely new regime has being very criticised by scholars.
18. The source of the equality principle is Art. 226, para. 5 of the Brazilian Constitution. Some scholars argue that the equality was already achieved by the former law: Statute of the Married Woman (*Estatuto da Mulher Casada*), Law 4,121/1962.
19. Article 1,704, sole paragraph. Scholarly opinion has criticised the use of words like guilty (*culpado*) and suggested the interaction among Arts 1,694, 1,702 and 1,704 of the Civil Code.

D. Cohabitation Out of Wedlock

Cohabitation is recognised under two forms: stable union (*união estável*) and concubine relationships (*concubinagem*). The latter is a residual form, applicable to relationships between man and woman who are prevented from marrying each other.

A stable union is the union between a man and a woman, configured by public, continuous and lasting cohabitation, and established with the goal of constituting a family. It is protected by the Brazilian Constitution, which states that the law should facilitate the conversion of a stable union into marriage. Such facilitation occurs as the Civil Code states that the conversion only requires that both partners in the stable union request the conversion before a judge and the registration of the union in the Civil Registry.[20] Suspending causes for marriage do not prevent the establishment of a stable union. The duties of each partner are those of loyalty, respect and assistance, as well as guardianship, support and education of children. The property regime is deed to be that of partial community.[21]

E. Termination of Marriage

Marriage will end if: (a) one of the spouses dies; (b) the marriage is voided by the courts; (b) through 'court separation' (*separação judicial*); or (d) through the issuing of a divorce decree. Either spouse may file an action for judicial separation, based on: (a) the fault of the other spouse for any action that amounts to a grave breach of any of the marital duties and makes cohabitation unbearable (such as adultery, abandonment of the marital house, conviction for an infamous crime or dishonourable conduct); (b) the fact that for over one year the spouses have not lived together and no longer intend to do so; or (c) based on the fact that one of spouses started suffering from a serious mental illness, manifested after the celebration of marriage, making the continuation of cohabitation impossible, as long as, after two years, the disease has been declared unlikely to be cured. The courts tend to overlook fault as cause of the judicial separation and declare that there is no liability on any party.

The judicial separation is a stage prior to divorce. It imposes the sharing of assets and the termination of the duties of cohabitation and reciprocal faithfulness. After one year of court-declared separation, or two years of proven de facto separation, the separation may be converted into divorce. Divorce does not change the rights of children born during the marriage, and a new marriage of either parent cannot harm the rights of these children.

A recent development in Brazilian Law enables separation and divorce to take effect in Civil Registries, as long as they are consensual.[22] This new law adds a

20. Article 1,726. The origin of this article is in Art. 8 of Law 278/1996.
21. Article 1,725. The origin of this article is in Art. 5 of Law 9,278/1996.
22. See Law 11,441/2007.

provision to the Code of Civil Procedure providing that a public document (*escritura pública*) can be used to determine issues relating to the change of the parties' marital name, the division of property and alimony. Prior to this law being passed, a court order was required.

F. Family Law in Relation to Children

The law regarding the protection of the child, as well as family law in general, has been influenced by fundamental constitutional rights and international human rights treaties. The protection of children has received special attention from lawmakers. At the constitutional level, Article 227 of the Federal Constitution provides: 'It is a duty of the family, society and the State to secure the child and the adolescent, with absolute priority, the right to life, health, food, education, leisure, professional education, culture, dignity, respect, freedom and the family and community livelihood, besides making them safe of all forms of negligence, discrimination, exploitation, violence, cruelty and oppression.'[23]

There is a clear message that the child (understood as every person under 18 years old)[24] is of vital interest to the State and society as a whole. This places the child in a special position, entitling him or her to special protection under the law, considering the child's particular condition as a person in development.[25]

1. The Basis for the Protection of Children as Vulnerable Beings

Brazilian Family law has historically focused on economic and parenting consequences of the traditional nuclear (married) family. The Federal Constitution of 1988 provides for equal rights for all children, whether born in or out of wedlock, biological or adopted. This anti-discrimination principle was a very important vehicle for change in Brazilian family law, abrogating a one-sided economic vision of the family. The most important constitutional values in this respect are the principles of protection for the dignity of the child and, in family issues, the priority ascribed to the best interests of the child. Family law has shifted its focus to include the regulation of non-marital family relationships and single-parent families as well as the human rights of all family members, especially children. Brazilian academic opinion is unanimous in agreeing that the new rules of Brazilian family law has at its centre the child, maintaining the possibility that any family (single-parent families, families by marriage or families without marriage) can give the child the opportunity for full development. The family is no longer seen as a rigid *institution*, but as a 'space' for the exercise of individual and collective human

23. This provision is repeated in Art. 4 the Child and Adolescent Statute.
24. This is the concept generally accepted internationally. See Art. 1 of the Convention on the Rights of the Child.
25. See Art. 6 of the Child and Adolescent Statute.

rights of its members. Indeed, the Child and Adolescent Statute (*Estatuto da Criança e do Adolescente*)[26] provides for the child's right to dignity and especially Article 16, V where a general anti-discrimination principle is secured.

A corollary to the special status of the child is the principle of best interest of the child, which implies that the well-being of the child must be of paramount consideration by the State and all other individuals.[27]

2. Civil Code Rules and Supplementary Legislation

Rules concerning protection of the child are present not only in the Civil Code, but also in other laws, mainly the Child and Adolescent Statute.[28]

a. Protection of Children

The Civil Code is concerned with the protection of children after termination of the marriage, providing that the spouses must ensure, upon termination of the marriage, custody (*guarda*) of the children. In case there is no agreement in this regard, the court must grant custody to the parent who shows the best conditions for exercising parental care, unless there are exceptional circumstances that prevent the application of this principle.[29] The parent without custody of the children still has visiting rights, to enjoy the company of the children and to supervise their maintenance and education, as agreed upon with the other parent or determined by the court. If the guardian enters into a new marriage, there is no automatic change of custody rights – there must be a change of circumstances to persuade the court that a change of custody should be ordered.[30]

b. Filiation

As explained above, all children, regardless of whether they were born in or out of wedlock or adopted enjoy the same status. However, filiation is still an important issue in determining who the parents of the child are. The Civil Code has several types of presumed filiation during wedlock: children born at least 180 days after the establishment of cohabitation; children born within 300 days after the termination of the marital status; children born out of heterologous artificial insemination; children born out of exceeding embryos of homologous insemination; and children born out of heterologous insemination, as long as previously consented to by the husband.[31]

---

26. Law 8,069 of 1990.
27. See Art. 3(1) of the Convention on the Rights of the Child.
28. Law 8,069/1990.
29. Article 1,586 of the Civil Code. These are discretionary matters for the court.
30. Articles 1,588 and 1,589 of the Civil Code.
31. C.L. Marques, 'Assisted Reproduction Technology in South America and the Effect on Adoption' (2000) 35 *Texas International Law Journal* 65.

Adultery committed by a wife is not sufficient grounds for shifting the presumption of paternity, but proof that the husband was infertile at the time of conception is. A father's right to challenge filiation is not subject to a statute of limitations, yet only the father has standing to file the challenge. The child has the right to prove paternity for as long as he or she lives and this action can only be filed by the child, unless he or she dies a minor or lacking legal capacity, in which case his or her heirs have standing.

c. Recognition of Children

The child born out of wedlock can be recognised by the parents, individually or jointly. The recognition of the children is irrevocable and can be achieved by filing a written document to this effect with the competent Civil Registry, by testamentary disposition or by sworn statement made before the court.

Brazilian law emphasises the right of the child to know his or her family background.[32] To this end, it allows for DNA evidence to be tendered and provides that the refusal of the suspect parent to provide samples for DNA testing is to be regarded as a presumption of truth of the allegation. The child who is no longer a minor cannot be recognised unless he or she consents to it and the minor can challenge the recognition within four years after cessation of his or her status as a minor.

d. Adoption

Brazilian Law recognises domestic and international adoption of children and of adults. The adoption of children is governed by the Child and Adolescent Statute[33] and by the Civil Code.[34] The adoption of Brazilian children by foreigners and people domiciled abroad is expressly provided for in the Brazilian Constitution in Article 227, paragraph 5. The article provides that '[a]doption shall be assisted by the Public Power, in accordance with the law, that will establish the cases and conditions where foreigners are involved'. The adoption of adults is allowed only according to the Civil Code rules, by foreigners and people domiciled in Brazil or abroad.

The Child and Adolescent Statute and the Civil Code provide for only one type of adoption – i.e., full adoption – through a court order. The adoption legally inserts the child totally in the adoptive family, with the same rights (including accessory rights) of the other children, disconnecting the child from any bond with his or her natural parents or relatives, except for impediments for marriage.

Adoption is irrevocable and will be effective once the court order is no longer subject to a possible appeal, enabling the adoptee to change his or her name,

32. Article 27 of the Child and Adolescent Statute. See the decision of the Federal Supreme Court in STF, HC 71373-RS/1994 and of the Superior Court of Justice, Resp. 234538-GO/1999.
33. Law 8,069/1990.
34. Law 10,406/2002.

including the first name, subject to the judge's discretion, if there is a request from the adopter.

The Child and Adolescent Statute has as a principle the maintenance of the children's bond with his or her biological parents, which will be attempted through positive administrative actions from the Guardianship Council (*Conselho Tutelar*), during provisional guardianship, by the court and placement in a substitute family.

Adoption through the Child and Adolescent Statute requires the loss of parental power or consent from the biological parents, but the regulation of these matters is found in the Civil Code.

All these adoption cases, and also in international adoptions, equally submit to the principles of the greater interest of the child contained in Article 43 the Child and Adolescent Statute and will only be granted if they present 'real advantages to the adoptee' and, mainly, to be founded upon 'legitimate reasons'. In this sense, the rule of Article 31 must be understood as establishing the inter-country adoption to be an exceptional measure. The major requirement for adoption is the best interest of the child. This major principle overrides the other requirements except for the principle of secondary liability, as we will see below.

As to the general requirements for the adoption of children and adults, those are primarily found in the Child and Adolescent Statute and secondarily in the Civil Code. They are: (a) minimum age of 18 for the adopters; (b) an age difference between the adopter and the adoptee of at least 16 years; (c) marriage or stability in the marital status of the adopters; (d) personal manifested will from the adopters; (e) psychosocial analysis of the adopters,[35] (f) biological parents' consent or a previous action to destitute parental power; (g) manifestation of the adoptee's will if the adoptee is over 12 years old; (h) temporary custody; and (i) the submission to the general principle of the best for the adoptee's welfare.

The adoption of Brazilian children by foreigners and people domiciled abroad is considered such an important issue that the Brazilian Constitution deals specifically with this issue. The principle of superior interest of the child is of particular interest to inter-country adoption. Two corollaries of this principle are the *principle of maintenance of the bond* and the *principle of subsidiarity*. According to the principle of subsidiarity, international adoption can only occur when it is not possible to keep the child within national borders, since an international adoption implies a total detachment of the child from its culture of origin, its language and implies the likelihood that the child will never again have contact with his or her biological family. According to Article 31 the Child and Adolescent Statute, the placement in a foreign substitute family is an exceptional measure, to be attempted only when an in-country adoption is not possible for that child. In other words, the Child and Adolescent Statute gives priority to adoptions within Brazil over international adoptions. This modern international adoption system of the 1990s became known as 'intercultural adoption', as opposed to the previous adoption system, which was known as 'humanitarian adoption'.

35. In the case of adoption of children, see Arts 50, 51 and 167 of the Child and Adolescent Statute.

The influence of the Hague Convention of 1993 on the issuing of Decree 3,087/1999, has had a great impact in the Brazilian legal system precisely for not being a convention with classic conflict rules, but rather a convention that prioritises administrative and procedural rules. From there it derives its great success, because it goes further than modifying national rules in Brazil, be it the rules present in the Child and Adolescent Statute or those of the Civil Code, the Hague Convention of 1993 consolidated national rules and the regime of centralisation and secondary application of international adoption rules currently in force in Brazil. It has also preserved the conflict rules, present in the Law of Introduction to the Civil Code (*Lei de Introdução ao Código Civil*),[36] and of civil procedure, present in the Child and Adolescent Statute and in the Code of Civil Procedure (*Código de Processo Civil*).[37] The result is a pluralism of sources to determine the regime of international adoption in Brazil.

The rules concerning international adoption of minors (0 to 18 years old) are currently found in the Child and Adolescent Statute. This statute provides for the adoption under State supervision, special rules for adoption by foreigners, equality of rights between adopted children and other children, responsible parenthood and priority for the child and his or her fundamental rights.

The Child and Adolescent Statute, only allows that Brazilian children leave the country after there is a final decision on the adoption and imposes criminal sanctions over any attempt that does not obey this prohibition.[38]

e. Administration of a Child's Assets by the Parents

The father and the mother, while exercising family power, can use children's property but must maintain it for the children under their custody. The parents must represent their children until they are 16 years old (i.e., until they are relatively capable) and assist them until they are 18 or emancipated (i.e., of full legal capacity).

Parents must jointly decide questions relative to their children's property and in any case of disagreement, either of them can resort to the courts. The parents cannot take any action beyond the mere maintenance of the child's property unless it is clearly in the best interests of the child or pursuant to a court order.

36. Decree-Law 4,657/1942.
37. Law 5,869/1973.
38. Arts 85 and 239 of the Child and Adolescent Statute. Under Brazilian law there are three crimes connected to the subject: illegal sending of children and adolescents abroad (Art. 239 of the Child and Adolescent Statute), pecuniary and criminal intermediation in adoption (Art. 239 of the Child and Adolescent Statute) and false birth register made by the adopter, provided in the Criminal Code (Art. 242 of the Child and Adolescent Statute).

f. Guardianship

Guardianship is imposed upon the children: when their parents die or are considered legally absent;[39] or (b) when the parents lose family power. The guardian must provide for the education, protection and food needs of the minor and fulfil all other parental duties. The child may testify if he or she is over 12 years of age to assist the court in relation to the guardianship decision. The guardian must also represent the minor under 16 years of age and assist the minor between 16 and 18 years old, receive all income and pensions of the minor and administer the child's money to provide for his or her subsistence and education, as well as the maintenance and improvement of his or her property. If authorised by the court, the guardian can pay the minor's debts, accept inheritance on behalf of the minor, sell movable property and file court proceedings. The guardian cannot, however, buy for himself or herself property belonging to the minor, gifts over the minor's property or become a creditor to the minor.

The guardian must also administer the child's property, and will be responsible for it, signing a document where all assets and their respective market values are listed. The guardian can be remunerated for his or her work, but he or she is liable for all economic losses he or she causes to the minor. The guardian cannot have under his or her possession any of the minor's money that is not necessary for the support, education and administration of the minor's assets, and must biannually render accounts of administration of the minor's funds to the court.

The guardian must be named by the parents in a will or any other notarised document (called testamentary guardians, *guardiães testamentários*). If the parents do not name a guardian, the minor's blood relatives are to exercise the guardianship in the following order: firstly the descendants, and in the absence or inability of these collateral relatives, until the third degree (called legitimate guardians, *guardiães legítimos*). The court will appoint a guardian in case there is no named or legitimate guardian, or these are excluded, excused or removed from guardianship.

Some people cannot be appointed guardians. These are: (a) those who cannot freely manage their own assets; (b) those who, at the moment of constitution of the guardianship, are debtors or creditors of the minor, or parents, children or spouses to these; (c) the enemies of the minor or of his or her parents; (d) those convicted of burglary, theft and certain other types of crimes; (e) those by the nature of their duties cannot be guardians. The following persons can be excused from the duty of guardianship: (a) married women; (b) persons over 60 years old; (c) those who already have three children under their guardianship or custody; (d) persons who live far from where the guardianship must be exercised; (e) military personnel on duty; and (f) persons who have already been guardians or curators. The excuse

39. The procedure for declaration of absence is provided in Arts 22 to 39 of the Civil Code. An absent person is person who is missing from her domicile and is not heard from, not leaving a person to look after her interests while away (Art. 22 of the Civil Code).

must be presented within ten days of the court appointment, and if the judge does not accept it, the guardianship will be deemed to be effective even while there is an appeal pending.

The guardianship ends: (a) when the minor becomes *sui juris* by reaching 18 years of age or being emancipated; (b) if family power is gained upon him or her through recognition or adoption; (c) when the guardian's term expires; or (d) when he or she is removed or legitimately excused. The guardian's term must last at least two years.

g. *Curatorship*

Curatorship is exercised in similar terms to guardianship, except when the curator is the spouse under the full community of property regime, who is exempted of rendering accounts of his or her actions, unless determined otherwise by the court. Those who are mentally ill and by virtue of the illness cannot exercise legal acts, who cannot express their will or who have incomplete mental development, are mentally handicapped, alcoholics or addicted to toxic substances, or even the prodigals, are subject to curatorship. Curators will also be appointed to an unborn child (*nasciturus*), if the father dies during the pregnancy and the mother for any reason cannot exercise parental power. A person with a physical disability can also have a curator appointed.

The declaration of incapacitation of those persons must be requested by their parents or guardians, the spouse, a relative or the Attorney General's Department (*Ministério Público*). The *Ministério Público* will only intervene in cases of serious mental illness, in the absence of other people entitled to seek the declaration of incapacitation or if those people entitled to seek the declaration of incapacitation are incapable. The interdiction must be declared by a court decision that will be effective once given, although an appeal can still be filed.

The legitimate curator is the spouse, or in the absence of a spouse, an ascendant or descendant, in this order. If there is no one in these categories able to exercise curatorship, the court will appoint someone at its discretion.

h. *Alimony to Children*

Alimony can also be owed to the children, as well as other relatives. The same provisions regarding spousal alimony are applicable.[40] In the case of judicial separation, each spouse must contribute to the maintenance of the children in proportion to their resources. When the person receiving alimony is a minor, however, the alimony must include the necessary funds for the education of the child.

---

40. See further above.

III. SUCCESSION LAW

A. Attribution of Successor Status

The process of succession takes place in the last place of domicile of the deceased (the deceased) and will be determined by law or with the directions provided in a will (subject to the mandatory provisions provided by the Civil Code).

The Brazilian Civil Code establishes two types of heirs: the legitimate heirs (*herdeiros legítimos*), who are also known as necessary heirs (*herdeiros necessários*); and the testamentary heirs (*herdeiros testamentários*). The legitimate heirs are presumed beneficiaries and inherit the deceased's estate in the absence of a will, or when part of the estate has not been included in the will, for that part, or in the event of a null or expired will.

Legitimate heirs must inherit at least 50% of the estate, regardless of the terms of the will. This provision aims at protecting the interests of children. However, this presumption can be rebutted if the beneficiary: (a) was the perpetrator, conspirator or accessory of wilful murder of the deceased, the deceased's spouse or de facto partner, ascendants or descendants; (b) criminally defamed the deceased or the deceased's spouse or de facto partner or otherwise offended the deceased's honour or that of his or her spouse or de facto partner; (c) inhibited or prevented the deceased from freely disposing of his or her assets as he or she wished.

The estate is treated as one property until the court orders its final distribution (*partilha*). The beneficiaries' right is merely an expectancy (*pretensão de direito*) that can be transferred to a third party, even though the other beneficiaries have a right of first refusal over the acquisition of these rights over non-beneficiaries.

The inheritance has to be accepted, either expressly, through a written declaration, or impliedly. A beneficiary can only waive his or her rights if a court so declares or if the beneficiary expressly renounces his or her rights in a document drafted by a notary. If the waiver affects the rights of the beneficiary's creditors, the creditors can, once authorised by a court, accept the inheritance in the name of the beneficiary/debtor.

If the deceased dies intestate or without a legitimate heir, the estate will be given to a curator, who will administer it until some qualified heir claims it or until it is declared as escheat (*vacante*), in which case it will become the property of the city or federal district, or of the Union, if the relevant assets are located in a federal territory.

B. Legitimate Succession

The legitimate succession occurs where the deceased dies intestate or with a will (a will can only deal with 50% of the deceased's total asset pool). The legitimate heirs, to whom 50% of the estate is necessarily reserved, are the descendants, ascendants and surviving spouse excluding the collateral relatives. The Civil Code establishes a hierarchical order of precedence of legitimate heirs.

The presence of heirs in one of the early classes described by the Civil Code excludes the rights of those in the lower ranked classes. In order, these classes are: (a) descendants, simultaneously with the surviving spouse, unless the matrimonial regime is that of complete separation of property or full communion of property; (b) the ascendants, simultaneously with the surviving spouse; (c) the surviving spouse; and (d) the collateral relatives, until the fourth degree.

The surviving spouse will only be regarded as an heir if at the time of the deceased's death the couple were not separated, judicially or in fact. The surviving spouse, regardless of what happens to the estate, is entitled to continue inhabiting in the residence where he or she lived with the deceased. And when the surviving spouse is in the same class of beneficiaries as the descendants, he or she is entitled to the same share as the descendants, as long as the share is not less than 25% of the total asset pool, a share that is necessarily reserved for the surviving spouse where the surviving spouse is an ascendant to the descendants of the deceased.

The descendants of the same line have the same rights; the ones in different lines have their rights to be determined in accordance with a formula that can be explained through the following example: if the deceased had four children and no spouse, and at the time of death one of the children had died, leaving behind two grandchildren, each of the surviving children is entitled to one-fourth of the estate, while the grandchildren share equally what would be the entitlement of their dead parent, that is, each grandchildren is entitled to one-eighth of the estate.

C. Testate Succession

The testate succession takes place when there is a will. Any capable person can dispose of his or her property after death, as long as it does not prejudice the legitimate heirs, as explained above. A will is a unilateral legal act, revocable, personal, which is used to alter the order of inheritance. It can be altered at any given moment, through the writing of a new will, regardless of the type, except when the will recognises parenthood over a child, in which case this part cannot be revoked by a new will.

Court proceedings are required to enforce a will, regardless of the type. The proceedings are required to make the will public. In a will drafted by a notary public ('public will' or *testamento público*), the court proceedings are used to formally appoint the executor of the will; if it is a sealed will (*testamento cerrado*), it serves to formally unseal and read the document; in case of a private will, the court proceedings confirm the will, as long as the witnesses to the making of the will can be found (or else the will will be deemed as void).

There are three types of ordinary wills allowed by law: public, sealed and private. There can be only one testator – joint wills, no matter what they provide, are expressly forbidden in the Civil Code.

The public will has several requirements. First of all, it has to be drafted by a notary public in a specific book, as dictated by the testator, as long as what is dictated does not contradict the law (the notary public must verify this); also, once written down, it has to be read out loud before the person making the will and two witnesses and only then can it be signed. In specific circumstances, the notary public can be replaced by ambassadors, aircraft captains or ship commanders. If the testator is deaf, he or she may read the will and then sign it. If the testator cannot sign the will, the notary can sign on the testator's behalf, as long as this is expressly declared in the will. This is the only type of will allowed for blind persons.

The second ordinary type of will is the sealed will. This type of will is written by the testator and then given to the notary public, who will examine it for formal errors and write down a statement of approval. This statement is then read before the testator and two witnesses. The statement will only provide that a will has been made but will not mention its content. The will must be sealed to ensure its validity until the time comes to have it opened. This type of will can be written in Portuguese or in any other language, by the testator or whomever he or she requests to do so. The will is returned to the testator and not kept with the notary public.

The third type of ordinary will is the private will and requires the least formalities of all three types. It can also be written in any language, as long as at least three witnesses sign it and can understand the language. After the testator's death, this will must be confirmed by at least one of the witnesses, unless none of the witnesses can be found, in which case it is up to the judge to decide whether the will can be confirmed or not.

Another type of will is known as codicil (*codicilo*) and it refers to assets of low value. A codicil merely needs to be in written form in a document which is dated and signed – there are no other formalities required.

There are only three types of special wills: the nautical, the aeronautic and the military. The nautical and aeronautic wills are drafted on board, before someone designated by the commander of the ship or aircraft, observing the requirements of the public or sealed wills discussed above – the commander acts as the notary public. These wills lose their efficacy ninety days after the completion of the journey during which they were prepared if the testator does not die within that time period. The military will is prepared for officers in the field and its validity also expires ninety days after the mission is completed or the opportunity arises for another will to be made through one of the ordinary means.

D. Succession Proceedings

1. Probate

Succession starts as soon as a person dies. Probate proceedings (when required) must be filed within sixty days of the person's death, even though the court has the discretion to extend this time period. It is the duty of the person who has possession and is managing the estate's assets to file probate proceedings. The estate is administered by an executor (*inventariante*). Up until the time when the executor signs a declaration (*compromisso*) to act as the executor, a temporary administrator will have possession of the estate. After that, the executor will manage the estate until the court approves the asset division (*partilha*), which is filed by the executor.[41]

All beneficiaries must provide information about the assets which belong to the estate, whether they have it in their possession or know that the assets be possessed by some other person (the non-provision of information is called *sonegação*). If the beneficiary does not do so, he or she will lose all rights over those assets. Such a penalty, however, can only be imposed through an action started by the beneficiaries or the creditors of the estate.

The estate will only be liable for the deceased's debts up to the amount of its total assets. If the assets have already been distributed, each beneficiary will be liable for these debts, up to the limit of and in proportion to what the beneficiary inherited.

In the case of descendants inheriting from an ascendant, all the gifts the former received from the latter during the latter's life must be taken into account when assessing the rights of that beneficiary. The gifts received from the deceased when he or she was alive will be reduced from the amount to be distributed to that descendant. This process of setting off assets is called *colação* and its purpose is to make equal the shares of the descendants and surviving spouse, in the proportions established by the Civil Code. The gifts are presumed to come out of the deceased's available assets (i.e., the 50% which is not reserved to legitimate and necessary heirs), if the heir who received the gift would not otherwise be considered a beneficiary (such as a grandchild who receives a gift from his or her grandparent and the parent is alive at the time of the deceased's death). In other cases, the donor must expressly state in a document or in the will that the assets of the gift are to be taken from the available part of the assets.

Various types of expenses are excluded from this process, such as those relating to the education and general upbringing of the children, the ones related to marriage and the payment of criminal defence lawyers, as well as those related to services rendered by the heir to the deceased during the deceased's life.

2. Asset Division

Once the asset list is compiled, the division of the assets (*partilha*) can be requested by any beneficiaries, assignees of the beneficiaries' rights or the estate's creditors. The testator can indicate in the will his or her desires on how the assets are to be divided, as long as the amounts determined are equivalent to the share incumbent to each beneficiary. Alternatively, the beneficiaries can themselves determine the sharing, either amicably (if they are all of full legal capacity and in agreement, in which case the sharing must be approved by a judge); or by court proceedings, if one of the beneficiaries is not of full legal capacity or if the beneficiaries are not in agreement as to how the division should be made.

---

41. Article 1,991 of the Civil Code. The approval of the *partilha* is loosely analogous to a grant of probate in common law jurisdictions.

The sharing must be done as equally as possible. If an asset of the estate cannot fit within the share of any particular beneficiary, it must be sold and its value split, unless there is an agreement to allow for joint ownership. Any asset deliberately not presented at of time the assets were to be listed or whose existence was discovered only after the division of the assets took place will be subject to a new division (*sobrepartilha*). Once the court orders the distribution (*formal de partilha*), the rights of each beneficiary are limited to their share of the estate. The court's order can only be annulled by factors that compromise generally the validity of the legal acts, such as error, coercion, fraud against creditors or similar acts.

Selected Bibliography

In English

A.A.S. de Camargo, 'The Revised Brazilian Civil Code' (2003) 11 *University of Miami International and Comparative Law Review* 65.

C.L. Marques, 'Assisted Reproduction Technology in South America and the Effect on Adoption' (2000) 35 *Texas International Law Journal* 65.

In Portuguese

W. de Barros Monteiro, *Curso de Direito Civil: Direito das Sucessões* (Saraiva, São Paulo, Saraiva, 2003).

M.H. Diniz, *Curso de Direito Civil Brasileiro: Direito das Sucessões* (Saraiva, São Paulo, 2006).

O. Gomes, *Sucessões*. (Forense, Rio de Janeiro, 2006).

R.M. Mariângela, *Atualidades do Direito de Família e Sucessões* (Notadez, Sapucaia do Sul, 2008).

S. Rodrigues, *Direito Civil: Direito das Sucessões* (Saraiva, São Paulo, 2006).

A. Wald, *O Novo Direto de Família* (16th edn, Saraiva, São Paulo, 2005).

Chapter 5
Property Law

*José Isaac Pilati**

I. INTRODUCTION

Brazilian Law real and personal property law follows the German system of codification of rules, which distinguishes between patrimonial personal rights (obligations, credit rights, civil liability and unjust enrichment) and rights in rem (possession, property or ownership and its sub-divisions).

Property Law (*Direito das Coisas* or 'Law of Things') is mainly found in Book III of the Civil Code and encompasses four major subjects: possession, property or ownership, rights in rem of enjoyment and security rights in rem. It includes provisions relation to possession, surface, servitudes, usufruct, use, habitation, rights of the promissor buyer, pledge, mortgage, antichresis, concession of special use for the purposes of residential occupancy and concession of the right of use.

Legal protection of these rights is based on three types of actions: possession is enforced by possessory actions; real property is enforced by claiming actions; and rights in rem over third-party property (enjoyment rights) are protected by *actio confessoria* and *actio negatoria*. Rights to quiet enjoyment are protected by specific types of actions, and so are condominiums and joint ownership.

---

* Associate Professor of Law (UFSC), LLD, LLM (UFSC) LLB (UFPR).

Fabiano Deffenti & Welber Barral (eds), *Introduction to Brazilian Law*, pp. 71–83.

II. POSSESSION

Following the Roman law tradition, the Brazilian Civil Code protects the de facto control of a thing regardless of ownership or another right in rem. *Possessor* is defined in the Civil Code as the person who holds (any or all) property rights over a thing. Any individual or legal entity may hold or possess something as owner, as usufructuary, as tenant or as a pledgee. There are many ways to express possession over an object.

Writs of possession are the actions that protect de facto possession. They are used to prevent any threats to the possessory situation before imminent aggression or burden.[1] The action to maintain possession is used to make sure that the possessor exercises his or her right when this right is being disturbed. The possessory action or 'repossession action' is used to restore possession that was unjustly taken. This type of action is a preventive measure, which may be preliminary or final. This preliminary decision may put an end to the dispute if the complaining party halts the legal action.

Some possession situations are not protected by writs. A person, who takes possession without proper title, either through violence, in an unlawful manner or through abuse of trust, cannot have a better possessory right over the person who suffered these abuses. Though a person may have custody of an object as an employee while at work because he or she has the permission of the owner, this does not give him or her the right to any possessory protection. Detention also does not provide any possessory protection.

The Civil Code also governs the effects of a situation in which the possessor loses possession by a possessory action or an *actio vindicatoria* (*ação vindicatória*). The Civil Code contains provisions regarding the consumed fruits of property (i.e., the benefits obtained from the property or profits a prendre), the improvements made, and the possible deterioration or loss of the enjoyment during the time the rightful possessor was displaced.

Good faith serves as the basic criteria in assessing possessory rights. The possessor in good faith (the person who possesses something and does not know that the property's ownership is in dispute) does not have to compensate the rightful possessor for the fruits he or she consumed. The possessor in bad faith, on the other hand, has to compensate even for the fruits that he or she was not interested in obtaining. The possessor in good faith has a right to be compensated and to retain the property until payment is tendered. The compensation may be related to necessary improvements[2] and valuable improvements (which make the property more valuable). The possessor in good faith also has the right to remove the voluntary improvements (the purpose of which is merely ornamental) for which he or she did not receive compensation, if he or she can do so without causing any damage to the property. The possessor in bad faith only has the right to be compensated in cases of necessary improvements, and he or she cannot retain the

1. Writ of *interdito proibitório* (Arts 932 and 933 of the Code of Civil Procedure).
2. Made to prevent the deterioration of property (Art. 1,220 of the Civil Code).

property until payment is tendered. That is, if he or she gives the property back because of a court order, then only after she or she complies with the order he or she may seek compensation.

If the property perishes while in hands of the possessor in good faith, he or she will only be liable if the perishing occurs due to deceit or negligence. The possessor in bad faith, on the other hand, is liable for damages to make good the damaged property even if the situation was one of force majeure, unless he or she can prove that the damages would have occurred even if the property was in possession of another party who faced the same situation.

The Civil Code makes only one exception in its severe stance against bad faith: unjust enrichment (*enriquecimento ilícito*). If the possessor *mala fide* has invested in the property, he or she must be compensated by the person who gathers fruits from the property. If the possessor *mala fide* is in possession of industrialised materials that he or she has to return to the rightful possessor, the wrongful possessor must be compensated for the investments made.

III. RIGHTS IN REM

In Book III, Title II of the Civil Code lists some rights in rem:[3] real property, surface, servitude, usufruct, use, habitation, rights of the promissor buyer of real estate, pledge, mortgage and antichresis. The list is not exhaustive; other laws deal with other rights in rem, such as concession of use[4] or concession of use for housing.[5] In this Title, the Civil Code provides that real property rights over movables, when created or transmitted by an act between two parties, are acquired by transfer. In the case of real property, it is necessary to register the title of the property in the real estate registry, except in those cases in which the law provides otherwise. These exceptions are: adverse possession, accession and inheritance, and marriage.

A. Ownership

Under Title III, Ownership (*Propriedade*), there are eight chapters: preliminary articles (concepts, contents, limitations, and social function), acquisition and loss of real and personal property, right of quiet enjoyment, traditional condominium (voluntary and necessary) and special condominium as well as ownership subject to a condition and fiduciary ownership.

The Civil Code defines the owner (proprietário) as the person who can use, enjoy and sell the property, and has the right to recover real estate from anyone who has or withholds it in an unjust way. It includes the airspace and the subsoil, where

3. Articles 1,225–1,227 of the Civil Code.
4. Decree-Law 271/1967.
5. Temporary Decree 2,220/2001.

there is an interest to prevent activities of third parties; however, it does not include mineral resources, potential resources for producing electricity, archaeological artefacts and other resources mentioned by special laws.

Ownership is acquired and lost depending on the type of property involved: movable or immovable, perpetual or subject to a condition subsequent, full or imperfect, and tangible or intangible. The Civil Code does not classify real estate as urban or rural, nor does it include special properties (such as the *quilombola* property,[6] indigenous property,[7] belonging to foreigners[8] or intellectual property, which are addressed in other statutes).[9]

The *quilombola* property, according to law, is the ownership of land that has been occupied since the historical resistance to slavery, owned by the members of communities (the *quilombos*) formed by run-away slaves. This type of property has priority over any other kind of occupational interests (public, private, environmental preservation, or even archaeological). It must be recognised by the government, and has a special legal regime. It cannot be sold, subdivided or divested of rights, and has a communitarian nature. The *quilombola* property is linked to traditional knowledge and the ethnic values of African ancestry. Indigenous property also exhibits some of these characteristics. The Brazilian Constitution recognises indigenous people's rights to the territory originally occupied by them, their social organisation, costumes, languages, beliefs and traditions.

Ownership of property generally is acquired by adverse possession (*usucapião*), registry of title (*registro do título*) or accession (*acessão*). There are other means of gaining ownership, such as inheritance, which are addressed by other titles in the Civil Code.

The acquisition of real estate through adverse possession may either be ordinary (*ordinária*) or extraordinary (*extraordinária*), which may be urban or agricultural. Acquisition of ownership by extraordinary adverse possession occurs when a person has possession over the estate for fifteen years without any challenges or complaints against the possessor's rights. The person can demand a court judgment declaring his or her rights. This lapse of time may be reduced to ten years if the possessor lives on that property or if he or she works on it. This is called possession-work. If the possessor, in addition to the requirements noted above, also possesses a just title in good faith, the acquisition may occur in ten or even in five years (should possession-work occur).

The special urban adverse possession, when it relates to real estate of up to 250 square metres, has a time lapse of five years, independent of title or good faith, if the property is used as a family dwelling and the possessor does not own any other dwelling. The special agricultural adverse possession also prescribes a

6. Article 68 of the Transitory Constitutional Dispositions Act of the Federal Constitution of 1988 and the Decree 4,887/2003.
7. Article 231 of the Brazilian Constitution of 1988 and Law 6,001/1973.
8. Article 190 of the Brazilian Constitution of 1988 and Law 5,709/1971.
9. Industrial Property Law (Law 9279/1996) and the Copyright Law (Law 9,610/1998), among others.

five-year period for acquisition. The property must be located in an agricultural zone, be no larger than 50 hectares and be kept in a productive state by the actions of the possessor or his or her family.

The Statute of the City[10] allows collective acquisition by right if possessors fall within the low income and if the portion of each joint owner does not exceed 250 square metres. This is also a type of special urban adverse possession.

The acquisition of property *inter vivos* most commonly occurs by the signing of a contract drafted by a public notary. This contract must then be registered at the real estate registry with jurisdiction over the area.[11] The register is *iuris tantum* proof of the right in rem, admitting evidence to the contrary.

Accession via adverse possession is the original form of acquisition of ownership. It occurs when something that belongs to a person joins itself and incorporates another element that belongs to someone else. The owner of the accessory loses all rights over the thing accessed by the other, subject to a right to be compensated.

Accession may be natural or artificial. The cases of natural accession are: formation of an island in common tides or private tides; alluvium (sediment deposited by flowing water within the margins); *avulsão* (dislocation of parts of land, by force of nature, which are joined and incorporated with each other) and abandonment of *álveo* (when the abandoned riverbed is divided between riparian owners).

Artificial accession occurs when there is a construction or plantation by one person on someone else's land, with materials or seeds belonging to the first person. If the doer acted in good faith, the owner of the main property (generally the owner of the land) acquires the personal property from the accessory by paying them their value. If the doer acted in bad faith, the owner may have the improvements undone and be compensated by the person who constructed or planted the personal property. If the construction or plantation, made in good faith, is more valuable than the land, then the owner of the land will lose the title over the property but will be compensated by the new owner.

The Civil Code also deals with the invasion of a building under construction. The invader has to pay damages and has to return anything he or she would have gained as a consequence of the invasion. There are intricate rules as to how the invader must compensate the rightful owner, depending on whether the invader acted in good faith, the value of the property and the extent of the land that was invaded.

There are five ways to lose title over real estate: transfer, renunciation, abandonment, destruction and dispossession. Tangible personal property may be acquired or lost as a consequence of: adverse possession of personal property (in three or five years, depending on the type, if ordinary or extraordinary); occupation (in the case of *res derelicta* or *res nullius*); transfer or *traditio*, when made *inter vivos* as well as specification, when the transformation of feedstock that

10. Law 10, 267/2001.
11. Law 6,015/1973.

belongs to someone else creates something new and more valuable, and it is not possible or there is no interest in restoring it to its original form.

Further, the personal property may be lost due to confusion. Confusion occurs when two or more pieces of personal property have become mixed, and when property rights can no longer be distinguished.

There are two more possible ways to acquire and lose tangible personal property: the finding of treasure (which will be divided between the owner of the land and the person who accidentally finds it) and the finding of the lost property of a third party. In the case of lost property, the finder must look for the owner or the authorities to return the property – he or she is entitled to compensation of the expenses and the payment of a reward of 5% of the value of the property found. If the owner is not found or interested in having his or her property back, it will, by right of possession, belong to the finder.

B. Neighbourhood Rights

The owner or possessor of a building has the right to stop any interference related to the usage of the neighbouring property that may affect its own security, peace and well-being – these are called neighbourhood rights (*direitos de vizinhança*). The prohibition takes into account the nature of the building's use, the location of the building, the zoning rules and the ordinary limits of tolerance between neighbours.

There are other conflicts related to neighbourhood rights, such as bordering trees (damages related to the growing of roots, fruits or branches), limited passage (to the neighbour whose property does not have an access to the road, harbour or fountain – in this case, the owner or possessor must pay compensation for any diminution in value caused by the passage), passage of cables, tubes or similar types of installations (of collective interest), water (rain water, aqueduct, stream), boundaries between buildings, and the right to build (distance between windows, between buildings, and sharing of walls). Neighbourhood rights are classified as onerous (forced passage, aqueduct) and gratuitous (all the others).

The protection of the neighbourhood rights occurs by means of possessory actions (*ações possessórias*) or comminatory actions (*ações cominatórias*),[12] and other specific actions, such as *damnum infectus* (the owner or possessor has the right to demand from the owner of the neighbouring building its demolition or repairing or a pledge in case of imminent damage). This action is called *ação de nunciação* and allows for the owner to demand the necessary guarantees[13] and can ask for a demarcating action (for instance, an action to demarcate the boundaries between two properties).

12. Articles 920–925 of the Code of Civil Procedure.
13. Article 934 of the Code of Civil Procedure.

C. CONDOMINIUMS

The Civil Code separates general condominium (voluntary condominium and necessary condominium) from special condominium. In voluntary condominiums, all owners have an equal right to enjoy the whole property, regardless of the fraction that each individual owner owns. Expenditures and profits related to the condominium are distributed according to the fraction that each person owns. Decisions about the property follow the same formula. When there is a sale of a fraction, other owners have a right of first refusal over third parties.

A necessary condominium occurs when there is joint property of walls, fences and ditches that divide two properties. The property must be maintained in the best interest of the neighbours.

A special condominium is the legal regime of apartment buildings, commercial offices, garages and even houses that share common areas (soil, water distribution, sewage, electricity, roofing, stairs, access areas, elevators, playgrounds) and where there are autonomous fractions of exclusive property of the owners. Each owner has a specific fraction of the whole, as a parameter for decisions made in meetings, to approve ordinary or extraordinary expenses and to establish the right that each owner has to the land or its value when the condominium is to be indemnified.

The condominium's convention (*convenção de condomínio*) describes the respective areas, common and private, establishes the rights and duties of joint owners' management rules, and procedures for the changes and termination of the condominium.

D. SURFACE

The owner of real property may grant to another person the right to build or plant on the land for a determined period of time. These rights are called surface rights (*direitos de superfície*). The Statute of the City[14] establishes the right of surface for urban properties, and it allows for the existence of this right for an undetermined period of time. The right of surface can be acquired by adverse possession, if its requirements are met.

E. SERVITUDES

A servitude (*servidão*) is a right over a real estate that imposes a burden that benefits another property belonging to someone else. There are restrictions *in patiendo* (to allow the passage of the owner of the dominant property through the servient property, for instance) and restrictions *non faciendo* (committing oneself to not build beyond a certain height in the servient property). These rights are

14. Federal Law 20,257/2001.

created for the benefit of an owner of another property and are intended for use by that owner.

Discontinuous servitude (*servidão descontinuada*) is a servitude that is renewed by each human act that exercises the right. This contrasts with a continuous servitude (*servidão continuada*), such as an aqueduct.

The dominant owner must enjoy his or her right in a reasonable manner and in the case of doubt, any situation can be interpreted against him or her. The servient owner must not disturb the enjoyment of the dominant owner's rights; he or she must allow the expansion of servitude if it is necessary for agricultural purposes, subject to payment of compensation.

Servitude rights may be extinguished by means of common property rights and two additional rights: confusion (*confusão*) and lack of use (*desuso*). Confusion occurs if the same person becomes owner of two buildings; lack of use occurs when the right is not used for ten years, as is true for the case of discontinuous servitude.

The protection of servitude occurs through possessory actions (in the case of apparent servitudes) and declaratory actions, against anyone who hinders its exercise; with regard to the servient property owner, there is a negating action to deny or prevent the abusive use of servitude. Possessory actions can also be used for these purposes.

F. Usufruct

Usufruct (*usufruto*) is a right in rem that encompasses possession, usage, administration and gathering of the profits from the property. In the case of fruits, the usufructuary may take possession of them, but, at the end of the usufruct, he or she must leave the remaining fruits.

Usufruct may be created via conveyance *inter vivos*, by registered will or by adverse possession. Family Law also establishes the possibility of usufruct of property belonging to a child by his or her parents, exercising parental rights.

Usufruct rights can be granted over one or more properties, real or personal. It can encompass all assets, or part of them, encompassing part or all of the property's profits and utilities.

At the end of the usufruct, the usufructuary will have to render information about the administration of the assets. The good or land must also be returned to its owner in the same condition the usufructuary received it, excluding fair wear and tear.

The Civil Code also establishes some cases for the termination of usufruct. These cases are: the resignation or death of the usufructuary, the deregistration of the legal entity or the end of a thirty-year period, the cessation of the cause that led to the usufruct, destruction of the asset, the consolidation of separate properties, the lack of use or enjoyment, and the breach or negligence of the usufructuary if he or she sells or spoils the property or allows it to be destroyed. Some of these cases lead to an automatic termination of the usufruct, and while others require a court decision to cause termination.

The Civil Code also establishes two other kinds of usufruct: use and habitation.

Use (*uso*) is right in rem which allows for the use of the property and the consumption of its fruits limited to the needs of the user and his or her family. For instance, if the property has an orchard, the user can consume the fruits, but cannot sell them. The personal needs of the user will be evaluated according to his or her social condition and the place where he or she lives, and the family needs will encompass the needs of the spouse, the children (minors) and those who work at his or her house. Other aspects of this right are similar to the usufruct, with respect to the nature of the right of use in rem.

Habitation (*habitação*) is also a right in rem. It is a type of right that has as its subject-matter another person's dwelling. The holder cannot rent it or lend it – he or she can only occupy it, gratuitously, but he or she can do so with his or her family. If more than one person has this right, none of them will pay rent, but they cannot obstruct the occupation of the house by the others.

G. Promissor Buyers

As explained above, rights over real property may only be transferred by an *escritura* (i.e., a conveyance contract drafted by a notary public), which is subsequently registered with the real estate registry.

However, it is often the case that parties enter into agreements to promise to make a purchase and sale agreement (*promessa de compra e venda*). A *promessa de compra e venda* is a contract where the promissor promises to sign the *escritura* upon the occurrence of a certain event, which is generally the outstanding consideration paid for the property. Unlike *escrituras*, the *promessas de compra e venda* may be drafted by the parties or by a notary public.

H. Pledge, Mortgage and Antichresis

There are many forms of security rights under Brazilian Civil Law. Security rights over property allow the debtor to separate an asset of his or her personal assets and set it aside for payment of a debt. Pledges (*penhores*), mortgages (*hipotecas*) and antichreses (*anticreses*) are security rights in rem. But we may also include in this list the so-called super security rights, such as the retention of title (fiduciary conveyance)[15] and lease,[16] including secured property construction used for low income earners.[17]

15. Federal Law 4,728/1965, Decree 911/1969, Federal Law 9,514/1997 and Arts 1,361 and 1,368-A of the Civil Code.
16. Federal Law 6,099/1964.
17. Federal Law 10,188/2001.

In the case of super security rights, the legal title is temporarily transferred to the creditor, who has a temporary ownership over the asset which is subject to the payment of the outstanding debt. Once the debt is paid, the holder of the legal title must transfer the asset to the (former) debtor.

Pledges, mortgages and antichreses involve the creation of a link between a property and the incurring of an obligation. When they are in place, the creditor cannot simply keep the secured asset if the debtor does not pay or otherwise defaults on his or her obligation. However, if the debtor does not pay the debt, and the debt matures, he or she can offer the asset as payment, yet where the sale of the property is insufficient to pay debts and expenses, the debt will continue to exist.

The pledge and the mortgage allow for the forced sale of the property, in an enforcement action, while the antichresis does not. In the antichresis, the creditor receives possession of the property in order to pay himself or herself with the income obtained from the property.

As rights in rem, these security rights are not exempt from the requirements of publicity which are given priority in the relevant registry (the real estate registry, the registry of titles and documents or the National Institute of Industrial Property). Repayments do not automatically extinguish the secured creditor's rights, even if the security is given over more than one property. There must be a release registered with the relevant registry.

In general terms, a pledge is a security right over a third person's tangible personal property who transfers possession to the pledge and offers the pledge the possibility of priority enforcement in case the debt is not paid by the pledgor. There are, however, some special cases of pledge, with different rules.

The common pledge is registered at Registry of Titles and Documents (*Registro de Títulos e Documentos*), while special types of pledges – rural, industrial and mercantile – are registered with the real estate properties register. In this case, and in the case of pledges of vehicles, the asset stays with the debtor and not with the creditor.

In addition to the duties of custody, protection and return of the benefits received from the property, the creditor also has the duty to refund the debtor if the price obtained through the sale of the secured property exceeds the debt, in the case of forced sales.

The pledge ends: (a) upon full payment of the debt secured by the pledge; (b) if the property perishes before the debt is paid in full; (c) if rights over the pledge are waived; (d) if the secured creditor becomes the owner of the secured asset (or vice-versa); and (e) via the sale of the property. Waiver of pledge rights over an asset is presumed if the creditor accepts the sale without questioning the price, when he or she gives possession of the asset to the debtor, or when he or she agrees to the replacement of the pledged property with another asset. The termination of the pledge only becomes effective after registration of the pledge is cancelled.

The pledge can be either common or special. One type of special pledge is the rural pledge (*penhor rural*), created by a document drafted by the parties or by a notary public and registered in the real estate registry in the jurisdiction where the property is located.

The rural pledge can be agricultural (*agrícola*) or related to cattle (*pecuário*). The agricultural pledge includes machines and agricultural instruments, pending harvests or the plantation itself, stored fruits, coal and firewood. The pledge *pecuário* covers animals that are part of pastoral or agricultural activity or dairy production. The sale or substitution of animals can only occur when the creditor consents in writing and subrogation will only be valid against a third party if the pledge is registered.

The other two types of pledges are industrial and mercantile. The industrial pledge (*penhor industrial*) includes pledges over machines, materials, instruments installed and working (with or without accessories), animals used in industries, salt, raw materials and others. The mercantile pledge (*penhor mercantil*) covers merchandise stored in warehouses. The creation of these pledges requires a document drafted by a notary public or by the parties themselves which must be registered in the real estate registry in the jurisdiction where the assets are located. In both cases, a pledge note issued by a bank may be the pledge over the property, if both parties agree.

The pledge over rights and negotiable instruments (*penhor sobre direitos e títulos de crédito*) is another type of special pledge. This kind of pledge is possible if the rights are allowed to be transferred. It can be created by a document drafted by a notary public or by the parties and registered with the registry of titles and documents or by endorsement and delivery. The pledgee has to preserve and defend the pledged right, by collecting interest and other payments that are specified in the document that establishes the debt. When the negotiable instrument is due, the pledge must immediately proceed to collect it and deposit the amount obtained from the debtor; if the negotiable instrument is overdue, the creditor can retain the amount of the loan plus interest, returning the rest.

The Civil Code also includes a pledge over vehicles (*penhor sobre veículos*), created through a document drafted by the parties or by a notary public registered with the registry of titles and documents located in the jurisdiction over the domicile of the debtor. A note must be attached to the certificate title of the vehicle. The pledge over vehicles is limited to a two-year term that can be extended. The debtor keeps the vehicle and the sale or exchange of the pledged vehicle, without previous authorisation, results in the anticipated maturity of the debt.

Certain pledges may also be imposed by law. A legal pledge (*penhor legal*) is established independently, by agreement between the parties. It applies for the benefit of hotel and restaurant owners for luggage and personal objects of guests and customers to cover expenses incurred by them or over a lessee's assets for the benefit of the landlord to secure unpaid rent.

Another type of right in rem set out in the Civil Code is the mortgage (*hipoteca*). The Civil Code lists the possible types of property rights that may be mortgaged: real estate (together with its accessories), direct domain, useful domain, railroads, natural resources found with the personal assets of a person, aircrafts and ships.

In mortgages over real estate, the debtor holds the property subject to a debt described in a public notation in the title document registered with the Real Estate Registry (*Cartório de Registro de Imóveis*) where the property is located. The debtor can sell the mortgaged property, but that may cause the anticipated maturity of the debt, if that is so provided in the mortgage instrument. There can be a second mortgage on the same property, benefiting a third person or the same creditor. The second mortgage can only proceed to enforcement if the debtor is insolvent.

The person who buys the mortgaged property can also redeem the mortgage within thirty days, counted from the day of registration of the purchase agreement on the title.

There are three types of mortgages: conventional, based on the parties' agreement; legal, used as a security; and judicial, formed as a result of a judgment pending enforcement. A conventional mortgage is created by a writing registered on the title with the real estate registry with jurisdiction over the area where the property is located. A legal mortgage is a mortgage established by law for the benefit of state entities in charge of managing certain funds (such as social security) over the assets of debtors, the children entitled to certain assets over the assets of the parent who marries again before distribution, the victims of crime over the assets of the perpetrator for payment of damages and court costs, heirs of assets transferred to another heir until the first heir receives his or her part of the inheritance and for the creditor of a court-ordered sale until the full sale price is transferred to the creditor. The Code of Civil Procedure also establishes court-issued mortgages[18] to benefit the prevailing party in legal proceedings.

Brazilian Law also has special types of mortgages, such as the mortgage over railroads,[19] ships[20] and aircraft.[21] However, these are not used very often. In the case of ships and aircraft, leasing arrangements have replaced the mortgage with some advantages.

A mortgage is terminated if: (a) the main obligation is fulfilled; (b) the property perishes; (c) the owner of the property loses title over it; (d) the creditor renounces the right of redemption; (e) the debt is paid; or (f) there is a sale of the property via auction or adjudication. The cancellation of the mortgage must be registered with the real estate registry. Creditors that did not take part in the collection of the debt must be notified prior to deregistering the mortgage.

IV. FIDUCIARY CONVEYANCE

Brazilian Law has other forms of security interests over property, such as fiduciary conveyance (*alienação fiduciária*).

---

18. Article 466 of the Code of Civil Procedure.
19. Article 1,502 of the Civil Code.
20. Federal Law 7,652/1988.
21. Federal Law 7,565/1986.

Fiduciary conveyance was inspired by the Roman principle of *fiducia cum creditore*. The debtor, in order to secure the payment of his or her debt, transfers to the fiduciary creditor the conditional title over the asset. The creditor keeps the legal title over the property while the debt is not paid. If the fiduciary debtor does not comply with its obligations, the fiduciary creditor can take possession from the debtor via an action of search and seizure; if the debt is not paid, the creditor can sell the asset in order to pay the secured debt. In the case of insolvency or bankruptcy of the debtor, the title given as security is not affected by claims of creditors in liquidation, because the asset is not deemed to belong to the wound up company or bankrupted person.

If the debtor transfers possession over the asset subject to fiduciary conveyance rights, the creditor may petition the court to change the action from one of search and seizure to an action of court deposit. If the order is granted, the debtor can become the fiduciary possessor of the asset and can be arrested if he or she deals with the property.

Selected Bibliography

In English

A. dos Santos Cunha, 'Informal Land Subdivision and Real Estate Regularization: A Comparative Study between Colombia and Brazil' (Winter 2009) 40 *The University of Miami Inter-American Law Review* 315.

S.L. Graham, 'Slavery's Impasse: Slave Prostitutes, Small-Time Mistresses, and the Brazilian Law of 1871' (1991) 33 *Comparative Studies in Society and History* 669–694.

J. Holston, 'The Misrule of Law: Land and Usurpation in Brazil' (1991) 33 *Comparative Studies in Society and History* 695–725.

In Portuguese

M.N. Chalhub, *Negócio Fiduciário: Alienação Fiduciária, Cessão Fiduciária, Securitização, Decreto-Lei n° 911, de 1969, Lei n° 8.668, de 1993, Lei n° 9.514, de 1997* (2nd edn, Renovar, Rio de Janeiro, 2000).

S. de Salvo Venosa, *Direitos Reais* (Atlas, São Paulo, 1999).

O. Gomes, *Direitos Reais* (19th edn, Forense, Rio de Janeiro, 2006).

A. Wald, *Direito das Coisas* (Revista dos Tribunais, 1995).

Chapter 6
Contract Law

*Luciano Benetti Timm**

I. INTRODUCTION

Traditionally, a contract was defined as the meeting of minds that is sufficient to confer rights and impose obligations on the parties to the bargain. A contract was also perceived as the place for self-regulation of private parties. More recently, however, a contract has been defined as the legal vesting of a social event that creates the conditions for a transaction involving economic exchange to occur, that is, it is the rule employed by society to make goods and services circulate in the marketplace.

Nowadays, it is widely accepted that a contract is subject to regulatory influences not only by the will of the parties but also from laws enacted by lawmakers in order to afford protection to collective concerns potentially threatened by the parties. The concept that a contract is 'socially embedded' (an act which should not be looked at in isolation separate from the interests of community) took shape in Brazil as an outcome from legal transplant from the European civil law system in a process started in Brazil's colonial period (in the fifteenth century).

Brazilian Contract Law, especially that set out in the now defunct Civil Code of 1916, received particular influence from the works of nineteenth century Brazilian legal scholars. These scholars were heavily influenced by classical Roman law, medieval Portuguese Law (the Manueline and Philippine Ordinances),

---

* Professor of Contract Law at the Pontifical Catholic University of Rio Grande do Sul. Visiting Scholar (UC-Berkeley), LLD, LLM (UFRGS) LLM (Warwick) LLB (PUC/RS).

Fabiano Deffenti & Welber Barral (eds), *Introduction to Brazilian Law*, pp. 85–104.

nineteenth century German jurisprudence (the Pandectist School of Windscheid and his followers) and the French codification (*Code Civil*). As a consequence of these influences, lawmakers adhered to notions of freedom of contract and the absence of laws to interfere in the parties' bargain, except in cases where consent might be vitiated. This became known as the liberal model of contract regulation.

The twentieth and twenty-first centuries saw the main influence in Brazilian Contract Law shift to continental European law (especially in relation to consumer relationships, urban real estate leases and the regulation of employment relationships), especially that from Italy and Portugal (which provided the models for the Civil Code of 2002) as well as from American law in the case of a number of specific types of contracts and their regulation (companies, trade regulation, capital markets, insurance, mortgage of chattels, franchising, leasing arrangements, among others).

From continental European law, Brazilian lawmakers transplanted the idea of contractual *dirigisme* by the state, thus broadening the scope for government intervention in the realm of the parties' will by having in place mandatory rules that cannot be excluded or changed by the parties. In this new regulatory paradigm (typically a phenomenon of 'publicisation' of private law through distributive or social welfare laws), the assumption of the liberal model of contractual relationships – based on the principle that freedom and formal equality of individuals would ascertain the balance and justice in private relationships whatever their economic and social status might be – was undermined. Hence, there was an understanding that the need arose for protection of the weaker party in the relationship with the goal of establishing a substantive, or positive, balance. This became known as the social or collectivist model of contract regulation, it being the offspring of socialist and collectivist influences.

The box below sets outs the differences between the two models:

Liberal Model	**Social Model**
Civil Code of 1916	Civil Code of 2002
Contract = agreement	Contract = cooperative social event
Justice = meeting of minds	Justice = balance between parties' rights and obligations
Basic tenet = freedom of contract	Basic tenet = solidarity, fairness
Pacta sunt servanda (the parties are free to regulate their contractual relationships)	Statutory and court control leading to review and modification in the will of the parties
Individual rights or civil rights	Social rights
Individualism (free bargaining of parties interests generates increase of public welfare)	Collectivism (prevalence of collective interests governed by legislation and court decisions)

In sum, it is clear more than ever that in Brazil it is not always that the terms of the contract that will govern the relationship of the parties.

II. FORMATION AND VALIDITY OF CONTRACTS

A. Generally

Brazilian Contract Law distinguishes between the existence (*existência*), validity (*validade*) and effectiveness (*eficácia*) of contracts. In the realm of existence, the test of whether a contract exists is connected with elements that, if present, will determine the status of contract to a particular relationship. The realm of validity deals with certain criteria that must be met for an act to be in the legal environment without being expelled on any relevant grounds. Finally, the realm of effectiveness is the environment in which a contract will generate its desired effects. Often, the effectiveness will be halted by either the parties' or the lawmakers' will.

Traditionally, the key element to determine the existence of a contract was consent, that is, a meeting of the minds (offer and acceptance).[1] However, nowadays the existence of a contract is subject to the presence of the following elements:

(a) bilateralism (two parties, an active and another passive party);
(b) subject-matter (an obligation to give, perform or refrain from performing).

It follows that under Brazilian law, wherever two (or more) individuals cause their assents to be manifested in a certain way as to create an obligation to either or both of them, a contract will exist. This is not to say that the contract, albeit existing, will be valid and enforceable. Since this issue deals with a type of bilateral legal transaction, the validity of a contract is subject to the satisfaction of the legal requirements for legal transactions in general contained in Articles 104 and 166 of the Civil Code, namely:

(a) the parties having the proper capacity to enter into the contract;[2]
(b) proper powers with respect to manifesting a third party's assent, as with an attorney (appointed by power of attorney), company officers (as provided in the company articles and by meetings), manager of a condominium (as provided in the declaration of condominium and by meetings of owners/tenants), insolvency trustee (as appointed by the insolvency court), administrator of an estate (as appointed by the probation court);
(c) any formalities required by law being observed[3] – as a general rule, Brazilian contract law does not impose any formality with regard to manifestation of

1. Articles 427 to 434 of the Civil Code.
2. Article 3 of the Civil Code for individuals, and Arts 44 and 45 for legal entities.
3. Article 104 and 107 of the Civil Code.

assent. Exceptions include contract for the sale of real estate, constitution of legal entities, chattel mortgage, franchising, and others;

(d) the purpose is lawful and reasonable;[4]

(e) no vitiating factors are present[5] – when such a defect exists in a legal transaction and it will render consent inadequate, as with the case of misrepresentation of reality by either party (error, *erro*), unfairness of either party (deceit, *dolo*), duress (*coação*) or fraud against the law (simulation, *simulação*);

(f) there is no force majeure (*caso fortuito e força maior*) that would otherwise lead to the termination of the contract on ground of frustration of its object;[6]

(g) the contract is not against public policy (mandatory rules such as labour legislation, for instance, cannot be excluded by the will of the parties; public order or *ordem pública*).[7]

Lastly, the effectiveness of the contract will usually be subject to what was agreed upon by the parties. They may agree that the effectiveness of the transaction is deferred in time,[8] or that the contract will be valid for a certain period of time only or, still, the parties may subject the transaction's effects to conditions precedent[9] (a *cláusula suspensiva*, which is a condition that puts the transaction in a state of 'idleness' until its occurrence, such as, for example, the required approval of a transaction by antitrust authorities or the granting of a licence from the food and drugs agency) or subsequent[10] (a *cláusula resolutiva*, which is a clause that provides for the termination of the contract upon fulfilment of its condition, for example, clauses that provide in anticipation for changes in tax or foreign exchange rules, etc).

B. Formation of Contracts

A contract is formed at the moment there is a meeting of the minds: offer (*proposta*) and acceptance (*aceitação*). Before this event, the law allows parties to freely engage in negotiation regarding their interests (the bargaining stage).

The bargaining stage consists of the preliminary understandings with regard to the contract, that is, the initial dealings that may result in obligations between the parties. These are preliminary talks, assessments, discussions in which the interests of each party will emerge and during which information is obtained with respect to the transaction that is to be made.

4. Articles. 104 and 166, II of the Civil Code.
5. Articles. s 138 and ensuing articles of Civil Code.
6. Article 393 of the Civil Code.
7. Articles 122, 123 and 166 of the Civil Code.
8. Article 131 of the Civil Code.
9. Article 125 of the Civil Code.
10. Article 127 of the Civil Code.

Under Brazilian law, at this moment, both parties are afforded the freedom to act under no obligation other than a duty to deal in good faith (*boa fé*). Failure to adhere with good faith principles during the bargaining stage may result in pre-contractual liability (*culpa in contrahendo*; *responsabilidade pré-contratual*). This would include, for instance, when untruthful information is presented by one party or unforeseeable or unreasonable disruption of negotiations.

Parties may, at the bargaining stage, resource to memoranda of understanding and letters of intent. Unless the terms of the agreement expressly or impliedly provide otherwise, the parties will not be bound to enter into the final agreement (the main contract). This is an exclusive feature of preliminary contracts or pre-contracts (*contratos preliminares* or *pré-contratos*), which under Brazilian law are governed by Article 462 of the Civil Code.

Pre-contracts will carry the obligation to execute the main contract. In other words, when a letter of intent is signed, the parties are not under any obligation whatsoever to enter into the contract; however, if a pre-contract is signed, such obligation will ensue.

An offer constitutes a unilateral manifestation of assent and, as such, it will in itself carry an obligation on the offeror. In order to be valid, the offer needs to be firm and include the basic obligations of the prospective transaction. If the offer complies with these elements, when made it will bind the offeror and become irrevocable, except if the contrary arises out of its own terms, the essence of the transaction or the circumstances of the transaction.[11]

The offer is also different from an invitation to treat, where an offer to conduct a certain business is not exactly put in place, but will rather be made to the market or to certain companies so that they submit an offer of their own (such as in the case of government tenders, in Brazil government by the Procurement Law).[12]

A private offer becomes irrevocable once it is received by the offeree.[13] The timing of the offer depends on whether it was made to a present or absent offeree. If the offer is made in the presence of the offeree (physical presence or through an electronic medium allowing immediate communication exchange such as telephone, peer-to-peer internet communication, videoconferencing, etc), it will expire immediately and be unenforceable if not accepted at that moment, except if otherwise agreed (such as where the offer terms give the offeree time to consider).[14]

On the other hand, if the offer was made to an absent person (because a communication time gap exists between the parties as in the case of the proposal being sent by post, fax, wire, e-mail or similar), then it will not expire until the time granted for acceptance has elapsed; if the offer does not contain a set time to accept, the law provides that reasonable time be allowed for acceptance to reach the offeror.[15]

---

11. Articles 427 and 428 of the Civil Code.
12. Law 8,666/1993.
13. Article 428, IV of the Civil Code.
14. Article 428, I of the Civil Code.
15. Article 428, II and III of the Civil Code.

With respect to form, the party may make an offer by e-mail, fax, by video, teleconferencing or even orally, unless the law requires a special formality.

A public offer (such as one made on a supermarket's website or advertised on a newspaper, for example, *oferta pública*) enjoys the same legal effect as if it was made to a specific person[16] and thus will bind the offeror.

There are no specific rules regarding how manifestation of *acceptance* must be made, except that it must be done in a timely manner – i.e., within the period of time fixed by the offeror or, if the offer does not provide for a specific time for acceptance, within a reasonable period of time taken for analysing the terms of the offer.[17] A manifestation of acceptance that does not strictly observe the terms of an offer, or that is made in an untimely manner, will be deemed equivalent to a counter offer.[18]

III. GENERAL PRINCIPLES OF CONTRACT LAW

The law of contracts rests upon two major principles and their corresponding sub-principles that make up the premises in which all rules relating to contracts in Brazilian law are based:

(a) the principle of freedom of contract (or freedom of will; *liberdade contractual*), which is subdivided into the sub-principle of sufficiency of consent, the sub-principle of sanctity of contract (*pacta sunt servanda*), the sub-principle of privity of contracts and the sub-principle of *incompleteness*; and

(b) the principle of *solidarity* (*solidaridade*), which is subdivided into the sub-principle of *strict good faith*; the sub-principle of social function; and sub-principle of fairness or contractual balance.

A. The Principle of Freedom of Contract (Freedom of Will)

The principle of freedom of contract (freedom of will) is a key principle in Brazilian contract law. It provides that the parties are free to enter into whatever contract they wish, with whosoever they desire and in whatever form they see fit. It means that the contract is the environment of freedom of will, in other words, of self-regulation of individuals. Therefore, the State cannot interfere with what is freely agreed between the parties.[19]

16. Article 429, of the Civil Code; Art. 30 of the Consumer Protection Code.
17. Article 430 e and following articles of the Civil Code.
18. Article 431 of the Civil Code.
19. Article 421 of the Civil Code.

1. Sub-principle of Sufficiency of Consent

This sub-principle provides that mere consent will suffice for entering into a contract; that is, additional formalities are not required. Under modern Brazilian law, no special formalities are required to verify whether there is assent (it can be evidenced by e-mail, telephone, fax, by an unmistakable behaviour denoting willingness to contract and similar means). Whilst it is true that consent will be a sufficient manifestation of assent to make a contract, this is not to say all contracts are purely consensual. The validity of some contracts is subject to the carrying out of certain formalities prescribed by law, while other contracts can only come into existence if a certain requirement is satisfied (in this sense, Article 108 of the Civil Code stands as the main exception to the rule of sufficiency of consent requiring that a contract be drafted by a public notary for transfer of title over real estate).

2. Sub-principle of Sanctity of Contract

This sub-principle provides that a freely agreed contract is deemed as the law between the parties (*força vinculativa dos contratos*). Where all requirements and formalities required for making a contract are fulfilled, the parties must abide to the terms of the contract as if its clauses were mandatory statutory provisions (this is based on the Roman law principle of *pacta sunt servanda*). Failure to comply with the terms of the contract will give ground to sue for compulsory enforcement in court or, if enforcement is not possible, a claim for damages.

3. Sub-principle of Privity of Contracts

This sub-principle provides that a contract can only bind the parties manifested their assent to the bargain (*força relativa dos contratos*). This sub-principle will be balanced against the social function of the contract sub-principle, which, according to some authors, will in some instances override privity and creates obligations on third parties.

This sub-principle does not bar parties to a contract from stipulating that benefits under the provisions of that contract be extended to third parties.

4. Sub-principle of Incompleteness

Since contractual obligations ultimately are an expression of the parties' free will, it is not legislation (law on the books) that will restrict what types of contract can be created. To this end, the sub-principle of incompleteness found in Article 425 of the Civil Code gives parties the right to create certain types of contracts that were not defined by legislation (*atipicidade*). This principle is based on the fact that custom and usage are sources of law.[20]

---

20. Article 4 of the Law of Introduction to the Civil Code and Art. 113 of the Civil Code.

B. Principle of Solidarity

Some scholars and even a significant part of Brazilian case law have maintained that the principle of freedom of contract gives prominent role in contractual relations on the individual and that this model of contract regulation needs to be tempered by another model that should emphasise the social relevance of the contract. This is called the principle of social solidarity (*pricípio da solidariedade social*).

The principle aims at bringing the contract closer to the model of welfare state structured in the Federal Constitution of 1988 and its concern with social justice by striking a balance between the interests of individuals and society values. Its supporters argue that the law allows for significant mechanisms for State intervention in the parties' will on account of social interests allegedly deserving protection.

The principle of solidarity restricts freedom of contract by making the relevant social interests more relevant than the private interests of the parties to the contract. This principle is used to justify the need of state intervention to protect the weaker party (as in the case of employment, consumer and lease agreements), enforce a minimum of solidarity and cooperation between the parties, protect community or collective interests (so as to prevent cartels or misuse of market power), spread the economic benefits of the relationship and even avoid abusive contractual obligations.

This highly interventionist approach has been targeted by sporadic criticism from scholars who applied an economic analysis to the law. Their studies show that the interventionist approach increases transaction costs. Nevertheless, many Brazilian courts have tended to apply this protective and interventionist stance in contractual interpretation, being concerned almost exclusively with social justice as between the parties with no regard to the economic consequences of their judgments.

1. Sub-principle of Good Faith

The sub-principle of good faith (*boa fé*) also puts a restraint on freedom of contract principles,[21] imposing on the parties the obligation to act reasonably. This principle imposes duties on the parties regardless of the terms of their bargain, taking into account the economic and social purpose of the contract, as well as the nature of the parties' agreement.

These implied duties, assessed by the courts when exercising their judgment over what is considered reasonable on a case-by-case basis, may be subdivided as follows: (a) duty of care and protection (*cuidado e proteção*) – for example, when dealing with passwords and client assets in banking contracts; (b) duty of information, loyalty and disclosure (*informação, lealdade e divulgação*) – for example, full, extensive disclosure of information in insurance contracts; (c) duty to render

21. Article 422 of the Civil Code.

accounts (*prestação de contas*) – for example, in management contracts; and (d) duty of confidentiality (*confidencialidade*) – for example in contracts that deal with the rendering of services.

This sub-principle also imposes limitations to the exercise of certain subjective rights. For instance, scholars and court decisions alike have favoured that the principle of good faith would guard against termination of a contract when there has been a substantial performance of its terms on the part of the defendant, whenever termination would emerge as an abuse of rights (doctrine of substantial performance; *adimplemento substancial*). The same applies to situations when the party wishes to enforce a provision that although formally incorporated to the contract it was never enforced nor complied with by either party in the course of their contractual relationship.[22]

2. Sub-principle of Social Function of Contracts

The sub-principle of social function of contracts (*função social dos contratos*) provides that subjective rights are recognised by the legal system not in an absolute manner, but rather taking into account a socially relevant purpose.[23] Therefore, a party is barred from exercising any given right with the purpose of harming the other party. Moreover, collective interests must be regarded by the contracting parties, and so they must not inflict any harm to the environment, market and similar consequences to society in general.

Brazilian courts have applied this sub-principle to mitigate the strict application of *pacta sunt servanda* principles in instances where the protection of certain rights overrides the private interests of the innocent party. For instance, based on the sub-principle of social function of contracts courts have reviewed bank contracts to cut down on interest rates charged by financial institutions, extended the coverage of health insurance policies (such as in the case of AIDS-suffering policy holders) and enjoined power utility companies from interrupting the distribution of power to a defaulting consumer.[24]

3. Sub-principle of Contractual Fairness

The sub-principle of *contractual fairness* (*justiça contratual*) provides that the contract must allow for a balance to exist in the exchange of goods and services. The economic equilibrium in the contract must be maintained, taking into account circumstances existing both at the beginning and end of the contract.[25] That is the idea of *synallagma* or contractual commutability that ancient classical jurists held in great esteem.

22. Article 187 of the Civil Code.
23. Articles 187 and 421 of the Civil Code.
24. Civil Appeal 70005790837, Court of Appeals of Rio Grande do Sul.
25. Articles 157, 317 and 478 of the Civil Code and Arts 4, III e 6°, VI of the Consumer Protection Code.

Therefore, a flawed contract may be annulled or even reviewed by the court when either party has undertaken an overly burdensome obligation due to inexperience or forced by extreme circumstances – as in the case of a farmer who sells his lands in the countryside for 10% of its market value to a real estate company located in the State's capital.

In other instances, the principle of contractual fairness allows a contract to be terminated or reviewed in court in situations where the undue burden imposed upon a party to the contract owes itself to an unforeseeable, unusual and unavoidable event (*onerosidade excessiva*) – although reviewing of consumer contracts can be effected regardless of events of such nature. Thus, contracts containing a clause that provided for payments linked to a foreign currency have been reviewed by courts so that a balance was achieved after changes in government policy brought about a plummeting devaluation in the domestic currency against the foreign currency.

IV. CLASSIFICATION OF CONTRACTS

Contracts can be arranged into different categories, each with their own set of rules. Therefore, the correct classification of contract types is essential under Brazilian law.

A. Typical and Atypical Contracts

A contract is said to be typical (*típico*) when it is outlined in statutory provisions; conversely, it is rendered atypical (*atípico*) when it is not regulated specifically by law.[26] For instance, the Civil Code of 1916 did not provide for freight contracts, and so this contract was regarded as atypical. Conversely, the Civil Code of 2002 contains provisions for this type of contract[27] and thus the freight contract is considered typical in the Civil Code.

There is a vast number of typical contracts in Brazilian law. These include purchase and sale contracts, lease contracts, agency and distribution contracts, insurance contracts, contract for gifts, mandate, insurance contract, commission contracts, loan contracts, deposit contracts and many others.

It is important to identify typical contracts under Brazilian law to understand whether a provision is mandatory or may be excluded by the will of the parties as well as to understand the relationship between these contracts and the general rules of the Civil Code applying to contracts.

26. The parties are free to make atypical contracts (Art. 425 of the Civil Code).
27. Article 730 of the Civil Code.

B. Unilateral and Bilateral Contracts

Bilateral contracts (*contratos bilaterais*) are agreements that set forth obligations to both parties (such as sale and lease agreements). Unilateral contracts (*contratos unilaterais*) will typically establish obligations to only one of the parties (such as gifts, mandates and loan agreements).

Under Brazilian law, every contractual relationship implies:

(a) main obligations (they indicate the nature of the agreement, whether bilateral or unilateral);
(b) accessory obligations (obligations implied from the duty of good faith in dealing such as the duty of disclosure of information, clarification and rendering of accounts);
(c) secondary obligations (such as the obligation to store and transport purchased goods, the lack of which will prevent performance of main duties).

Insofar as a bilateral agreement is concerned, the general rule is that neither party has a claim to the performance of the other party before that first party has fulfilled its own obligations. In such an event, the innocent party may raise an excuse to withhold performance based on the rule of *exceptio non adimpleti contractus*.[28] It is exceptionally admitted that a party may withhold performance if after the contract is made circumstances arise where the other party's assets are compromised to such an extent that reasonable doubt is raised as to that party's ability to perform according to its promise.[29]

Also, in bilateral contracts the thing or service which makes up the subject-matter of the contract may be rejected if a hidden defect (*vício oculto*; a flaw or imperfection that cannot be reasonably detected by a person under normal circumstances) is found to exist that will diminish its value or render the thing unusable or the service useless (*vícios redibitórios*).[30]

Similarly, in bilateral contracts, the seller of a thing has a duty to guarantee clear title to the thing being sold. The seller further warrants the buyer against third-party claims as to ownership over the thing in question and must hold the buyer harmless against eviction (*evicção*).[31]

C. Gratuitous and Onerous Contracts

An onerous contract (*contrato oneroso*) is a contract that will include an exchange of consideration (something of value or an exchange of obligations). On the other

28. Article 476 of the Civil Code.
29. Article 477 of the Civil Code.
30. Article 441 of the Civil Code.
31. Article 447 of the Civil Code.

hand, in gratuitous contracts (*contrato gratuito*) one party will always carry a burden in favour of the other party (i.e., gift or free loan).

D. Commutative and Risk Contracts

A commutative, or synallagmatic contract (*contrato comutativo* or *signalagmático*) is one that establishes a balance between performances (such as purchase and sale or lease agreements). A risk contract (*contrato aleatório*) is such a contract where one party will assume the full risk of non-performance of the counterparty (such as a contract for the purchase of future harvest of a farmer by a factory or trader).[32]

E. Consensual, Formal and Real Contracts

Consensual contracts (*contratos consensuais*) are established according to the free manifestation of the parties' assent, with no further requirement of form or substance being necessary to its making or validity. They stand as the general rule since Brazilian law only requires that few contracts be in written form.[33]

Formal contracts (*contratos formais*), on the other hand, are agreements which the law requires to be in writing or follow specific formalities. Contracts for the sale of real estate, for instance, must be made by a contract drafted by a notary public (called a *escritura pública*).[34] Real estate contracts are a legacy from classic Roman law where the delivery of possession of the thing was an essential element to the existence of the agreement and, in the case of land, the formality of delivery is a fiction which the law deems as effected when the *escritura pública* is signed.

F. Instant, Deferred and Long-Term Contracts

In instant performance contracts (*contratos de execução instantânea*), legal obligations are carried out as soon as the contract comes into being – its formation is almost simultaneous to its termination (such as ordering, taking and paying for a chocolate bar at a shop).

Deferred performance contracts (*contratos de execução diferida*) are agreements where performance will take place later in time as provided for in the contract (i.e., delivery of furniture occurring thirty days after purchase).

Long-term contracts (*contratos de execução continuada*) are contracts where payment is made in instalments, the fulfilment of each does not constitute

32. Article 458 of the Civil Code.
33. Article 107 of the Civil Code.
34. Article 108 of the Civil Code.

discharge from the whole obligation (such as house mortgage contracts and lease agreements).

G. Standard Contract Forms/Contracts of Adhesion

Methods of pro-forma contracting are now prevalent in just about all contractual relationships between companies and individuals. As a matter of economic rationality, streamlining, feasibility and even safety, nowadays companies lay down contractual terms in advance and set them out for the mere acceptance (adhesion) by offerees.

The contract of adhesion is not a new and independent kind of contract. In fact, it is a contract used to buy and sell goods, for the provision of services and for difference relationships sharing a common method of entering into a binding agreement.

1. Concept

A contract of adhesion (*contrato de adesão*) can be defined as a contract where the terms are unilaterally set out by the party with greater bargaining power and where the other party is not in position to negotiate or significantly modify the content of the written document, being limited to a mere acceptance of its terms. Brazilian law recognises the formation of such contracts not only in consumer relationships but also in business relationships such as those of franchising and distribution, for as long as there is no actual opportunity for bargaining the terms of the contract.[35]

2. Characteristics

A contract of adhesion is presented to offerees in a standard, generally printed, form or document that needs only to be filled out with some details about the party, the subject-matter and the price. Thus, those who wish to enter into contract with a supplier will be presented with an already formalised and adjusted binding relationship without scope for striking a bargain or negotiating the most important terms and conditions of the contract.

The distinctive characteristic of adhesion contracts, therefore, is the absence of an ultimate bargaining stage, the lack of previous negotiation with respect to the clauses of the contract and their unilateral imposition on the offeree, insomuch that he or she is not able to modify the contract in any relevant way. The offeree's consent is manifested by the mere adherence to the contract as drafted by the offeror.

Despite the limited bargaining possibilities under a contract of adhesion, there usually remains a minimal freedom of contract. Ordinarily, there will exist an economic advantage between the parties, which may lead to abuse. Brazilian law provides for protection against these abuses – for instance, through abuse of

35. See Arts 423 and 424 of the Civil Code.

economic power principles (Article 20 of Law 8,884/94) and abusive clauses (see below).

3. Interpretation and Regulation

As a general rule, the terms set out in contracts of adhesion, especially those with clauses that are ambiguous, are to be interpreted against the party who drafted the document.[36] Furthermore, the prevailing view from both scholars and case law is that clauses agreed upon separately, usually written by hand or machine, will prevail over boilerplate or printed clauses (although the existence of these clauses will not per se exclude the contract as being deemed a contract of adhesion).

There is special attention given to abusive clauses (those which lay an excessive burden on the weaker party). Article 424 of the Civil Code provides that clauses determining waiver in advance of offerees' rights arising out of the nature of the transaction (such as, for example, an insurance contract that provides a reimbursement scheme that in practice will render indemnity impossible) are regarded as null and void. Additionally, Brazilian courts will tend to grant protection to offerees of contracts of adhesion and may rule void clauses deemed as abusive especially in consumer relationships (see Article 51 of Consumer Protection Code).

V. ASSIGNMENT OF CONTRACTUAL RIGHTS AND OBLIGATIONS

A. Generally

Assignment of contractual rights and obligations may occur in three ways. Firstly, by an assignment of credits (*cessão de créditos*) which is a kind of transfer whereby only the benefits to be received from the contract are assigned.[37] Secondly, by assumption of debt (*assunção de dívida*), where only the passive position in a contract (the obligations owed or the 'debt'), will be assigned.[38] Finally, the assignment may be an assignment of a contractual position (*cessão de posição contratual*) which is an assignment of the whole contractual relationship with its full entitlements and obligations thus leading to a complete substitution of one party by a third party.

B. Assignment of Credits

An assignment of credits occurs when an agreement is made where the creditor (i.e., the party to which the obligations are owed) assigns the whole, or part, of its

36. Article 423 of the Civil Code.
37. Article 286 of the Civil Code.
38. Article 299 of the Civil Code.

benefits under the contract to a third party with or without the consent of the debtor (i.e., the party which owes the obligations). An assignment of credits agreement only requires assent from the assignor and assignee – the remaining debtor (i.e., the party which owes the obligations) is not required to manifest its assent to the assignment – even though it is advisable to do so in anticipation of the duty to give notice to the debtor of change of beneficiaries.

A necessary causal connection exists between the assignment agreement and the original contract. If any obligation contained in the original contract is found to be null, void or unenforceable, such will affect the ensuing assignment – much to the contrary to what happens in the case of a promissory note, for instance, where an abstract or autonomous obligation to perform exists.

In order for the assignment to be valid, apart from the normal requirements, the corresponding contract must fulfil other requirements specially provided by law: the benefits form the contractual obligations must be allowed to be assigned (as when there is no contractual provision to the contrary), the benefits in question must not be personal and non-assignable due to its nature (the relevant obligation must not be *intuito personae*) and the benefits must be free from any pending court attachment. Furthermore, the law also requires that the assignment of the benefit be made in writing.

If an assignment is made, the assignor does not remain liable for the benefit of the obligations assigned to the third party, except if the assignment agreement provides otherwise.

C. Assumption of Debt

In an *assumption of debt agreement* a third party will commit to performing contractual obligations in lieu of the debtor of the original agreement.[39] In other words, a debt assumption agreement will cause a transfer of an obligation by means of a contract.

This occurs by means of a contract that will necessarily include the original creditor, who must appear as consenting to the transaction (known as a consenting third party; *interveniente anuente*). Hence, a debt assumption agreement is not valid without the creditor's consent and in this sense, such contract greatly differs from that of credit assignment.

With regard to its effects, a debt assumption agreement may: (a) discharge the original debtor, unless an express term provides otherwise (if the original debtor is to take part in the assignment agreement as co-debtor, such provision must expressly appear in the assignment document); (b) release all encumbrances over assets and guarantees provided by the original debtor, unless an express term provides otherwise (i.e., if the new assignment requires any security, the security must be expressly described in the new agreement).[40]

---

39. Article 299 of the Civil Code.
40. Article 299 and 302 of the Civil Code.

With regard to any formalities prescribed by law, a debt assumption agreement must satisfy the same elements as explained above in relation to the credit assignment agreement.

D. Assignment of Contractual Position

An assignment of contractual position (*cessão de contrato*) is the assignment, in full, of all rights and obligations of the assignor in the original contract. In other words, it is the complete substitution of one party to a contract by a third party. In this case, the subject-matter of the assignment is not simply a right of or an obligation but the whole set of rights and obligations that comprise a contractual position.

This type of agreement is not expressly regulated by the Civil Code. However, the substantive rules and formalities which govern the assignment of a contractual provision are drawn from those which regulate assumptions of debt, which are stricter than those provided for credit assignments under the Civil Code.

VI. INTERPRETATION OF CONTRACTS

To interpret a contract is to ascertain the intention of two distinct manifestations of assent that comprise the contract. In a broad sense, legislation determines that the person interpreting the contract must take into account more the parties' underlying intentions than the literal meaning of the language.[41] In Article 113, the Civil Code states that 'legal transactions shall be interpreted according to good faith and custom in the place of making'. In Article 114, the Civil Code further states that 'beneficial legal transactions and waivers are to be interpreted strictly'. In addition to this, the Consumer Protection Code (in Article 47) states that the clauses of a contract shall be construed in such a way as to afford the greatest possible benefit to the weaker party in the contractual relationship.[42]

In pursuing equilibrium within the contract environment, Brazilian contract law and its social model will emphasise the role of the law as a limiting one and the true authoritative source of freedom of contract. The law (mandatory and indefeasible by the will of the parties) is perceived to afford protection to certain social interests, thus valuing reliability and good faith among the parties to bargain. This ultimately lends a great deal of discretionary power to the Brazilian Judiciary when interpreting contracts in light of the written law.

41. Article 112 of the Civil Code.
42. A similar statement is found in Art. 423 of the Civil Code.

VII. TERMINATION OF CONTRACTS

A. Termination by Performance

Performance (*adimplemento* or *execução*) is the usual manner of terminating a contractual relationship. Performance occurs when the relevant obligor performs that obligation which the obligor agreed to incur. Discharge, in certain circumstances, may be effected by third parties – the Brazilian legal system allows for any person to agree to pay for another person's debt.[43]

There are alternative ways to substitute a party's obligation to pay that will essentially bear the same effect, such as in the case of a party who consents the other party to perform in a different manner or deliver a different chattel than that which was agreed upon in the first place (known as giving in payment or *dação em pagamento*).

B. Nullity and Avoidance

Under Brazilian law, a voidable (*anulável*) contract is a contract that whose parties' consent has been vitiated by mistake, unfairness, duress or wrongdoing.[44] Such issues can be raised as exception or excuse only by the innocent party.

The contract is said to be void (*nulo*) when it suffers from a more serious vice in degree, such as the case when an essential formality required by law was neglected, when it was entered into by a person lacking capacity or when its subject-matter is unlawful.[45] The law does not require a specific motion in the proceeding from the party seeking to void the contract; a court may declare it on its own motion.

C. Unilateral and Bilateral Termination

Under Brazilian law, termination which is effected by one party or by mutual consent is called *resilição*. A *resilição* may be effected by a meeting of the minds (a bilateral termination or *distrato*) or exceptionally by the will of one of the parties (a unilateral termination or *resilição unilateral*).

Bilateral termination is also called abrogation (*abrogação*), meaning that the contractual relationship was terminated by the same intention that caused it to come into being.[46] It is an agreement that brings a former contractual relationship to an end. The law requires no other formality to the abrogation than that which is required for the enforceability of the original contract; that is, if the law prescribes

43. Article 304 of the Civil Code.
44. Article 138 et seq. articles of the Civil Code.
45. Article 166 of the Civil Code.
46. Article 472 of the Civil Code.

a deed drafted by a notary public as a condition of validity of a contract (as in the purchase sale of real estate), then the abrogation will only be effected by the same type of agreement.

Unilateral termination (or *denunciação*) is seldom allowed as the legal system forbids that a legal transaction rely solely on the will of one party to continue to exist (such provisions are known as a *cláusulas leoninas* or *cláusulas abusivas*). Because the unilateral termination is an exception to the rule, it must be provided by law or expressly under the terms of the contract.[47] Care is needed when anticipating or exercising the right to terminate, since the Brazilian legal system protects the party that is harmed by unilateral termination. Courts may issue injunctions to keep the contractual relationship on foot and/or award damages on grounds of wrongful termination.[48]

D. Dissolution

Dissolution (*dissolução*) is a manner of termination of a contractual relationship due to breach of contract.[49] Dissolution may take place along with the payment of damages to the innocent party (*indenização*), so as to compensate for the losses suffered and also for what that party would reasonably have earned if the party in breach had not breached its obligations (*perdas e danos*).

There are no strict rules as to how the courts calculate damages, but the damages must have a causal connection to the breach and put the victim in the position it would be if the agreement was fully performed. In lieu of seeking an order for dissolution of the contract, the innocent party may instead file a motion asking the court to compel the other party to perform, in which case the court may pre-emptively order the payment of *astreintes* (daily fines to enforce performance on the part of the non-performing party).[50]

Dissolution may be express or implied. Express dissolution (*cláusula resolutiva expressa*) needs to be provided for in the contract itself and does not require an order be handed down by a court to produce effects. However, a dissolution clause that is implied (*cláusula resolutiva tácita*) will depend upon a court decision before it has legal effects.[51] In this sense, even oral contracts may be dissolved on grounds of implementation of such an implied dissolution clause.

The doctrine of substantial performance (*adimplemento substancial*) prevents the innocent party from dissolving the contract when a substantial part of the obligations stemming from the contract have been fulfilled (for instance, where thirty-nine instalments of a total of forty agreed in a sale have already been paid).

---

47. Article 473 of the Civil Code.
48. Article 473, single paragraph or Art. 720 of the Civil Code.
49. Articles 474 and 475 of the Civil Code.
50. Articles 461 and 461-A of the Code of Civil Procedure.
51. Article 474 of the Civil Code.

A mere delay in performance when the creditor still has interest in that the obligation be fulfilled is called arrears (*mora*) or relative default (*inadimplemento relativo*).[52] Being in arrears will not necessarily give ground to dissolution of the contract but can lead to a claim for damages in case where the innocent party suffers damages as a consequence of the delay. Delay in payment will cause the party to incur in the duty to pay monetary readjustment (*correção monetária*) according to official indexes (the debt will be readjusted according to the measured inflation for the period) and also the payment of interest at the maximum monthly rate of 1% per month (except in banking contracts, in which the interest rate can be higher).

E. TERMINATION BY EXCESSIVE ONEROUSNESS

For contracts where performance is continuous or deferred, a party may be able to have the contract terminated or the terms of the agreement modified where there is excessive onerousness or hardship (*onerosidade excessiva*). Excessive onerousness will occur where due to extraordinary and unforeseen events make an obligation excessively onerous to one party and excessively advantageous for another.[53]

If the elements required for establishing excessive onerousness are established, the court will be allowed to change the terms of the agreement applying general concepts of equity (*ex aequo et bono*) and decide on now the obligations are to apply as between the parties on general contract law principles.

VIII. PREVENTING CONTRACT TERMINATION

In Brazil, the typical way to prevent default is the stipulation of a penalty or fine (*multa*).[54] This is achieved by the inclusion of a penalty clause (*cláusula penal*)[55] in the contract. The penalty clause is an attempt from the parties to exert some influence on the other party in order to persuade that party to comply with the terms in agreement or else be subject to paying an amount that has been previously agreed upon by both parties.

In contrast with Anglo-American law, prima facie the only legal restraint to the use of a penalty clause has to do with the amount set, which cannot be greater than the total consideration exchanged in the contract. Furthermore, the party who feels harmed may resort to the courts and seek to obtain reduction of the amount of the penalty set by agreement of the parties (even though it has been stipulated within the limits provided under the law), on the basis that it is an excessively onerous clause. Penalties may be imposed in addition to the damages which are suffered by the innocent party.

---

52. Article 395 of the Civil Code.
53. Article 478 of the Civil Code.
54. Article 409 of the Civil Code.
55. Article 408 of the Civil Code.

Another way to ensure performance of contractual obligations is to require the payment of a deposit (*arras* or *sinal*).[56] *Arras* are often used in purchases of land and vehicles so that if the party who paid the deposit calls off the transaction, the deposit will be forfeited. If, however, the person who received the deposit chooses not to proceed, then that party must reimburse twice the amount deposited to the innocent party.[57]

Finally, an effective way of protecting obligors' rights is via having security or personal guarantee in place. The parties may agree that the obligees have security rights granted over property (such as a mortgage over land or a pledge over chattels – *hipotecas* for real estate or *penhor* for goods) or that third parties give personal guarantees (*fiança*) to ensure the obligations of a party to an agreement. It has also become very common in Brazil that large transactions are backed up by performance bonds (*seguro adimplemento*).

Selected Bibliography

In English

P.M.B. Avallone, 'The Award of Punitive and Emotional Distress Damages in Breach of Contract Cases: A Comparison Between the American and the Brazilian Legal Systems' (2002) 8 *New England International and Comparative Law Annual* 253.

A. Franco, *Brazilian Contract Law Contextualized in Three Globalization Periods* (Thesis, Harvard Law School, 2004).

E. Grebler, 'The Convention on International Sale of Goods and Brazilian Law: Are Differences Irreconcilable?' (2005) 25 *The Journal of Law and Commerce* 467.

D. Stringer, 'Choice of Law and Choice of Forum in Brazilian International Commercial Contracts: Party Autonomy, International Jurisdiction, and the Emerging Third Way' (2006) 44 *Colombia Journal of Transnational Law Association* 959.

M. Trebilcock and L. Jing, 'Role of Formal Contract Law and Enforcement in Economic Development' (2006) 92 *Virginia Law Review* 1517.

In Portuguese

A.V. Azevedo, *Teoria Geral dos Contratos Típicos e Atípicos: Curso De Direito Civil* (Atlas, São Paulo, 2002).

O. Gomes, *Contratos* (26th edn, Forense, Rio de Janeiro, 2007).

S. Rodrigues, *Direito Civil* (29th edn, Saraiva, São Paulo, 2003).

A. Wald, *Obrigações e Contratos* (16th edn, Saraiva, São Paulo, 2004).

56. Article 417 of the Civil Code.
57. Article 418 of the Civil Code.

Chapter 7
Civil Liability

*Cláudio Filkenstein**

I. INTRODUCTION

In Brazil, civil liability may arise both from civil and criminal legal rules, as well as from rules of moral, religious and social nature. Civil liability is also divided into contractual liability and extra-contractual liability.

There are two main types of liability: *strict liability* and *subjective liability* (known as 'fault' or *culpa* in Portuguese). *Fault* is the general rule under Brazilian law and will apply to every situation, except for entrepreneurial risk and consumer related cases where *strict liability* applies.

To determine the duty to redress and pay damages in relation to a wrong, the following elements must be present: (a) damage; (b) causation (i.e., the *nexus* between the event and the damage); and (c) fault (which encompasses the notion of negligence, recklessness or lack of skill as well as a wrong wilful act with intent).

The duty to pay damages to third parties stems either from operation of law or a legal fact (acts, dealings, contracts, a unilateral declaration of will, an illicit act or even a licit act).

Civil liability can thus be defined under Brazilian law as the field of law that studies, analyses and understands the legal aspects of the obligation to redress and

* Professor of International Law, Pontifical Catholic University of São Paulo. LLD (PUC/SP), LLM (Miami), LLB (USP).

Fabiano Deffenti & Welber Barral (eds), *Introduction to Brazilian Law*, pp. 105–111.

indemnify material and moral damages (which under the Brazilian system includes pain and suffering), caused by third parties.[1]

II. APPLICATION

A. The Obligation to Repair

According to the Brazilian Civil Code,[2] anyone who, by an illicit act,[3] causes damage to someone else has the obligation to redress and repair the damage, regardless of fault in the cases specified by law or where the activity usually developed by the agent of the damage implies, by its nature, a risk to the rights or assets of another (which is known as the *theory of risk*). Hence, civil liability is found in every situation where some loss is caused by any activity to a person or to assets. The issue of liability does not apply if there is no damage, since the illicit act as a matter of civil law applies only if it causes losses to someone.

The principles that guide civil liability intend to put the injured party in its original position (*status quo ante*) or the status one was in before the damage was suffered. The principle establishes a duty to indemnify, transferring the costs of the damage suffered by the harmed party to the person that caused the damage and who, as established by law, bears these costs.

Leading scholarly writings are unanimous in considering the duty to indemnify as a means to re-establish a balance between the party that suffered the damage/injury and the party that inflicted it. The existence of the illicit act, pain and suffering or material damages are necessary to characterise and identify the liability to secure the protection of the harmed party's rights.[4]

B. Causation

The causal connection or causation (*nexo causal*) is the link that connects the behaviour of the agent to the damage.[5] The requirement of causation aims to establish that there was a breach of someone else's right and damage. As Brazilian law does not allow for trials by jury, the trial judge is responsible for deciding whether there is causation based on the evidence presented.[6]

---

1. It is worth pointing out that all civil matters within Brazil are decided by a court, be it in final or summary judgment. There is absolutely no trial by jury for civil and commercial matters in the Brazilian legal system.
2. Article 927.
3. Articles 186 and 187 of the Civil Code.
4. See, for instance, Civil Court of the State of São Paulo, Appeal 786.921-6, 9th Chamber (1998).
5. S. de Salvo Venosa, *Direito Civil* (5th edn, vol. 4, Atlas, São Paulo, 2005), 42.
6. C.M. da Silva Pereira, *Responsabilidade Civil* (9th edn, Forense, Rio de Janeiro, 1999), 82.

Within the area of civil liability, where the defendant can establish that the reason for inflicting the damage was because it was a fortuitous case (*caso fortuito*) or a case of force majeure (*força maior*) the obligation to indemnify is extinguished. Force majeure is established by natural circumstances that are ordinarily unpredictable, without fault of any party.

C. Return to the *Status Quo Ante*

The reason for making good the damages suffered by the injured party is connected to the concern to return the victim to the state he or she was in before the illicit act occurred. To that end, in many cases it becomes simply impossible to reach such a result because the act or accident resulted in irreversible consequences. Should this happen, the courts must resort to an alternative solution, through the payment of monetary damages.

Damages are limited to the amount of sufficient to compensate the plaintiff for the losses suffered. Brazil does not recognise the concept of punitive damages; therefore, only actual and moral damages (pain and suffering) can be granted by a court. Actual damages include identifiable losses and loss of profits.

D. Illicit Acts

In the civil liability context, an illicit act, according to Maria Helena Diniz, 'constitutes an action (act or omission), attributable to the agent, harmful to the harmed party and contrary to the legal order. The said action may be performed by the harming party or by a person, animal or thing that is under one's custody or care'.[7] Silvio de Salvo Venosa considers an illicit act as the act proven to have directly or indirectly originated from one's will resulting in legal effects contrary to the applicable legal system. The voluntary behaviour that violates a duty is said to be the main concern of civil liability.[8]

E. Damages Inflicted on Property

The duty to pay damages will not necessarily arise where damage is inflicted on property alone. The duty arises in the cases set out in Article 188 of the Civil Code, which provides that the obligation to pay damages will be excused if the damages were inflicted: (a) as legitimate defence or in the regular exercise of a recognised right; or (b) with the absolute necessity of avoiding imminent danger to the extent that it was reasonable.

---

7. M.H. Diniz. *Curso de Direito Civil Brasileiro* (19th edn, vol. 7, Saraiva, São Paulo, 2005), 24.
8. S. de Salvo Venosa, *Direito Civil* (6th edn, vol. 4, Atlas, São Paulo, 2006), 20.

III. CIVIL VERSUS CRIMINAL DAMAGES

Damages awarded in a civil action cannot be confused with criminal sanctions. A criminal sanction arises from criminal acts, with a penalty previously contemplated and set out in law. Civil liability, on the other hand, only calls for an illicit act with damages caused to someone else and causation between the two or more subjects in question. As the first Civil Court of São Paulo put it: 'criminal law requires, in order to apply its sanctions, the integration of the most severe conditions and, besides, included in well defined standards – *nulla poena sine lege*. [. . .] On the other hand, civil law starts on different assumptions. It mainly considers the damage [suffered by the plaintiff] and that a priori state of mind turns to the benefit of the victim of the loss.'[9]

Civil and criminal illicit acts do not overlap in the sense of preventing the coexistence of a civil claim with criminal consequences in one same duty to repair. However, criminal consequences and assessment can only be asserted in a criminal court, as the civil judge does not have jurisdiction over criminal matters, even if the crime committed is also a civil wrong.

According to Maria Helena Diniz,[10] as civil liability gives rise to private law damages, the law seeks to re-establish the changed balance of a factual situation, resulting in the resetting of the *status quo ante* or in a monetary award to compensate for the losses. In a civil case, the law is compelled to repair the position of the harmed party, indemnifying for the damages suffered, therefore tending only to redress the damages because it intends mostly to help the victim and its interests, compensating for the violated rights.

Professor Diniz mentions as examples 'the strict liability based on the theory of the risk; accidents resulting from the exercise of dangerous activities, such as the use of a vehicle; embezzlement of amounts performed by an employee in hotels, the indemnification for which will be the responsibility of the hotel manager (Articles 932, IV and 933 of the Civil Code); wrongs committed by a subordinate or servant, since the employer will be liable for the errors or mistakes of theirs (Articles 932, III and 933 of the Civil Code); falling of objects from a house or its throwing into an undue place, causing damage, which gives rise to strict liability to the house occupant (Article 938 of the Civil Code); payment of phony check by a bank (Digest 28 of the Federal Supreme Federal Court); wilful governmental behaviour that impairs the rights of the individual, which establishes the responsibility of the State (Federal Constitution, Article 37 paragraph 6); [and] acts performed in the exercise of certain rights (Articles 1285, 1289, 1293, 1251 and 1313 of the Civil Code)'. These clearly explain the importance of the study, adequacy and development of social aspects of civil liability in relation to day-to-day life in society.

---

9. 1st Civil Court of São Paulo, Appeal No. 259,837 (1979). See also Special Appeal 2002/0143357-4 (2006).
10. M.H. Diniz. *Curso de Direito Civil Brasileiro* (19th edn, vol. 7, Saraiva, São Paulo, 2005), 23.

IV. CONTRACTUAL, EXTRA-CONTRACTUAL, AND CONSUMER-RELATED LIABILITY

Modern Brazilian law increasingly highlights the existence of civil and criminal liability in acts that do not cause actual damage but that give rise to the right to receive reparations due to mere exposure to *possible* danger and injury. In addition to the scholarly writings that classify civil and criminal liability as the two elements of the law enacted to mandate rectifying injustice and/or bringing about satisfaction for those who suffered wrongdoing or loss, and the division of fault and strict liability, this principle becomes simple when two further classifications are used: (a) contractual and extra-contractual liability; and (b) liability in consumer relations.

According to Cavalieri Filho,[11] contractual liability occurs when there is a prior binding obligation and the duty to repair results from fault, whereas the liability in consumer relations is characterised when such duty results from a threat to a subjective right, without there being any prior legal relationship between the offender and the victim.

The liability established in the Consumer Protection Code is strict (*responsibilidade objetiva*), based on the duty imposed on the supplier to ensure safety of the product in relation to the products and services put in the market. Strict liability, which was an exception in Brazilian law, has extended its scope of application to cover even more areas than subjective liability (liability based on a *reasonable person standard*) itself. Cavalieri Filho states, in relation to the Consumer Protection Code,[12] that the appearance of a new strict liability concept in the legal system has created a significant increase in the factual circumstances which fall within the scope of liability without fault.[13]

The Consumer Protection Code[14] specifies, in Articles 12 to 14, that the liability for product and service results from malfunctions in the product or service that may cause physical damage or pain and suffering to the consumer. Articles 18 to 20 provide for the liability for defective products and services where there is a defect that partially or fully prevents its operation without physically harming the consumer.

Mario[15] explains that 'the evolution of the civil liability theory revolves around the need to aid the victim. This has propelled academic writings and case law beyond the written codes, because having restrictive principles hinder the development and rendering of good justice. It was necessary to resort to alternate technical ways and accept, by-passing daily resistance, that in many cases the damage is indeed subject to a remedy without existence of fault'.

11. S. Cavalieri Filho. *Programa de Responsabilidade Civil* (2nd edn, Malheiros, São Paulo, 2000, 31 et seq.).
12. Law 8,078/1990.
13. S. de Salvo Venosa, *Direito Civil* (6th edn, vol. 4, Atlas, São Paulo, 2006), 22.
14. Law 8,078/1990.
15. C.M. da Silva Pereira, *Instituições de Direito Civil* (7th edn, vol. 3 Forense, Rio de Janeiro, 1984), 390.

This determination should and indeed does go beyond the consumer-related cases to accept liability without fault.

Disregarding fault, the theory of subjective liability (*responsabilidade subjetiva*) takes into account the dangers involved in the activity performed by the wrongdoer, be it due to its nature or the nature of the means in which it is undertaken. Therefore, if the wrongdoer intends to obtain advantages or benefits, it is for this very reason that he or she must indemnify any party for all damages his or her acts or omissions cause.

Therefore, even before it was entered into Brazil's substantive law, via Article 927 of the Civil Code of 2002, the courts had already recognised the theory of risk. Under this theory, it would be deemed fraudulent not to anticipate foreseeable events or facts. From such acts follow the need to place responsibility and the need to pay damages.

Under the theory of risk, the element of fault becomes unnecessary in order to determine liability. Risk, alongside with causation, is enough to characterise the need to repair the wrong. Therefore, whoever creates a risk must bear its consequences should the risk cause damages to any party, even without fault or intent to cause damages. Given this, Brazilian courts have extended the theory of risk in order to order the payment of damages for certain wrongs even where there is no fault.

V. PROFESSIONALS' LIABILITY

The work of certain professionals is subject to a special set of rules, increasing the standard when assessing liability. This is the case, for instance, as damages caused by medical malpractice.

The vast majority of scholarly writings stands for the proposition that the relationship is based on a contract to advise made between the physician and the patient, which establishes an obligation to provide services with the intention to advise the patient and not to guarantee the cure. Under this theory, there will only be professional malpractice when lack of skill, recklessness or unjustifiable negligence, the reason why the courts are strict in applying the elements for showing lack of skill or neglect of the physician in a patient action seeking to hold that professional liable for the damage suffered.[16]

Selected Bibliography

In English

P.M.B. Avallone, 'The Award of Punitive and Emotional Distress Damages in Breach of Contract Cases: A Comparison Between the American and the

16. S. Rodrigues, *Direito Civil, Responsabilidade Civil* (20th edn, vol. 4, Saraiva, São Paulo, 2003, 248 and 249).

Brazilian Legal Systems' (2002) 8 *New England International and Comparative Law Annual* 253.

J. M. Iturraspe, 'Part III: "General Themes: General Trends in South American Product Liability Law: An Overview" ' (2003) 20 *Journal of International and Comparative Law* 115.

In Portuguese

A.V. Azevedo, *Teoria Geral das Obrigações: Responsabilidade Civil: Curso de Direito Civil* (10th edn, Atlas, São Paulo, 2004).

C. M. da Silva Pereira, *Responsabilidade Civil* (Forense, Rio de Janeiro, 1998).

C. M. da Silva Pereira, *Instituições de Direito Civil* (7th edn, vol. III, Editora Forense, 1984).

S. de Salvo Venosa, *Direito Civil* (5th edn, vol. 4, Atlas, São Paulo, 2005).

S.C. Filho, *Programa de Responsabilidade Civil* (2nd edn, Malheiros, 2000).

S. Rodrigues, *Direito Civil, Responsabilidade Civil* (20th edn, vol. 4, Saraiva, 2003).

Chapter 8
Corporate and Insolvency Law

*Fabiano Deffenti**

I. INTRODUCTION

The Brazilian legal system underwent substantial changes with globalisation and the consequent growth of foreign direct investments. These changes were especially felt in the Brazilian securities market. In this context, Brazil has been developing a more comprehensive and institutionalised regime of regulation, which was implemented by the amendments made to the Corporations Law (*Lei das Sociedades Anônimas*)[1] in 2001[2] and in the passing of the new Brazilian Civil Code in 2002.[3]

As a civil law country, the Brazilian Civil Code plays a key role in establishing the rules that govern the types of enterprises allowed to conduct business. The Civil Code sets the different enterprise types as well as the rules that govern them. One key exception applies to corporations (*sociedades anônimas* or *anonymous partnerships*), whose rules are provided in the Corporations Law.[4]

---

* BBus (International), LLB (Hons) (QUT). Attorney-at-Law (New York), Legal Practitioner (Queensland and Australian Capital Territory), Barrister and Solicitor (New Zealand), Lawyer (Brazil).

1. Law 6,410/1976.
2. Law 10,303/2001.
3. Law 10,406/2002.
4. Law 6,410/1976.

Fabiano Deffenti & Welber Barral (eds), *Introduction to Brazilian Law*, pp. 113–137.

The improvements to the statutes applicable to enterprises did not end with the changes to the Corporations Law and the new Civil Code. In 2005 a radically improved Bankruptcy and Recovery Law[5] was passed, bringing Brazil in line with the most advanced jurisdictions in relation to dealing with insolvent enterprises.

II. ENTERPRISES AND PARTNERSHIPS

In order to understand the Brazilian business enterprise system, one must understand the structure of the Civil Code. Book II of the Civil Code is titled Enterprise Law (*Direito Empresarial*). Book II is divided into Title I, which deals with sole traders (*empresários*), and Title II, which deals with partnerships (*sociedades*). Title III is titled The Business Unit (*O Estabelecimento*) and deals with the principal place of business of business entities. Finally, Title IV addresses registration, naming issues, company representatives (attorneys, managers and accountants) and company records. The division between sole traders and partnerships is the cornerstone of Brazilian enterprise laws.

A. PARTNERSHIPS (*SOCIEDADES*)

The notion of legal entity under Brazilian law is directly linked to the notion of partnership. With the exception of wholly owned subsidiaries of corporations, there must be at least two persons (natural or legal) for an entity to become separate from its shareholders. The term 'shareholders' is used here loosely, as partnership 'quotas' is the term of choice used in all applicable laws and regulations for the sharing of ownership of business entities, except in the case of corporations where the word 'share' (*ação*) is used.

Brazilian law has never accepted the idea that an administrative act (such as registration) is sufficient to create a legal entity. Instead, it adheres to the concept that there must be a signed contract between at least two parties as a precondition for the formation of a legal entity. The traditional notion of partnership permeates throughout Brazilian law relating to business associations. It affects how partners relate to one another the role they play in controlling the legal entity and personal liability for the business entity's liabilities.

A partnership will generally become a separate legal entity upon registration of the signed partnership documents. It is a precondition for the existence of a separate legal entity that the partnership contract be registered. Among other advantages, upon gaining legal entity status, the partnership will be able to enter into obligations and acquire rights and will be able to sue and be sued. With the exception of corporations, partners of partnerships are deemed to owe fiduciary duties to one another, unless the partnership is deemed to be one of a 'capital nature' only (i.e., one where there are no services provided by shareholders and

5. Law 11,101/2005.

due to its very nature it is simply a business enterprise). Prima facie, the partnership is based on *affectio societatis*: a personal commitment from the partners to a common goal.

The definition of partnership is provided in Article 981 of the Civil Code, which states that: '[a] partnership contract is made by the people who reciprocally obligate one another to contribute, with goods or services, for carrying out economic activity and sharing, among them, the results'. Therefore, pursuant to the Civil Code, there must be an intention to join efforts for the purpose of achieving a common goal for a partnership contract to exist. The partners must contribute with something – goods, services or anything of value – and have the goal of sharing the results from the venture.

Another corollary of the Brazilian contract-based legal entity system is that contract law principles will apply to company formation. Only persons with the required legal capacity will generally be allowed to enter into partnership agreements. Hence, minors under 16 years of age must be represented by their parents and between 16 and 18 years of age they must be 'assisted' by their parents (unless emancipated).[6]

Mentally ill persons who have been found by the courts as lacking the capacity to perform civil acts must be represented by their court-appointed attorneys. If, however, a party enters into a partnership agreement having full capacity, then for whatever reason he or she is declared as lacking capacity, the person will be allowed to remain as a partner (represented by an attorney). A judge may declare that the partnership should be wound up or a manager be appointed to represent the incapacitated person. Further restrictions may apply to certain persons. Sole traders declared bankrupt will not be allowed to become partners in business enterprises, neither will spouses married under the universal joinder of assets regime.[7]

Unless the contrary intention appears in a special law, partnerships that are subject to registration are deemed to be business partnerships (*sociedades empresárias*), while other entities are deemed to be simple partnerships (*sociedades simples*). Corporations will always be regarded as business entities and cooperatives as simple partnerships.

B. Sole Traders (*Empresários*)

Articles 966 to 980 of the Civil Code provide the rules for sole traders (*empresários*). In accordance with Article 966, a sole trader is the one 'who professionally carries out organised economic activity for the production or circulation of goods or services'. This provision is very wide in scope. However, the Civil Code expressly excludes certain professionals from the definition of sole trader, so

6. See Arts 1–5 of the Civil Code and the chapters on Contract Law and on Family and Succession Law. Please note that Brazilian indigenous people are only regarded as having 'relative capacity'. See Art. 3 of the Civil Code.
7. See the chapter on Family Law.

that those who practise an 'intellectual profession of a scientific, literary or artistic nature'. Lawyers, doctors, accountants and other similar professionals are, thus, not prima facie regarded as entrepreneurs.

Any person with full capacity and who is not prohibited by law to do so may be a sole trader. Sole traders can only be registered by one person, and they cannot have subsidiaries. However, sole traders may set up branches in other Brazilian States. Sole traders must be registered in the Public Registry of Commercial Enterprises (*Registro Público de Empresas Mercantis*). In order to obtain registration, sole traders must provide personal details, a sample of their signature as well as the address, objects and capital of the enterprise. The trader will be allowed to dispose of the business assets regardless of spousal approval, even if they are married under the full community of property or the partial community of property regimes.[8] Any pre-nuptial agreement, donations, inheritances and assets that will not make part of the marital assets must also be registered with the Public Registry of Commercial Enterprises.

Despite the sole trader's right to dispose of the enterprise's capital as he or she thinks fit, a sole trader does not become a separate business entity upon registration. The sole trader's liability is unlimited, so creditors will be able to enforce their rights against all of the sole traders' personal assets.

C. Personified and Non-personified Partnerships

The Brazilian Civil Code divides partnerships into two types: non-personified partnerships (*sociedades não personificadas*) and personified partnerships (*sociedades personificadas*).

1. Non-personified Partnerships

Brazilian law provides for two types of non-personified partnerships: partnerships in common (*sociedades em comum*) and partnerships in participation (*sociedades em conta de participação*). While the former is more often seen in litigious settings, the latter is commonly used for certain business deals where one of the shareholders neither wishes to appear in the business dealings of the entity nor to incur any liabilities.

a. Partnerships in Common (sociedades em comum)

Prima facie, all partnerships are partnerships in common (*sociedades em comum*). These include partnerships whose terms have been put in writing or are just de facto partnerships. Until the partnership documents are registered, all partnerships are governed primarily by the provisions relating to partnerships in common and,

8. See the Family and Succession Law chapter.

to the extent that they are not inconsistent with those provisions, by the provisions applicable to simple partnerships.

A third party may prove the existence of a partnership in common by any means permitted by law. Insofar as the partners are concerned, if they wish to prove that the partnership exists, there must be some written evidence tendered with the court, whether for the purposes of establishing the existence of the partnership among themselves or vis-à-vis third parties.

Regarding management rights, the general rule is that all partners are presumed to have management powers over the assets of the partnership in common. Partnership assets are deemed to be held by the partners as owners-in-common. The partners in partnerships in common are jointly liable for the partnership's obligations.

The assets of partnerships in common will be available to creditors to meet any liability incurred by 'management acts practised by any of the partners', unless the third party was, or should have been, aware of the relevant partner's limitation of powers.[9] Creditors must first seek remedies against the partnership before seeking to enforce their rights against the partners individually. The partner who entered into the contract on behalf of the partnership will be excluded from this rule and creditors may enforce their rights against him or her at the same time as against the partnership (he or she is jointly and severally liable for the partnership's liabilities).

b. Partnerships in Participation (sociedades em conta de participação)

Partnerships in participation (*sociedades em conta de participação*) are governed by Articles 991 to 996 of the Civil Code only to the extent that they are inconsistent to the provisions applicable to simple partnerships. In partnerships in participation one of the partners is the ostensible partner (*sócio ostensivo*), while the other is the participating partner (*sócio participante*). Unless the partnership agreement provides otherwise, all liability will lie with the ostensible partner, even though the profits from the partnership will be shared with the participating partner and the ostensible partner is not allowed to admit new partners without the participating partners' express consent.

In partnerships in participation, partnership assets will be regarded as being held in a 'special account'. These assets will be divided among the partners in accordance with the partnership agreement, which will only bind the partners, not third parties.[10] If the ostensible partner is liquidated, then the *sociedade em conta de participação* will be automatically dissolved and any credits of the participating partner will be deemed as unsecured and rank alongside other unsecured creditors.[11] If the participating partner is liquidated, then the partnership contract

9. Article 989 of the Civil Code.
10. Article 994, para. 1 of the Civil Code.
11. Article 994, para. 2 of the Civil Code; in relation of the ranking of credits, see also Art. 83 of the Bankruptcy and Recovery Law.

will be treated like a bilateral contract is treated in the Bankruptcy and Recovery Law.[12]

The existence of a partnership in participation may be proved by any means allowed by law and there are no formalities for setting it up. Partnerships in participation, even if registered, are still not regarded as independent legal entities.

2. Personified Partnerships

Pursuant to the Brazilian Civil Code, the following are personified partnerships: (a) simple partnerships (*sociedades simples*); (b) partnerships in a joint name (*sociedades em nome coletivo*); (c) simple commanditaire partnerships (*sociedades em comandita simples*); (d) limited liability partnerships (*sociedades limitadas*), (e) corporations (*sociedades anônimas*); (f) commanditaire share partnerships (*sociedades em comandita por ações*); and (g) cooperative partnerships (*sociedades cooperativas*).

The most common types of business entities are the limited liability partnership and the corporation. The first is governed by the Brazilian Civil Code. Corporations are the closest type of entity to an English company or United States corporation, and they are governed by a specific piece of legislation (the Corporations Law) in addition to the general provisions in the Civil Code.

a. Simple Partnerships (sociedades simples)

Simple partnerships are general partnerships. At the partners' choice, a simple partnership may either become a business partnership (*sociedade empresária*) or remain as a simple partnership. Certain activities must be carried out through simple partnerships. Legal services fall into this category and so do cooperatives.

A simple partnership will only become an independent legal entity once it is registered. If the partnership is to remain as a non-business partnership, registration will be effected at the Public Registry of Natural and Legal Persons (*Registro Público de Pessoas Físicas e Jurídicas*). Business partnerships will be registered at the Public Registries of Commercial Enterprises (commonly known as *Juntas Comerciais*).

b. Partnerships in a Joint Name (sociedades em nome coletivo)

Partnerships in a joint name can only have natural persons as partners. Partnerships in a joint name are governed by the rules applicable to simple partnerships, as modified by Articles 1,039 to 1,044 of the Civil Code. All partners are jointly liable for the company's obligations vis-à-vis third parties, but may set up among themselves (in the partnership agreement or by unanimous agreement by partners) limits to each partner's liabilities. Only partners may act as managers of the partnership and the partnership's name must only contain the partners' names (if any of the

12. See below under Insolvency, below.

partner's names is omitted, then the words '*e companhia*' must be added to the name).

Partnerships in a joint name are dissolved like simple partnerships. If they are business partnerships, they may also be liquidated in accordance with the terms of the Bankruptcy and Recovery Law.

c. Simple Commanditaire Partnerships (sociedades em comandita simples)

Simple commanditaire partnerships are somewhat analogous to limited partnerships that exist in some common law jurisdictions. In these partnerships, there are two categories of partners: the *sócios comanditados* and the *sócios comanditários*. The *sócios comanditados* are natural persons and are jointly liable for the partnership's obligations. *Sócios comanditários*, on the other hand, may be individuals or legal entities whose liability will be limited to the value of their shares. The partnership agreement must set out who the *sócios comanditários* are and who the *sócios comanditários* are.

The *sócios comanditários* must not have any management rights, if they do, their liability will be the same as the *sócios comanditados*. The *sócios comanditários* are not liable to return dividends paid to them in good faith, unlike *sócios comanditados*. Unless provided otherwise in the partnership agreement, the death of a *sócios comanditário* does not dissolve the partnership.

d. Limited Liability Partnerships (sociedades limitadas)

Limited liability partnerships (*sociedades limitadas*) are the most common legal entities in Brazil. *Limitadas* (as they are commonly known) are primarily governed by Articles 1,052 to 1,087 of the Civil Code and secondarily by the provisions that apply to simple partnerships.

The key advantage of limited liability partnerships is the partners' limitation of liability. Once all partners have fully paid-up their share of the *limitada*'s capital, their liability is extinguished.

Although the liability of *limitada*'s partners is established in the Civil Code, many Brazilian laws allow for lifting a *limitada*'s corporate veil. Breaches of the Consumer Protection Code, the Labour Law, the Environmental Code and of the Antitrust Law will generally lead to a partner being held liable for the *limitada*'s debts. Moreover, Article 50 of the Civil Code will allow for the veil of a *limitada* be lifted where there is 'abuse of corporateness, characterised by the deviation from its objectives' as well as in the case of fraud.

The *limitada*'s partnership agreement must contain: (a) the partnership name; (b) the partnership capital, the share of each partner's capital, the manner in which the shares were, or will be paid-up, and the term for paying up the capital (if not yet paid-up in full); (c) head office address and the addresses of any branches; (d) detailed description of the partnership's objects; (e) the term of duration of the partnership; (f) dates for assessing profits, when different to the calendar year;

(g) the individuals responsible for managing the partnership, together with their personal details; (h) share of each partner's profits and losses; and (i) choice of law or arbitral clause.

Partners are free to include other clauses in the partnership agreement. The clauses provided for in the Civil Code include clauses relating to: (a) rules for partnership meetings; (b) whether the partnership be governed secondarily (*subsidiariamente*) by the Corporations Law (instead and in addition to the provisions set out in the Civil Code; (c) rules for the exclusion of partners for just cause (*justa causa*); (d) of the right to appoint partnership managers who are not partners; and (e) the establishment of an audit board.

Although at the beginning there were some doubts as to whether *limitadas* could be exclusively controlled by foreign entities, in practice the registration offices have clearly accepted the position that a *limitada* can have foreign entities as the *limitada*'s partners. It is common nowadays to find subsidiaries of foreign entities that have the holding company as the main shareholder and one foreign subsidiary holding 1% or less of the shares. There is no general requirement that the *limitada* have a local partner.

There is little maintenance required for *limitadas*. However, those *limitadas* whose assets are greater than BRL 240 million, or whose revenues are greater than BRL 300 million in a given year, must audit, publish and register their accounts with the Companies Registries. They are deemed as corporations for these purposes.

e. *Corporations (sociedades anônimas)*

The corporation (*sociedade anônima,* commonly known under the abbreviation *S.A.*) is the legal entity type generally chosen for large businesses. While *sociedades anônimas* are partnerships (the literal translation of the term is 'anonymous partnerships'), they are governed by rules which are not dissimilar to English companies and United States corporations. *Sociedades anônimas* are regulated by the Brazilian Corporations Law, as well as the general provisions set out in the Civil Code.

For a corporation to be set up the following must be complied with: (a) at least two individuals or legal entities must subscribe to all of the corporation's shares; (b) at least 10% of the price of the issued shares must be paid-up; and (c) a deposit must be made into a bank account for all funds used for paying the issued shares. One exception applies insofar as the minimum number of two shareholders – wholly owned subsidiaries of corporations registered in Brazil may be single shareholder companies. The deposit must be made by the corporation's founder within five days after receiving the funds. Once the minimum number of subscribers is attained, they must meet in general meeting. A draft Articles of Association/by laws must be initialled by all subscribers. The corporate name must include the words *sociedade anônima* or *companhia* or their respective abbreviations, *S.A.* and *Cia.* More detailed rules apply for those entities that intend to seek funds from the general public.

A corporation's capital may be paid-up either in cash or with any other assets that can be valued in cash terms. Where a shareholder pays up the capital through assets other than cash, the assets must be valued by three experts or by a company which specialises in valuations. These are appointed in the subscribers' general meeting. The valuation will also need to be approved at the general meeting.

A corporation can only commence doing business once its Articles of Association/by laws have been registered at the Companies Registry and published in the Gazette. In most cases, the following documents must be provided to the Companies Registry: (a) original Articles of Association/by laws signed by all subscribers; (b) details of all subscribers and the amount of capital paid-up by each; (c) the receipt of the initial bank deposit; (d) copies of the minutes of meeting (where the payment of capital was effected with assets other than money); (e) a copy of the minutes of the subscribers' meeting which decided on the incorporation of the entity. If registration is refused, the first directors of the corporation must immediately hold a general meeting to rectify any problems with the documents. The documents must be published in the Gazette within thirty days after registration is obtained.

Corporations must keep in their head office the following books: (a) the book of Registry of Nominative Shares which must contain, among other things, the details about shareholders, shared conversions and redemptions, and existing encumbrances over the shares; (b) the book of Transfer of Nominative Shares, which provides the details of the transfers and must be signed by the parties effecting the transfers; (c) the book of General Meetings; (d) the book of Shareholders Roll Call; (e) the book of Advisory Board Meetings (if any) and Directors' Meeting; (f) the book of Minutes and Advices of the Audit Board.[13] Any shareholder, or group of shareholders, with 5% or more of the corporation's issued shares has the right to inspect the corporation's books.

Shares are generally nominative, although the Corporations Law allows for a company to issue bearer shares. Bearer shares are very rare nowadays. Nominative shares, for private entities, are registered in a book which is kept in the corporation's head office.

Pledges, usufructs, *fideicomissos* (trust-like structures), fiduciary conveyance (*alienação fiduciária*) and any other security interests or obligations must be registered on the shareholders register or with the custodian in the case of public companies.

Only corporations may have their shares traded on the stock exchange (if so, the corporation will be regarded as a public or 'open' company). If the shares are not traded on the stock exchange, the corporation will be regarded as private ('closed'). For corporations to have their shares traded, they must be registered with the Brazilian Securities Exchange Commission (*Comissão de Valores Mobiliários*). A number of specific rules apply to publicly traded companies.

---

13. An additional book is required for corporations which issue a type of negotiable instrument called 'beneficiary party' (*parte beneficiária*). These only apply to private corporations and are not common.

The corporations' Articles of Association/by laws (*estatuto*) provide the entity's rules of governance. Shares are given par value, which is used as the minimum amount for which shares may be issued. The amounts over and above par value paid to the company are deemed to be capital reserves. Shares without par value may have their value set when the company is being set up by its founders or when there is an increase of capital in the general meeting of shareholders or by the advisory board.

Corporations provide for three types of shares: ordinary (*ordinárias*), preference (*preferenciais*) or of fruition (*de fruição*). Ordinary shares may be divided into various classes, based on: (a) the convertibility into preference shares; (b) the requirement that the shareholder be a Brazilian citizen; and (c) the separate right to vote for the purposes of certain administrative bodies. The rights of each class may only be changed if the corporations' *estatuto* provides so – otherwise, it will require the approval of all members affected by the changes. As for classification under citizenship status, this is often used in specific sectors reserved for Brazilian control – such as media and aviation.

Preference shares may provide the following advantages over other shares: (a) priority for receiving dividends, whether fixed or minimum; (b) priority in having capital reimbursed, with or without a premium; or (c) both of the above. Holders of preference shares with or without restricted voting rights in corporations traded in the stock exchange must have one of the following advantages set out in the corporations' Articles of Association/by laws: (a) the right to receive at least 25% of the net profits in the year as dividends; (b) the right to receive dividends at least 10% greater than those given to ordinary shares; or (c) the right to be included in the public offer for the sale of control as provided in Article 254-A of the Corporations Law, with dividends at least the same as those available to shareholders who own ordinary shares. Article 254-A provides that the direct or indirect sale of the controlling block of public corporations may only be carried out subject to a condition precedent or subsequent providing that the other voting shares are also to be acquired for 80% of the value of those shares which are part of the controlling block. Additionally, the corporation's Articles of Association/by laws may also provide that holders of preference shares may elect one or more members of the corporation's board. Preference shares may not be more than 50% of the total issued capital of a corporation.

General shareholders of corporations also have certain mandatory minimum rights. These are: (a) to share in the profits; (b) in the case of liquidation, to receive the remaining proceeds; (c) to examine management; (d) preference to subscribe to shares, *partes beneficiárias* convertible into shares, debentures convertible into shares and subscription bonuses.[14]

Controlling shareholders are given special attention in the Corporations Law. 'Controlling shareholder' is defined as 'the individual or legal entity, or a group

14. The rights set up in (c) are subject to certain conditions, such as an exclusion to preference rights (*direitos de preferência*, which are similar to rights of first refusal) for public listed companies.

of these bound by a block voting agreement, or under a common control who: (a) holds shareholders' rights which permanently ensure the majority of votes in general meetings [. . .] and the power to elect the majority of the corporation's directors; and (b) effectively uses his or her power to direct the business of the entity and to direct the workings of the corporation's bodies.'[15]

Controlling shareholders have a duty to use their powers to make the company attain its objectives and to 'comply with its social function'. Additionally, the controlling shareholder also owes to the other shareholders of the corporation a duty of loyalty. Controlling shareholders must also pay damages whenever they abuse their power. Acts which amount to abuses of power set out in the Corporations Law include: (a) to direct the company to do things other than those in its objectives or favour another company to the detriment of minority shareholders, the company itself or the Brazilian economy; (b) liquidate a prosperous corporation; (c) change the corporation's Articles of Association/by laws, or merge, split or allow the company to be acquired by another, to obtain undue benefits, to the detriment of the corporation's shareholders, employees or investors; (d) elect as manager or auditor a person who is inapt; and (e) enter into a contract with the corporation, directly or through another person, in favoured or inequitable conditions.

Companies that are controlled by a common holding entity may be organised as a group. The holding entity must be a Brazilian registered company and must control, directly or indirectly, on a permanent basis, the related entities. Control may be affected via direct voting rights or through shareholders' agreements. Once registration as a group is effected, the group's name must contain the words 'group of companies' (*grupo de sociedades*) or simply 'group' (*grupo*). Although a specific type of registration is available for company groups, in practice the courts are ready to find liability over any group of entities that have a common controlling shareholder. This is particularly the case in relation to employment law, consumer protection, environmental law, competition law and taxation-related obligations. While some of these obligations stem from specific statutes, the liability of companies within the same corporate group has been substantially extended by court decisions to the extent that it is now quite difficult to persuade a court not to make the whole corporate group liable for liability arising from any of the companies within the groups. This is a peculiar characteristic of Brazilian corporate law and makes the corporate veil substantially weaker than in other jurisdictions.

Brazilian companies may also be organised as consortia (*consórcios*). Under Brazilian law, consortia are contractual joint ventures. A consortium does not have independent legal capacity and the insolvency of one of its members does not extend to the others. The consortium agreement must be registered at the Companies Registry. Consortia are often used for the purposes of participating in international public tenders, where one Brazilian company is the leader and foreign suppliers are made members of the consortium, as provided by the Procurement Law.[16]

---

15. Article 116 of the Corporations Law.
16. Law 8,666/1993.

Shareholders' agreements must be kept at the corporation's head office. Once registered in the corporation's books, then any obligations arising from the shareholders' agreement will bind any third parties. Shares which are subject to a shareholders' agreement cannot be traded on the stock exchange.

Foreign shareholders must appoint a person in Brazil to act as their attorney with at least the power to be served with legal proceedings. Until this requirement is met the foreign shareholder cannot be registered. Article 119, sole paragraph of the Corporations Law also contains a deeming provision: where a person exercises any of the shareholder's rights, that person is deemed to have the powers to be served with legal proceedings on behalf of the foreign shareholder.

The supreme decision-making body of the corporation is the shareholders in general meeting. Changes to the Articles of Association/by laws, the appointment and removal of directors and auditors, the approval of the corporation's accounts, the issuing of debentures, the suspension of any shareholder's rights, mergers, splits as well as seeking insolvency protection and winding up, among others, are powers reserved to the shareholders in general meeting. One notable exception is that the corporation's managers, with the agreement of the controlling shareholder, may seek insolvency protection or decide for the winding up of the corporation where there is an immediate need to do so. The managers must immediately organise a shareholders' meeting if this decision is taken.[17]

The quorum for general meetings of shareholders is one fourth of the voting capital for the first roll call and any number for the second (private corporations may provide for higher quorums in specific circumstances). Shareholders without voting rights will be allowed to participate in the deliberations. The higher quorum of 50% of the voting shares will be required (unless a higher quorum is provided in the corporation's Articles of Association/by laws) where: (a) new preference shares are to be issued other than proportionate to the number of those already issued (unless it is already provided for in the corporation's Articles of Association/by laws); (b) changes are to be made in preferences, advantages and redeeming or amortisation conditions of one or more classes of preferential shares or in the creation of a new less favoured class; (c) the mandatory dividend is to be reduced; (d) the merger or split of the corporation and similar types of transactions; (e) the formation of a company group; (f) changes to the objects of the company, among others.

Brazilian corporations may managed by a board of directors alone or by board of directors and an advisory board. If the corporation is to have an advisory board, this must be set out in the corporation's Articles of Association/by laws. All public corporations must have an advisory board.

The advisory board must have at least three members, who are called advisors (*conselheiros*). Advisory board members are elected by the shareholders in general meeting for a maximum three-year term, with the possibility of reappointment. Shareholders in general meeting may also remove board members. The advisory board's obligations include: (a) providing general advice in relation to the

17. See further under Insolvency, below.

corporation's business; (b) appointing, removing and setting the responsibilities of executive directors; (c) authorising the sale of the corporation's fixed assets and the granting of security interests over the corporation's assets; and (d) choosing and removing independent auditors (if any).

The board of directors is responsible for the day-to-day operations of the corporation – it is an executive board. It must have at least two directors, who are appointed for a maximum term of three years, with the possibility of reappointment. Up to one third of the members of the advisory board may be appointed as directors.

Only individuals may be appointed to the advisory board or the board of directors – no legal entity may be act as a director or advisor. Further, only permanent residents may be appointed to the board of directors. Members of the advisory board must be shareholders of the corporation. Persons who have committed certain types of crimes are prohibited from being appointed to the boards. Members of the advisory board must not hold any management role in a competing corporation or otherwise have any conflicts of interest with the corporation. The shareholders in general meeting must set the remuneration payable to members of the boards.

Board members owe to the corporation a duty of care and diligence 'that any active and prudent man customarily employs in the management of his own businesses'.[18] Board members must also act in the best interests of the corporation in light of the 'demands of the public good and the social function of the corporation',[19] and owe a duty of loyalty to the company (which includes an obligation not to profit from their position and a duty to maintain the secrecy of commercially valuable confidential information) as well as a duty to refrain from acting in a position of conflict of interest and a duty to disclose the 'nature and extension' of their personal interest in directors' meetings (even if there is disclosure, any transaction with directors must be made in 'reasonable or equitable conditions' in terms that are 'the same as those in the market or which the company would make with third parties').[20] Executive directors of listed companies also have to disclose material facts to the market – this is in addition to the obligations imposed by the Stock Exchange's rules.

In accordance with the Corporations Law, executive directors are not liable for the company's obligations when the obligations are incurred on behalf of the company 'and as a consequence of a normal management action'. Executive directors will be liable, however, in the case of an intentional or negligent act or when acting 'against the law or the company's Articles of Association/by laws'. The personal liability of an executive director only goes as far as his or her acts are concerned. Where one executive director breaches his or her obligations, the liability will not extend to another directors if: (a) the latter is not in collusion with the former; (b) if the latter 'does not neglect to become aware' of the

18. Article 153 of the Corporations Law.
19. Article 154 of the Corporations Law.
20. Article 156, first paragraph of the Corporations Law.

breaches; and (c) if the latter, being aware of the breach, expressly states in the minutes that he or she disagrees with the actions being taken or, if not possible, promptly gives written notice of the breach to the executive board, to the audit board (if in place) or to the shareholders in general meeting.

Executive directors are jointly and severally liable for the damages caused by breaches of duties 'imposed by law to ensure the normal functioning of the company', regardless of the terms contained in the Articles of Association/by laws. An exception applies to those executive directors of publicly listed companies – only executive directors who are expressly made responsible under a public company's Articles of Association/by laws for the particular task will be held personally liable. Each executive director will be liable, however, where he or she becomes aware of a prior director's breach and neglects to report the breach to the shareholders in general meeting.

Insofar as derivative actions against the directors are concerned, a corporation is not automatically bound to commence legal action against a director who has breached his or her duties. Legal proceedings may only be filed if the shareholders in general meeting approve it. A quorum of 5% of shareholders applies to these meetings, where members have the discretion to decide whether or not to proceed against the director. Where the directors acted in good faith and in the best interests of the corporation, the director will not be held liable. Shareholders and third parties may file proceedings directly against directors for the damages caused by the directors' acts and omissions.

The provisions relating to director's duties and derivative actions applicable to executive directors also apply to technical and advisory bodies responsible for assisting executive directors.

Corporations must have an audit board. The audit board is responsible for auditing the acts of the executives of the companies and verifying compliance with their respective obligations. The audit board's responsibility also includes providing opinions relating to annual management reports as well as proposals put by the management bodies to the shareholders in general meetings that relate to capital increases, issues of debentures and similar instruments, investment plans, payment of dividends, mergers and spin-offs. Members must also audit the corporation's accounts and inform shareholders where the directors have breached their duties.

The corporation's Articles of Association/by laws must set out the regulations for the audit board. The audit board may be permanent or be appointed by shareholders in a general meeting for a set term. The audit board must have at least three members and no more than five members. Audit board members do not need to be shareholders of the corporation. Where the audit board is not permanent, 10% of those shareholders holding voting shares or 5% of those shareholders holding non-voting shares may have one set up. A temporary audit board will remain in place until the next ordinary meeting of shareholders. Holders of preference shares, or with voting restrictions, can appoint one audit board member by separate vote. Also, where at least 10% of the corporations' shares in aggregate are held by minority shareholders, these may appoint one audit board member.

Audit board members must reside permanently in Brazil. Members of the audit board must receive reimbursement of transportation and hotel expenses, and receive a salary of at least 10%, on average, of the salary received by each director. Members of the audit board are also bound by the duty to act diligently, the duty to act in the best interests of the corporation, the duty of loyalty and the duty to avoid conflicts of interest as are executive directors.

Regarding changes of corporate status, there are four types of changes set out in the Corporations Law: (a) transformation (*transformação*); (b) incorporation (*incorporação*); (c) merger (*fusão*); and (d) split (*cisão*). Transformation is the change of the type of entity other than through dissolution or liquidation. Incorporation occurs when one company is absorbed by another. A merger, on the other hand, is a transaction where two entities are joined, creating a new company. Finally, a split is a transaction where the company transfers part of its assets to one or more other companies.

A transformation can only occur with the unanimous approval of shareholders, except if it is provided otherwise in the entities' constitution documents.

Incorporation, merger and split may occur in and between companies of different types. Incorporations, mergers and splits must be approved by shareholders in general meeting. During the meeting, the entities' shareholders must be informed of the reasons for the transaction and whether the entity is interested in making the transaction, the number of shares that the holders of preference shares will receive and the reasons for changing their rights (if any), what the shareholder composition will be after the transaction and the compensation that dissident shareholders will receive. These transactions may only be effected after valuers determine that the added net assets of the entities is at least the total that will be paid out to shareholders and creditors of the existing entities (this is to ensure that creditors are made whole).

Where a corporation has issued debentures, debenture holders will need to approve the change of status in a debenture holder meeting set up specifically for this purpose. However, no approval is required if the change of status allows for debenture holders to redeem their rights within six months after the minutes of meeting approving the change of status are published.

Creditors are given specific rights where companies change their status. In transformations, those creditors whose liability arose prior to the change will continue having the same rights against the shareholders as if the transformation had not occurred until they are paid in full. In the case of incorporations and mergers, creditors may file court proceedings seeking to nullify the change of status within sixty days after the minutes of meeting relating to the incorporation or merger are published, where the change of status unduly affects the creditor's rights. In the case of splits, the companies that acquire the assets will be jointly and severally liable for the splitting company's obligations to creditors. If, however: (a) there is only a partial split; (b) more than one entity acquires the splitting company's assets; and (c) the contracts which formalised the split provide that the companies (including the splitting company) are not to be jointly and severally liable for the debts, then creditors can file proceedings within ninety days after the minutes are published seeking to have this provision voided.

A corporation may be dissolved as of right if: (a) the corporation has a set term, once the term expires; (b) dissolution is provided for in the Articles of Association/by laws; (c) in the case of private companies, 50% of shareholders with voting rights vote in favour of the dissolution (unless the Articles of Association/by laws provide for a greater quorum); (d) the corporation is left with only one shareholder, unless a second shareholder is added in the following year (this does not apply to wholly-owned subsidiaries of corporations); or (e) it is specifically provided by the law which authorised the corporation to operate. A corporation may also be dissolved by a court order where: (a) its registration is held to be null and void, through a court action filed by any shareholder; (b) its objects cannot be attained, through a court action filed by at least 5% of the corporation's shareholders; (c) in the case of liquidation due to insolvency, as provided in the Bankruptcy and Recovery Law. Corporations may also be dissolved in specific circumstances by administrative bodies. A corporation will remain as a separate legal entity until it is finally liquidated.

Unless the corporation's Articles of Association/by laws provide otherwise, once the decision to dissolve the corporation is made, the shareholders in general meeting will appoint a liquidator and the audit board will remain in place while the company is being liquidated. For those corporations that have an advisory board, the advisory board may appoint the liquidator. The liquidator may be removed at any time by the same corporate body that appointed him or her. Where the corporation's winding up is ordered by the court, the court will appoint a liquidator of its choosing.

Liquidators of corporations must: (a) file and publish the shareholders' general meeting or the court order that decided for the liquidation; (b) gather the corporations' assets as well as books and documents wherever they are located; (c) promptly prepare the corporations' balance sheet; (d) demand payment from those shareholders who are yet to pay up the corporations' capital; (e) set up shareholders' meetings required by law or whenever the liquidator deems necessary; (f) file for bankruptcy or judicial recovery; (g) at the end of the liquidation, submit a report to the shareholders in general meeting with the steps taken and transactions made during liquidation, as well as the corporation's final accounts; and (h) file and publish the minutes of shareholders' meeting which decided for the liquidation to be ended.

Liquidators have wide powers. They can carry out any acts required for the liquidation, including selling of any of the corporation's assets. However, unless otherwise authorised to do so by shareholders in general meeting, liquidators must not encumber any assets or borrow money on behalf of the corporation. They may do so when these acts are 'indispensable for the payment of debts which cannot be postponed'[21] or are required to facilitate the corporation's liquidation. Corporations in liquidation must have the words *em liquidação* ('in liquidation') in their

21. Article 211, sole paragraph of the Corporations Law.

name. While in power, liquidators owe the same duties to the corporation as its executive directors.

f. *Commanditaire Share Partnerships (sociedades em comandita por ações)*

A commanditaire share partnership operates similarly to corporations. However, directors must be shareholders and will be jointly and severally liable for all obligations incurred by the partnership. Commanditaire share partnerships are also not obliged to have advisory boards and are very rarely used in practice.

g. *Cooperative Partnerships (sociedades cooperativas)*

Cooperative partnerships are regulated both by the Civil Code as well as by Law 5,764/1971. Cooperatives do not need to have any issued or paid-up capital and do not have a limitation as to the number of partners they may have. Shares in cooperative partnerships may not be transferred to any party other than those that expressly adhere to the cooperative's partnership agreement. There are limitations as to the number of shares that a member may hold. Partners' liability may be limited or unlimited. Cooperative partnerships may not be organised with a view to obtaining a profit.

D. Branch Offices of Foreign Entities

Branch offices of foreign entities are given special treatment under Brazilian law. These are not to be confused with subsidiaries or similar entities with 100% foreign ownership, which are regarded as Brazilian entities.

Branches of foreign entities need a Presidential decree to operate.[22] Branches of foreign entities appoint a person with powers to 'resolve any issues and to be served with legal proceedings' on behalf of the foreign entity.[23]

Given the difficulties involved in obtaining a presidential decree to commence operations in Brazil, branch offices of foreign branches are uncommon.

E. Brazilian-Argentine Bi-National Companies

Legislative Decree 26/1992 and Decree 619/1992 implemented the Treaty for the Establishment of a Statute for Brazilian-Argentine Bi-National Companies. These entities require at least 80% of the capital to belong to Brazilians and Argentines,

22. The rules pertaining to foreign branches are set out in Chapter VIII of Decree-Law 2,627/1940. This was the sole chapter survive and continue in force and effect after the passing of the Corporations Law.
23. Article 1,138 of the Civil Code.

with at least 30% of the shareholders being nationals or permanent residents of either country. These companies are extremely rare as there are next to no advantages over other types of corporate structures.

F. Stock Exchange

The São Paulo Stock Exchange (*Bolsa de Valores de São Paulo*, Bovespa') is Brazil's only stock exchange. In 2007, the Bovespa was listed on its own stock exchange and is now publicly traded. Commodities and futures trading currently takes place in the Mercantile and Futures Exchange (*Bolsa de Mercadorias e Futuros*, 'BM&F'). The BM&F also had its initial public offering on the Bovespa in 2007. In early 2008, the Bovespa and the BM&F merged and the joint exchange is now called BM&FBovespa.

In recent years, the BM&FBovespa has brought about changes to allow smaller companies to access the market through the introduction of the 'Bovespa Mais' programme. The BM&FBovespa has also implemented a system for differentiating levels of corporate governance that companies adhere to – Level One, Level Two and the Novo Mercado. To be accepted into the New Market (*Novo Mercado*) companies must comply with the highest standards of corporate governance, including having only one class of shares. The Bovespa has also set up an arbitration body for the resolution of disputes that relate to the market. The 'Bovespa Mais' has had limited success, due to the relatively high regulatory costs involved in keeping a company listed on the BM&FBovespa.

The BM&FBovespa rules also allow for trading of foreign securities on the Brazilian exchange. This is effected through the issuing of Brazilian Depositary Receipts (BDRs).

G. Registries

Enterprise-related registries are responsible for both analysing whether documents comply with the relevant legislation as well as to control the process of registration of enterprises. Registration is a condition for obtaining tax numbers and for setting up bank accounts, for instance.

1. Companies Registries (*Juntas Comerciais*)

Companies Registries are institutions administered by States which are responsible for the registration of business enterprises. From an administrative viewpoint, Companies Registries are subordinated to government of the State where they are located. Companies Registries issue their own regulations. Yet these are subordinated to the National Registry of Commerce Department's rules. Companies Registries are responsible for the registration of auctioneers, public translators and interpreters, managers of general warehouses and marine managers. Companies

Registries are also responsible for registration of sole traders, business partnerships (including corporations), cooperatives and branch offices of foreign legal entities.

Companies Registries will only allow for the registration of documents which comply with all applicable laws. This means that documents which are submitted for registration are carefully analysed by Registry staff. Whenever a document is non-compliant, the document will be returned for amendment (via a requisition process) or its registration will be refused altogether.

2. Civil Registries of Legal Persons (*Registros Civis de Pessoas Jurídicas*)

Civil Registries of Legal Persons are responsible for the registration of contracts and regulations (including Articles of Association/bylaws) for civil, religious, scientific and literary partnerships, as well as for foundations and public interest associations. They are also responsible for registration of political parties.

Professional partnerships (such as law firms) are registered at the Civil Registries of Legal Persons. Civil Registries of Legal Persons are subordinated to the relevant State where they are located. Unlike Companies Registries, there are often many Civil Registries of Legal Persons in any given State, with limited territorial jurisdiction.

III. INSOLVENCY

On 9 February 2005, the Brazilian President signed the new Bankruptcy and Restructuring Law. The Law marks a radical change to the previous way courts dealt with companies in financial trouble, drawing heavily from United States' laws. The Law does not apply to individuals (other than sole traders), government-owned or government-controlled companies, as well as to financial institutions.

Under the new Law, there are three procedures available for insolvent companies: judicial recovery (*recuperação judicial*), non-judicial recovery (*recuperação extra-judicial*) and bankruptcy (*falência*).

A. Judicial Recovery (*Recuperação Judicial*)

Judicial recovery is a court-controlled procedure where the debtor files voluntary insolvency proceedings aiming to reorganise the company and have it emerge from bankruptcy. Judicial recovery is only available to those enterprises that have not undergone judicial recovery in the previous five years (or eight years in certain circumstances).

The initial petition for judicial recovery must contain: (a) the reasons for the current financial situation of the business and for its financial difficulties; (b) the business accounts for the previous three years, together with a cash flow forecast; (c) a list of all creditors, together with the nature, classification and amount of the debt owed; (d) a list with all employee names, roles, salaries, termination entitlements and overdue pay; (e) the certificate of good standing from the Companies Registry, together with the business Articles of Association/by laws and the minutes of meeting that appointed the business directors; (f) a list of the controlling shareholders' and directors' assets (in the case of companies); (g) bank statements (including statements from financial institutions relating to the business' investments in funds and publicly traded corporations); (h) certificates from the Protests Registries (*Cartórios de Protestos*, where creditors may register negotiable instruments which are in default) where the business' head office is located and where it has branch offices; and (i) a list of all court actions to which the business is a party with an estimate of the amounts claimed against the business.

If the petition is properly filed, the judge in charge of the case will immediately appoint a judicial administrator (*administrador judicial*) and order that court actions against the business be stayed. Those actions against the business' shareholders who may be jointly and severally liable for the business' debt will also be stayed. The stay will remain in place for a period of 180 days. Actions for unliquidated damages or for the enforcement of tax-related obligations are not subject to the mandatory stay and continue normally as if no judicial recovery proceedings had been filed (however, courts have been giving companies some leniency in relation to tax-related obligations).

Where an enterprise obtains an order for judicial recovery, the court will have the power to allow the enterprise greater time to pay its debts, change payment conditions for overdue debts (as well as payments due in the future), force mergers, change shareholding control, replace directors, grant creditors the power to veto certain decisions, issue new shares, set a special purpose company to deal with the business' assets, among other things.

The judge will also order that the business be exempted from having to present certificates regarding absence of debts (generally social security, workers' guarantee fund and tax, which are often demanded by other parties as a condition for companies to enter into contracts). This exemption does not apply to government tenders and to benefit from tax incentives that may be available. Additionally, the court will order that the business present monthly accounts and, if this is not complied with, the directors will be immediately removed. Finally, the court will issue notices to the Public Ministry and all State and Municipal authorities where the business' head office or branches are located and order that a notice containing a summary of the request for judicial recovery, a creditors' list (with value and class of credit) and a warning for the creditors to file proofs of debt, be published in the Gazette. Proofs of debt must be filed with the judicial administrator within fifteen days from the day the notice is published.

The business must file a plan, the 'judicial recovery plan' (*plano de recuperação judicial*), within sixty days from the publication of the decision which allows for judicial recovery to proceed. The plan must contain: (a) details about the means to be applied for the business' recovery; (b) evidence of the financial viability of the business; and (c) an expert's report on the financial situation of the business and of the business' assets. The plan must also provide for payments of overdue employment entitlements (including damages arising from employment relationships) within one year prior to the filing date. Additionally, the plan must provide for the payment of all employees' wages relating to the three months prior to the plan being filed (this exception applies only to those employees who earn up to five minimum wages per month).

Upon receiving the plan, a court will publish a notice to creditors informing that the plan has been filed. The notice will also set the time period for creditors to file objections, which must be within thirty days. If any creditor objects, then the court will set up a date and time for a meeting of creditors. The meeting must take place within 150 days from the decision approving the start of the judicial recovery proceedings by the court. At the meeting, creditors may request changes to be made to the plan. These changes must be approved by the enterprise (i.e., by those in charge of the enterprise's management). If the plan is rejected, the business will be declared bankrupt and the process will continue as a bankruptcy. If the plan is approved, then the court will allow for judicial recovery to proceed and the creditors will appoint the members of the creditors' committee.

All creditors will prima facie be affected by the judicial recovery plan and subject to its terms. However, fiduciary creditors, creditors of currency swap agreements made in relation to export transactions, holders of retention of title rights and sale of real estate containing irrevocable obligations to sell will not be affected by the judicial recovery plan.

The creditors' committee will be responsible for: (a) checking the judicial administrator's accounts and activities; (b) ensuring that the proceedings are conducted lawfully and properly; (c) informing the court whenever any creditors' rights are violated during the proceedings and about anything that may damage the creditors' rights; (d) reviewing and issuing an opinion about any complaints made by interested parties; (e) seeking a court order for a general meeting of creditors to be held; (f) checking the business activities and preparing a progress report on these every thirty days; (g) ensuring that the plan is complied with; (h) seeking the court's authorisation, in certain circumstances, for the sale of fixed assets, encumbrance of assets or granting of security rights over the assets and guarantees of the enterprise and incurring debt for the purpose of the enterprise continuing to operate.

The creditors' committee will be comprised of three representatives. One will be appointed by the holders of employment-related credits; one will be appointed from the creditors holding security rights or specific priority rights; and one will be appointed by the unsecured creditors and those with general priority rights. Each representative will be appointed by the majority of the creditors of his or her respective class of creditors.

Both the judicial administrator and the members of the creditors' committee owe certain obligations to the enterprise. Each will be held liable for any damages incurred by the business as a consequence of his or her intentional acts or fault (negligence, recklessness or lack of skill), unless they expressly disagree with the decision being taken by the committee and the decision is recorded in the minutes of meeting.

B. Non-judicial Recovery (*Recuperação Extrajudicial*)

Non-judicial recovery allows enterprises to negotiate directly with some of their debtors. Once the negotiation is finalised, the troubled enterprise merely needs to obtain the court's approval of the settlement reached with its debtors. The same requirements that apply to judicial recoveries also apply to non-judicial recoveries. This procedure has rarely been used in practice.

Unlike judicial recoveries, tax and employment-related debts cannot be extinguished via non-judicial recovery proceedings. Fiduciary creditors, creditors of currency swap agreements made in relation to export transactions, holders of retention of title rights and sale of real estate containing irrevocable obligations to sell, like in judicial recovery proceedings, are not affected by non-judicial recovery proceedings. Moreover, non-judicial recovery proceedings do not provide for a stay of any court actions against the business.

Non-judicial recoveries are filed with the court for recognition and approval. Any creditor that is not part of a non-judicial recovery plan filed with the court will be allowed to seek the winding up of the enterprise. However, this exception does not apply where three fifths of all creditors of each class approve the plan. There can be no discrimination of creditors within the same class of creditors.

C. Bankruptcy (*Falência*)

The court will declare the bankruptcy of an enterprise where: (a) the enterprise does not pay a liquidated, due and owing, debt of over forty Brazilian minimum wages arising from a judgment, negotiable instrument or contract witnessed by two persons (*títulos executivos*);[24] (b) the enterprise, when having a debt for a liquidated debt enforced against it, cannot provide guarantees within the time set by law; (c) the enterprise precipitously sells its assets or uses of ruinous or fraudulent means to make payments; (d) the enterprise enters, or clearly tries to enter, into sham transactions for the sale of any assets to delay payments to creditors or to defraud creditors; (e) the enterprise transfers any of its business units to a third party without full consent of all creditors and without keeping sufficient assets to pay the creditors in full; (f) the enterprise falsifies the transfer of its main business unit with a view to avoiding the law, the parties responsible for auditing its actions or to negatively affect a creditor; (g) the enterprise encumbers assets or provides further collateral or guarantees for previously incurred liabilities without keeping unencumbered assets to pay for its debts; (h) the enterprise's manager absconds without leaving a person holding sufficient assets to pay for the enterprise's debts; (i) the enterprise's managers leave the business unit or try to flee from their domicile, the enterprise's head office or the enterprise's main business unit; and (j) the enterprise does not comply with an obligation set out in the recovery plan.

24. Refer to our Civil Procedure and Arbitration chapter.

Moreover, the enterprise may file for bankruptcy itself when its managers consider that the enterprise would not meet the requirements for filing for judicial recovery. Article 105 of the Bankruptcy and Restructuring Law further imposes on the managers the obligation to provide reasons for not continuing with the operation of the business. This emphasises the Congress' intention to make all reasonable attempts to have the enterprise continue in business. The documents to be presented by the enterprise at the time of filing are similar to those required for filing for judicial recovery proceedings.

As soon as bankruptcy is declared, the court will appoint a judicial administrator, order the stay of court actions against the enterprise and set the bankruptcy period, among other things. The bankruptcy period cannot go back further than ninety days from the time the enterprise filed for bankruptcy, from the time the enterprise filed for judicial recovery or from the time the first protest was registered against the enterprise due to lack of payment.

Once the judicial administrator accepts his or her appointment, he or she will proceed to gather all of the enterprise's assets and documents and carry out valuations on the enterprise's assets. The same notice as for judicial recovery will be published where a bankruptcy petition is filed. The creditors will also have fifteen days from publication to file their proofs of debt.

Those contracts to which the enterprise is a party will not be automatically terminated by the bankruptcy. The judicial administrator will have the discretion to keep the obligations in effect if: (a) by doing so the liabilities of the bankruptcy estate would be reduced or not increased, or (b) it would be necessary for the maintenance and preservation of the enterprise's assets. The judicial administrator must obtain prior approval from the committee of creditors before making a decision. The parties to the contract (other than the bankrupt enterprise) within ninety days from the appointment of the judicial administrator may seek a court ordering the judicial administrator to make a decision as to whether the contract is to remain in place or be terminated. Once served with the initial petition and court summons, the judicial administrator will have ten days to decide. If a contract is terminated, the innocent party will be able to file court proceedings seeking damages. Any damages awarded as a consequence will be deemed to be unsecured debt and rate accordingly for final distribution purposes. Specific rules will apply to a variety of contracts, such as those for the delivery of goods which are in transit, for instalment contracts, for the purchase and sale of real estate, as well as others.

Certain transactions may also be clawed back by the judicial administrator. These include all of those transactions that intended to defraud creditors (*fraude a credores*) and those specifically set out in the Bankruptcy and Recovery Law. The Bankruptcy and Recovery Law provides that the following transactions will be voidable by the bankrupt enterprise: (a) the payment of debt not yet due made by the bankrupt enterprise within the bankruptcy period; (b) the payment of any debt due and owing made within the bankruptcy period by any means other than as provided in the contract; (c) the granting of any security rights over any assets for debts incurred prior to the bankruptcy; (d) the carrying out of any gratuitous acts, or the renunciation of any inheritance or gifts, within two years prior to the bankruptcy being declared; (e) the sale or transfer of the enterprise's business unit without the express consent or the payment of all creditors unless sufficient assets were left for the enterprise to meet its obligations or if within thirty days no creditors oppose the transaction after being given notice through the court or through the Contracts and Documents Registry; and (f) the registration of security rights or the transfer of assets *inter vivos* after the bankruptcy is declared. All of these transactions require a court order prior to being voided by the enterprise.

As soon as all assets are gathered by the judicial administrator, the bankrupt enterprise's assets will be sold. The sale of the assets will be effected in the following order of preference: (a) sale of the enterprise as a whole; (b) sale of the separate businesses of the enterprise separately; (c) sale of all the assets of each business unit as a whole; (d) sale of the assets separately. The court has a discretion to consider more than one method if it is in the best interests of the creditors. The assets will be sold through live auctions, closed bids or a hybrid of the two. Once again, the provisions reflect the intention of Brazil's lawmakers to keep the enterprise operating.

Once all assets have been sold, all of those creditors not subject to the effects of bankruptcy have been paid and funds have been deposited into court as reserves of capital (if any, as determined by the judge in charge of the bankruptcy), the creditors will be paid in the following order of preference: (a) creditors holding employment-related credits up to 150 minimum wages; (b) secured creditors up to the amount secured; (c) tax credits with the exception of tax penalties; (d) preferred creditors (holders of 'special privilege' – *privilégio especial* – followed by other holders of specific rights); (e) preferred creditors (holders of 'general privilege' – *privilégio geral* – followed by creditors who supplied goods or services during the judicial recovery period, then followed by holders of other preferred creditors); (f) unsecured creditors (including employment-related credits above the 150 Brazilian minimum wage limit); (g) contractual, tax and administrative penalties; (h) subordinated credits (*créditos subordinados*), which include shareholders and directors who were not employed by the enterprise. Any creditor who sought to prove a debt greater than the actual credit owed by the enterprise intentionally or in bad faith will be liable for twice the amount that creditor receives.

Once all monies have been distributed to the creditors, the judicial administrator, within thirty days, will file the final accounts with the court. After these are reviewed by the Public Ministry (the Brazilian equivalent of the Attorney General's Department and/or the Crown), the court will hand down its judgment in relation to the accounts. After that, the judicial administrator will file his or her final report pertaining to the bankruptcy and the court will order that the bankruptcy proceedings be closed.

Selected Bibliography

In English

B.S. Black, 'Strengthening Brazil's Securities Markets' (2001) 7 *Revista de Direito Mercantil, Economico e Financiero.*

B.B. Black, A.G. de Carvalho and E. Gorga, 'The Corporate Governance of Privately Controlled Brazilian Firms' (2009) *University of Texas Law, Law and Economic Research Paper* 109.
S. Claessens, D. Klingebiel and M. Lubrano, Corporate Governance Reform Issues in the Brazilian Equity Markets (World Bank, 2001).
T.B. Felsberg, 'Cross-Border Insolvencies and Restructuring in Brazil' (2003) 31 *International Business Lawyers* 109.
E. Gorga, 'Does Culture Matter for Corporate Governance? A Case Study of Brazil' (2003) 257 *Stanford Law and Economics Olin Working Paper*
T. Nevona, 'Control Values and Changes in Corporate Law in Brazil' (2006) 9 *Latin American Business Review.*
M.S. Poulter, 'My Client's Going to Brazil: a U.S. Practitioner's Guide to Brazilian *Limitadas* Under the New Civil Code' (2005) 11 *Journal of Law and Trade in the Americas* 133.
A.R. Roth, 'Capital-Market Development in Israel and Brazil: Two Examples of the Role of Law in Development' (1967) 19 *Stanford Law Review.*
F.M. Rabelo and F.C. Vasconcelos, 'Corporate Governance in Brazil' (2002) 37 *Journal of Business Ethics* 321
P.R. Wood, *Comparative Law of Security Interests and Title Finance* (2nd edn, Sweet & Maxwell, United Kingdom, 2007).
R.A. Ziad, 'Bankruptcy Policy: A Review and Critique of Bankruptcy Statutes and Practices in Fifty Countries Worldwide' (2008) 16 *Yeshiva University Cardozo Journal of International and Comparative Law* 279.

In Portuguese

M. Carvalhosa, *Comentários à Lei de S/A* (Saraiva, São Paulo, 2007).
F.S. de Souza and A.S.A. de Moraes, *Comentários à Lei de Recuperação de Empresas e Falência: Lei 11.101/2005* (Revista dos Tribunais, São Paulo, 2005).
F. Martins, *Curso de Direito Comercial* (27th edn, Forense, Rio de Janeiro, 2001).
R. Requião, *Curso de Direito Comercial* (26th edn, Saraiva, São Paulo, 2005).

Chapter 9
Taxation Law

*Cristiano Carvalho & Eurico Marcos Diniz de Santi**

I. TAX LAW IN THE BRAZILIAN CONSTITUTION

Brazilian tax law presents a distinctive feature that sets it apart from the majority of other tax systems: its framework is provided by the Brazilian Federal Constitution. The 1988 Federal Constitution contains a chapter named 'Brazilian Tax System', which contains dozens of provisions on limitations and guarantees for taxpayers, tax immunities, powers to create taxes, and the characteristics that Brazilian taxes should have, leaving little creative freedom for the ordinary lawmaker.

This 'constitutionalisation' of Brazilian tax law has positive and negative sides. The positive is that, at least in theory, it provides greater predictability for the taxpayer, as crucial changes to the tax system require changes to the Constitution itself, which are difficult due to the complex legislative procedures required for the approval of constitutional amendments. The negative side is the difficulty of implementing the required changes to tax laws. Bills stay for many years before the Congress, despite the need for quick changes.

---

* Cristiano Carvalho, Professor of Law at the Brazilian Institute of Tax Studies. President of the Tax Academy of the Americas. Visiting Scholar (UC–Berkeley), LLD LLM (PUC/SP) LLB (UNISINOS). Professor of Law at FGV School of Law. Coordinator of the Center of Tax Studies (NEF – FGV). Eurico Marcos Diniz de Santi, LLD LLM (PUC/SP) LLB (FDSBC).

Fabiano Deffenti & Welber Barral (eds), *Introduction to Brazilian Law*, pp. 139–151.

One of the biggest difficulties in implementing changes to the tax system is the federative nature of the Brazilian State, which cannot be abolished even by Constitutional amendment.[1] The powers to impose taxes are constitutionally shared among all the members of the Federation, namely: (a) the Federal Union; (b) the States; (c) the Federal District; and (d) the Municipalities.

The Federal Constitution sets out important guarantees for the taxpayer vis-à-vis the State. The principle of legality (*princípio da legalidade*)[2] restricts the institution of taxes by law, and forbids executive decrees to create new taxes. The principle of non-retroactivity (*princípio da não-retroatividade*)[3] disallows taxes to reach tax events prior to their creation. The principle of precedence (*princípio da precedência*),[4] as a general rule, postpones the application of new taxes for the fiscal year following their creation or increase (or, in the case of certain levies, to ninety days after approval by the legislature). The principle of non-confiscation (*princípio do não-confisco*)[5] bans the use of taxation as an instrument to expropriate taxpayers assets.

Further, the Federal Constitution sets out that the taxation must be, as far as possible, proportional and gradual as compared to the personal conditions of the taxpayer, in a way to respect his or her capacity to pay.[6] We say 'as far as possible' due to the impersonal and objective character of certain taxes incident on consumption and production of certain goods and services.

II. THE NATIONAL TAX CODE AND GENERAL TAXATION RULES

The Federal Constitution assigns to Declaratory Statutes the important prerogative of centralising tax law. Section 146 of the Constitution sets out three functions for a Declaratory Statute: (a) to determine jurisdictional conflicts among federated States and Territories; (b) to regulate the constitutional limitations to the taxing power; and (c) to set out general rules regarding tax law, especially on: (i) the definition of the taxes and their types (as well as of the taxes classified by the Constitution), the taxing events, the calculation formulas and entities on which taxes will be imposed; and (ii) tax rates, tax levying, credit, prescription and limitation periods.

The main Declaratory Statute that governs the Brazilian taxation system is the Brazilian Tax Code (*Código Tributário Nacional*, 'CTN').[7]

---

1. Only by the promulgation of a new constitution altogether.
2. Enshrined in Art. 150, I of the Federal Constitution.
3. Enshrined in Art. 150, III(a) of the Federal Constitution.
4. Enshrined in Art. 150, III(b) and (c) of the Federal Constitution.
5. Enshrined in Art. 150, IV of the Federal Constitution.
6. This is so provided in Art. 145, 1st para. of the Federal Constitution.
7. Law 5,172/1966. Despite having been passed in 1966 and being previous to the 1988 Constitution, it has been received by the current constitutional framework as it does not opposite to any current constitutional provision.

The CTN aims to perform the important function of homogenising the Brazilian tax system, setting out general rules that bind all the federated entities, and making Brazilian Tax Law a structure organised in a way that rationalises the taxation process, avoiding excessive contractions in tax rules among the federated entities.

To this end, the CTN establishes major general rules applicable to taxation, such as: (a) the definition of tax (*tributo*), which is defined as every pecuniary consideration that does not originate from any wrongful act, that is instituted by law and that is imposed by a fully bound administrative activity;[8] (b) that the obligation to pay tax arises from the occurrence of a tax event and its object is the payment of the tax or a pecuniary penalty, which are extinguished once the debt is paid;[9] (c) that the administrative authority has powers to perfect tax debts through levying (*lançamento*), which is defined as the administrative procedure applied to verify the occurrence of the tax event against the related corresponding obligation, to determine the taxable matter, to calculate the amount of the tax due, to identify the taxpayer and, if applicable, to set out the applicable tax penalty;[10] (d) to define the methods which extinguish the obligation to pay tax, which are: (i) payment; (ii) offsetting of credits and debits between the State and the taxpayer; (iii) transaction (*transação*), which is a settlement over a tax-related dispute; (iv) remission (*remissão*), which is waiver of the tax debt; and (v) the expiration of the limitation periods for the loss of the right to file proceedings (*prescrição*) or extinguishment of a right (*decadência*).[11]

The right of the State to commence proceedings against the taxpayer for unpaid taxes occurs upon the elapsing of the period during which the tax authorities could perfect tax credits through the tax assessment. In other words, the tax authorities have both the legal duty and the right to enforce tax obligations on taxpayers through a procedure named 'tax assessment' (*lançamento tributário*). The authorities can effect this either following the original procedures for some taxes that require it or alternatively, in those cases where the taxpayer carries the obligation to calculate the taxes, inform to tax authorities and pay the tax, but for any reason does not do it. However, the CTN sets out a term for the tax authorities to comply with these obligations, which occurs after five years from the tax event.[12] After this term expires without taxes being imposed on the taxpayer, the tax authorities will not be able to enforce their rights, since the right to do so has been extinguished. Time barring on a cause of action has a similar effect, but it extinguishes a different kind of right, that is, the right of the tax authorities to enforce the tax obligation in court.

Even though the State has the power to inspect and collect taxes from individuals, it cannot unilaterally and automatically take away private property to

8. Article 3 of the CTN.
9. Article 113, para. 1 of the CTN.
10. Article 142 of the CTN.
11. Article 156 of the CTN.
12. Article 174 of the CTN.

ensure that the taxes are paid other than through a specific judicial proceeding called tax foreclosure (*execução fiscal*).

Pursuant to the tax foreclosure proceedings, if the taxpayer does not pay the tax debt after being served with notice, the only way the Tax Authority can receive the tax owed is via court proceedings, and penalties may be added to the tax debt owed by the taxpayer. The tax foreclosure proceedings have the purpose of complying with the due process of law principle enshrined in the Federal Constitution.[13]

The five-year term for the State filing the tax foreclosure starts to run from when the administrative review procedure is finalised.[14]

General rules on exemptions are also provided by the CTN. Among these rules, there are important constraints regarding the creation of exemptions by the federated entities. Section 178 sets out two limitations for the revocation of exemptions: (a) If a law revokes an exemption, such revocation is deemed equivalent to a new tax for the purposes of validity and commencement; and (b) if the exemption is conditional and it was granted for only a set period of time, the CTN forbids its revocation in order to preserve legal certainty.

III. TAXATION ON INDUSTRY, TRADE AND SERVICES

Business entities are liable for different taxes depending on the type of activity they carry on. Various taxes which apply to taxed activity are levied by the Federal, State and Municipal governments.

A. Income Tax on Legal Entities and Social Contribution on the Net Profits

There are two methods of calculation for a company's income: (a) the actual profit method; and (b) the deemed profit method.

The first method reflects, strictly speaking, the concept of income, that is, the positive gain or profit found in the balance sheet calculated in a given fiscal year. Based on the earned income and on the expenses accepted as deductible by law, a profit or loss is made. The same occurs with the Social Contribution over Net Profits (*Contribuição Social sobre o Lucro Líquido*, 'CSLL') that, similar to Company Income Tax (*Imposto de Renda de Pessoas Jurídicas*, 'IRPJ'), is levied on the positive result on the balance sheet, referred as 'net profit'.

The 'deemed profit' method deems a certain percentage of a company's gross income as its net profit. Depending on the cost structure of the company, the deemed profit method of calculation can be of great benefit to the company. Under the deemed profit method, the percentage of the gross revenue received

13. Article 5th, LIV and LV of the Federal Constitution.
14. Article 174 of the CTN.

by the company will be deemed as the company's profit, regardless as to whether the company makes an actual profit or not. For the sale of goods, the law deems 8% on the monthly gross revenue as income. If the company provides services, 32% on the monthly gross revenue will be deemed as the company's income.

However, there are limitations for the deemed profit method. Companies that exceed the yearly revenue of BRL 48,000,000 must have their income tax calculated in accordance with the actual profit method. Likewise, banks, stockbrokers, leasing companies, credit cooperatives, private insurance companies and pension funds must apply the actual profit method. Moreover, companies that hold shares in foreign entities also are bound to apply the actual profit method.

IRPJ is levied at 15%, an additional 10% will be payable where the company makes a profit of more than USD 20,000 per month. CSLL is levied at 9%, over the company's income, calculated in accordance with the deemed or actual profit methods as provided by the rules applicable to the IRPJ.

The framework of both taxes is basically the same, with the difference that the product levied by the last has is solely intended to finance the social security system.

B. Excise Tax and State Tax on the Sale of Goods and Services

Both Excise Tax (*Imposto sobre Produtos Industrializados*, 'IPI') and the State Tax on the Sale of Goods and Services (*Imposto sobre a Circulação de Mercadorias e Serviços*, 'ICMS') are very similar. They are imposed on business transactions and have some basic differences: (a) IPI is a Federal tax and ICMS is a State tax; (b) IPI is imposed on manufacturers (or anyone who laws deem as their equivalent), while ICMS is imposed on taxpayers' referred to as 'traders'. Exceptionally, ICMS is also applied on two specific services:[15] communication services and inter-State and intercity transportation services.

Both taxes are governed by two constitutional principles: (a) principle of non-accumulation; and (b) principle of selectivity.

1. Non-accumulation

IPI and ICMS are 'multi-phase' taxes, that is, they occur in several stages of an industrialisation or commercialisation chain of a good. The non-accumulation principle prevents that the taxes accumulate throughout the whole productive chain, whose economic effect would be an excessive increase in the production costs and, finally, in an increase in the final prices to consumers.

This is to be compared with the Value-Added Tax (IVA), adopted in various Latin American and European countries, which take the added economic value in each stage of the productive chain in order to avoid tax accumulation. IPI and

15. Since the general rule is that the provision of services be taxed by means of the municipal tax on services – see further below.

ICMS, on the other hand, are based on the total revenues obtained from the relevant sales, requiring the use of a system of credits and debits in order to avoid accumulation.

The system of credits and debits operates as follows, for exemplification purposes: (a) manufacturer W sells a component to manufacturer X for BRL 100. IPI is imposed at 10% hence there is a BRL 10 debit; (b) manufacturer X incorporates the component to its product, selling it to manufacturer Y for BRL 200. IPI is imposed at 10% hence there is a BRL 20 debit. Yet, there was a BRL 10, credit from the former transaction, thus there is a BRL 10 debit to be charged to the manufacturer Y incorporates the product into the equipment that is sold to manufacturer Z for BRL 300. Ten percent IPI times BRL 300 = BRL 30 (debit) minus BRL 20 (credit from the former transaction), equals BRL 10 (a debit). The same systematic applies to ICMS as well.

The Federal Constitution forbids credits when former transactions are ICMS exempt.[16] However, insofar as IPI is concerned, credits can generally be offset.

2. Selectivity

IPI and ICMS are also known as taxes on consumption due to their direct effect on the price of goods. Strictly speaking, the tax event is not the purchase of the good by the end buyer, but its onerous transfer of title to a third party.

The Constitution determines that IPI an ICMS tax rates be selective according with the 'essentiality' of the good, understood as the degree of necessity that people have to acquire them. Therefore, superfluous consumption goods should have a higher tax rate than essential goods.

Due to the selectivity principle, IPI and ICMS contain varying tax rates. IPI has tax rates that range from 0% to 330%.[17] Since it is a State tax, ICMS is governed by the laws of the twenty-seven different States of the Brazilian Federation. Nevertheless, due to inter-State agreements, the specific tax rate on sale of goods is usually 18%, as is the case, for example, in the State of São Paulo.

C. PIS and Cofins (Employees' Profit Participation Program and Contribution for Social Security Financing)

Companies, regardless of the field in which they operate, are bound to pay employees' 'Social Integration' Program (*Programa de Integração Social*, 'PIS') and Contribution for Social Security Financing (*Contribuição para o Financiamento da Seguridade Social*, 'Cofins'). These taxes are imposed on the companies' revenues from the sale of goods, the provision or services, gross revenues from all sources, regardless of the sector they operate or whether they sell goods or provide services.

16. Article 153, paras 2, II(a) and (b).
17. This rate is levied on cigarettes.

Since these taxes are imposed on gross income, historically they have had a cumulative (i.e., without credits) feature that was authorised (or at least not prohibited) by the Constitution. However, the Federal Congress has recently enacted legislation providing for the non-accumulation of taxes in order to provide stimulus to companies. The Law 10,637/2002 provides for the credit of expenses such as: leasing of buildings, machines and equipment paid to legal entities and used for performing company activities; machines, equipment and other goods incorporated to fixed assets, acquired or manufactured to be leased to third parties or for the production of goods meant for sale or for the provision of services; buildings and improvements to third parties' real estate when the costs, including labour, have been borne by the lessee; returned goods, whose sale revenue has integrated the current or previous month's income and has been taxed; and electric power consumed in legal entities' production facilities.

Companies that choose or are bound to apply the deemed profit method will not be entitled to the non-accumulation of taxes, thus being taxed under the cumulative system (i.e., tax no credits are allowed).

PIS and COFINS are imposed under two systems: (a) the non-accumulation system (actual profit method): PIS (levied at 1.65%) and COFINS (levied at 7.6%), both imposed on the monthly gross revenues; or (b) the accumulation system (deemed profit method): PIS (levied at 0.65%) and Cofins (levied at 3%), both on the revenues originated from the company's provision of goods and services.

D. Services Tax

Companies and contract workers that provide services must pay municipal services tax (*Imposto sobre Serviços*, 'ISS'). ISS' general rules are provided by Complementary Law 116/2003, while specific statutes are enacted by the over 5,000 Municipalities around Brazil.

The taxed services are those provided under a private law regime, that is, contractual and for consideration, and must not be confused with the public services provided by the State, or with the services provided by the employee to his or her employer, which are governed by employment laws. Nevertheless, the Complementary Law 116/2003 has created a list setting out the relevant services subject to ISS, meaning that if any services that are not listed will not be subject to ISS.

The tax collecting location has always been controversial within the Brazilian tax system. Complementary Law 116/2003, and prior laws that governed the same matter, establish that the Municipality where there service provider has an establishment or domicile is entitled to the tax collection. Thus, if the provider has his or her establishment registered in the city of São Paulo but provides services in other cities, as per the law São Paulo will be entitled to charge the ISS.

However, precedents from the superior courts, especially from the Superior Court of Justice and from the Federal Supreme Court, have consistently found that ISS is due in the location where the services are *provided*. The discrepancy between what statutes State and what the courts have decided brings problems for the taxpayer, who faces the possibility of being liable for twice the amount of ISS for the same tax event. This problem has been partially resolved by the application of withholding tax according to the service hired, when the services are provided in a Municipality different from the one where the company's establishment is located. The solution is only partial because the services that are subject to the withholding tax system are exceptions.

The ISS payable is calculated in accordance with the price of the service provided. The tax rate, except for some exceptions, is usually 5%. In no circumstances may the Municipalities impose a rate above the 5% rate.

IV. TAXATION ON FOREIGN TRADE

The Brazilian tax system taxes both imports and exports. It must be pointed out the intrinsically 'non-fiscal' nature of the taxes on foreign trade since they operate much more as an intervention of the State in certain sectors of the economy in order to regulate it than mere revenue raising.

A. Import Tax and Export Tax

Import tax is traditionally charged on goods and products imported from abroad. It is payable when the product or foreign good enters Brazilian territory.[18] The tax is either charged on the customs value of the imported good or on the number of items imported. The method used to determine it follows two specific criteria:[19] (a) when the tax rate is specific, the measurement unit adopted by tax law, as, for instance, BRL 10 for each litre of liquor; and (b) when the tax rate is *ad valorem*, the criterion is the customs value determined as per the General Agreement on Tariffs and Trade.

The import tax rate is based on the Common External Tariff (*Tarifa Externa Comum*, 'TEC'), which applies to all members of the Common Market of the South.

B. Export Tax

Export Tax is one of an non-fiscal nature, meaning that its function is not to burden, but to stimulate or to discourage the taxpayer to act in some way that is regarded as important for the common good of the country.

As with IPI, with the Tax on Financial Operations (*Imposto sobre Operações Financeiras*, 'IOF') and with the import and export taxes, the principle of legality

18. Article 19 of the CTN.
19. Article 20 of the CTN.

and the principle of precedence associated to the tax rate increase does not apply to Import Tax and Export Tax. This exception to the taxpayers' fundamental rights results from the belief of the legislator that the federal government sometimes needs to intervene in the economy.

The maximum rate that the Customs Regulations set out for the export tax is 30%. However, due to the incentive that the government has been providing to the exports in the last years, the vast majority of the goods are classified with having a zero export tax rate.

C. IPI on Imports

Even though this tax shares its name with IPI, it is not levied on the transfer of title of industrialised products, but on their importation.

The CTN establishes some general rules about IPI on imports,[20] defining customs clearance as the moment when the tax event occurs. This means that, for the purposes of this tax, the moment immediately after its customs clearance is considered 'as if' the good had come into the country.

Still according to the CTN, the formula for calculating import tax is the value used to determine it, plus the customs duties and the exchange rates owed by the importer and added to the formula. The rate applied to this base is published in the TIPI-IPI Table.[21]

The relevant taxpayer[22] is the individual or legal entity that imports any product, even if their end activity is not importing goods.

D. ICMS on Imports

The Federal Constitution sets out in section 155, 2nd paragraph that ICMS will be levied 'on the entry of the good or merchandise imported by any individual or legal entity, even if they are not usual taxpayers of this tax, whatever its purpose, as well as on any service provided abroad, being the tax owed to the State where the domicile or establishment of the addressee's merchandise, good or service is located'.

Complementary Law 87/1996 sets out general rules that bind all States. According to the law, like IPI on imports, the obligation to ICMS arises at the time customs clearance of the good coming from abroad is carried out, and also upon the reception of the services provided abroad, and finally, upon the acquisition, in a public tender, of seized or abandoned imported goods.[23]

---

20. Articles 46–51.
21. Decree 4,542/2002.
22. Article 51, I of the CTN.
23. Article 12, IX to XI of Complementary Law 87/1996.

The applicable formula is the value of the good or product Stated in the import declaration plus the Federal import tax, IPI on imports and any customs expenses.[24] There are various tax rates which apply, due to the constitutional principle of selectivity.

E. PIS and COFINS on Imports (*PIS-Importação* and *COFINS-Importação*)

The social contributions explained above are also payable on the importation of goods and services. Despite having the same name, they are different taxes levied specifically on imports.

The structure of PIS and COFINS on Imports is very similar to the ones levied on imports. The taxpayer is the importer and the tax event is the moment when the merchandise enters Brazilian territory.

The applicable formula is the customs duty plus the ICMS value on the import and the value of the contributions.[25] Different rates may apply, yet generally, the rates applicable are 1.65% and 7.6% for PIS on Imports and COFINS on Imports, respectively.

V. SELECTED TAXES ON PROPERTY AND ASSETS

A. Tax over Buildings and Land

The Tax over Buildings and Land (*Imposto Predial e Territorial Urbano*, 'IPTU') is levied on any real estate (land or buildings) located in urban areas. The taxpayer is the owner of the real estate, the holder of its useful ownership or any possessor or the real property type.

The formula for calculating IPTU considers the market value of the property. The rate charged on the value of the property is, on average, 1%. The Federal Constitution authorises two kinds of progressive levying for this tax: (a) non-fiscal progression: Article 156 of the Constitution provides that the progression should be used as a means to encourage the productive use of property. If that does not occur, the municipal district will be entitled to tax progressively over time, that is, the more the real estate remains abandoned or misused, the greater is the progression that may be levied; (b) tax progression: Constitutional Amendment 29/2000 created the possibility of progressive taxes based only on the nominal value of the property. This same Amendment has established the differentiation of the rates may be applied to property merely due to their location. This distinction allows Municipalities to tax real estate in different ways, depending on the zone in which

---

24. Article 13, V of Complementary Law 87/1996.
25. Article 7, I of Law 10,865/2004.

they are located. For instance, a property located in a commercial zone can have a lower IPTU rate than a property located in a residential zone.

Most of the Municipalities have not instituted the progression system permitted under the Constitution and tax real estate with a fixed rate.

B. RURAL LAND TAX

Rural land tax (*Imposto Territorial Rural*, 'ITR') is a federal tax applied to properties located outside the urban zones of municipal districts, or 'rural zones'. The Stated purpose for ITR is to stimulate productivity of rural land. The taxpayer is the owner of the real estate, the holder of its useful ownership and any possessor of rural land.

The formula used to determine the ITR payable is more complex than for IPTU. It requires a calculation method that takes into account:[26]

(a) the value of the rural property, excluding the amounts associated to: (i) construction, facilities and improvements; (ii) permanent and temporary crops; (iii) cultivated and improved pastures; and (iv) planted forests;
(b) the taxable area (the total area of the property), except for areas: (i) of permanent environmental preservation and legal reserves; (ii) with environmental interest provided in the previous paragraph; or (iii) proved to be improper for any agricultural use, cattle breeding, chicken farming, aquaculture or forestry uses;
(c) the value of the taxable empty land, which is obtained multiplying the value of the rural property by the rate between taxable area and the total area;
(d) the serviceable area, which is taken to be as the area that is object of agricultural exploitation, cattle breeding, chicken farming, aquaculture for forestry projects, excluding the areas: (i) occupied by improving waste and repairs; (b) covered in paragraphs (b)(i) and (ii), above;
(e) effectively used areas, which is taken to be the portion of the property that in the previous year: (i) was planted with vegetable products; (ii) served as pasture, native or planted, in accordance with the occupation rates per cattle breeding zone; (iii) was object of extractive exploitation, in accordance with the production rates per product and environmental legislation; (iv) served to exploit chicken farming and aquaculture activities; (v) was object of implementation of a technical project; and
(f) the degree of use, which is the percentile between the area effectively used and its total useful area.

26. See Law 9,393/1996.

C. Intervivos Real Estate Transfer Tax

Intervivos Real EState Transfer Tax (*Imposto de Transferência de Bens* Intervivos, 'ITBI') is a municipal tax levied on real estate transfers for consideration and the granting of security rights over real estate, as well as assignment of rights for the acquisition of real estate. Transactions (with some few specific exceptions) involving transfer of property in exchange for consideration, such as the purchase and sale of real estate, will be taxed.

The taxable basis is the market value of the real estate, which assessed by the municipal tax authorities. Even if the buyer and the seller agree on a price lower than the market price, the tax will be charged on the value assessed by the Municipality. The rate varies from Municipality to Municipality, but is generally 3%.

The Constitution[27] exempts the transfers of properties or rights incorporated to the legal entity, assets transferred to pay up capital, or the transfer of goods and rights originating from mergers, incorporations, spin offs or deregistrations of legal entities.

Selected Bibliography

In English

R.G. de Ferreira Souza, 'Form Versus Substance: A Comparison of Brazil's Tax System to the Tax System of The United States of America' (Spring 2004) 35, no. 2 *The University of Miami Inter-American Law Review* 311–343.

W.R. Dillinger, *Urban Property Taxation: lessons from Brazil* (World Bank, Infrastructure and Urban Development Dept., World Bank Publications, 1999).

K. Dimancescu, *International Business Publications – Brazil Tax Guide* (World Country Study Guide Library, 2009).

K. Dimancescu (ed.), *Brazil Tax, Law and Business Briefing* (World Trade Executive, 2008).

A. Estache and V. Gaspar, 'Why Tax Incentives Do Not Promote Investments in Brazil', in A. Shah (ed.), *Fiscal Incentives for Investment and Innovation* (Oxford University Press, Oxford, 1995).

R. Mitchell, 'United States-Brazil Bilateral Income Tax Treaty Negotiations' (1997) 21 *Hastings International and Comparative Law Review* 209.

M. Mora and R. Varsano, *Fiscal Decentralization and Subnational Fiscal Autonomy in Brazil: Some Facts of the Nineties* (IPEA Working Paper No. 854, December, 2001).

W.A Selcher, 'The Politics of Decentralized Federalism, National Diversification and Regionalism in Brazil' (Winter 1998) 40 *Journal of Interamerican Studies and World Affairs* 25–50.

A. Shah, *The New Fiscal Federalism in Brazil* (World Bank Publications, 1990).

27. Article 156, 2nd paragraph.

In Portuguese

P.A. Barreto, *Imposto sobre a Renda e Preços de Transferência* (Dialética, São Paulo 2001).
P. de Barros Carvalho, *Curso de Direito Tributário* (22nd edn, Saraiva, São Paulo, 2010).
A.R. Carrazza, *Curso de Direito Constitucional Tributário* (26th edn, Malheiros, São Paulo, 2010).
A.R. Carrazza, *ICMS* (14th edn, Malheiros, São Paulo, 2009).
C. Carvalho, 'Comentários à Lei Complementar n. 116/03' in M.M. Peixoto and R.S.M. Lacombe (eds), *Comentários ao Código Tributário Nacional* (2nd edn, MP, São Paulo, 2008).
C. Carvalho, *Teoria do Sistema Jurídico – Direito, Economia, Tributação* (Quartier Latin, São Paulo, 2005).
A.J. Costa, *Estudos sobre IPI, ICMS e ISS* (Dialética, São Paulo, 1999).
E.M.D. de Santi, *Decadência e Prescrição no Direito Tributário* (3rd edn, Max Limonad São Paulo, 2004)
E.M.D. de Santi, *Lançamento Tributário* (2nd edn, Max Limonad, São Paulo, 2001).
R.G. de Souza, G. Ataliba and P. de Barros Carvalho, *Comentários ao Código Tributário Nacional. 40 anos do Código Tributário Nacional* (2nd edn, Quartier Latin, São Paulo, 2007).

Chapter 10
Labour Law

*Estêvão Mallet**

I. SOURCES OF LABOUR LAW

In the Brazilian legal system, as in other legal systems of the civil law family, the main source of law is legislation. Other sources, such as customs and usage, regulations and administrative rulings, play a subordinate and ancillary role (albeit in no way negligible) and are, as a rule, subject to the limits established by legislation. The administrative authorities, for instance, cannot impose on employees or employers an obligation that is not contemplated by legislation. Even agreements entered into with unions (collective bargaining agreements or collective labour conventions), which are so important when it comes to shaping labour rights in countries such as Great Britain and the United States, are relegated to a lesser role in Brazil, serving essentially to broaden the rights already provided for in the legislation.

It is incumbent on the Federal Government to legislate on Labour Law. As a general rule, labour laws promulgated by the States or Municipalities are unconstitutional. One of the very few exceptions refers to minimum wages, which may be established by the States under Complementary Law 103/2000. Few Brazilian states, however, have adopted the prerogative granted in Complementary Law 103/2000. As a result, Labour Law is substantially uniform throughout Brazil.

* Professor of Labour Law at the University of São Paulo School of Law. Post-Doctorate, LLD, LLM, LLB (USP). Advisor to the Brazilian Bar Association, São Paulo Chapter.

Fabiano Deffenti & Welber Barral (eds), *Introduction to Brazilian Law*, pp. 153–182.

Labour law is dealt with mainly in the Consolidated Labour Laws (*Consolidação das Leis do Trabalho*, 'CLT'), which make up a Code containing over 900 articles, many of them amended by different laws along the years. Other laws not included in the CLT also address labour issues, such as Laws 4,090/1962 and 4,749/1965, which provide for payment of a mandatory annual bonus (Christmas bonus or thirteenth salary); Law 7,783/1998, which regulates the exercise of the right to strike; and Law 8,036/1990, which regulates the Unemployment Guarantee Fund (*Fundo de Garantia do Tempo de Serviço*, 'FGTS'). There are also laws that regulate certain professions or activities, such as those of lawyers,[1] aircraft pilots,[2] professional athletes,[3] domestic workers,[4] rural employees,[5] musicians,[6] travelling salespersons,[7] among others. When labour laws are silent on an issue, other ordinary laws, including the Civil Code, will operate as a secondary source.

Several labour rights are set out in the Brazilian Constitution itself, especially in Articles 6 through 11. Article 7 of the Constitution lists the most important labour rights, such as minimum wage, salary irreducibility, remunerated weekly day of rest, vacation, thirteenth salary and the right to strike.

Case law, which draws on the interpretation and application of labour rules, is summarised in propositions called case law abstracts (*súmulas*) and case law statements (*orientações jurisprudenciais*). These rulings are frequently mentioned and consulted to resolve issues yet to be settled by case law.

II. SCOPE OF APPLICATION OF LABOUR LAW

A. GOVERNING LAW

In Brazil, employment contracts are governed by the law of the place where the service is provided (*lex loci executionis*).[8] The place where the employee was hired, the place of domicile of the company, or even the existence of another applicable law in the employment contract itself, are immaterial. The parties are not free to elect the law that will govern the employment contract. As a result, if the employee has worked in Brazil, Brazilian law will apply even if he or she was hired abroad or the employer is a foreign company.

The application of labour laws does not depend on the will of the parties to the employment contract (employee and employer). These parties cannot resolve that a certain right imposed by law (such as, for instance, the payment of the thirteenth

1. Law 8,906/1994.
2. Law 7,183/1984.
3. Laws 6,354/1976 and 9,615/1998.
4. Law 5,859/1972.
5. Law 5,889/1973.
6. Law 3,857/ 1960.
7. Law 3,207/1957.
8. Case Law Abstract 207 which states: 'Legal labour relations are governed by the laws in force in the country where the service is provided and not by the laws of the place of hiring.'

salary or otherwise) will not be applied to their employment contract – labour rights cannot be waived. This rule was set forth in Article 9 of the CLT, which provides: 'The acts performed with the purpose of sidestepping, impeding or defrauding the application of the precepts set out in these consolidated laws shall be void by operation of law.'

B. The Contract of Employment

The contract of employment is the legal bond established between employee and employer – also called the employment relationship – which entails the application of labour rules. It may be entered into either in writing or orally. In any event, it is imperative that the employee register the new position in the employee's Work and Social Security Card (*Carteira de Trabalho e Previdência Social*, 'CTPS'), a document that must be submitted by the employee to the employer upon hiring and which will be kept in the employee's possession, as well as in the book of registration of employees, a corporate document that must be submitted to the administrative bodies overseeing the enforcement of labour rules.

Given that labour rights cannot be waived, the existence of an employment contract does not depend on the will of the parties. The courts have adopted a clear stance on the matter, stating that '[i]t is the manner in which the services will be provided that will determine whether [an employment] relationship exists, since the employment contract is a reality-based contract'.[9]

In order to characterise an employment contract so as to give rise to an employment relationship subject to the CLT, it is essential that: (a) the work be performed by an individual; (b) subordination by the employee to the employer; (c) the work be performed on an ongoing and regular basis; (d) remuneration; (e) the work performed be on a personal basis.

The first element (*work performed by an individual*) means that only an individual may be an employee, pursuant to Article 3 of the CLT. Therefore, if the activity is performed by a company rather than by an individual, there is no employment contract.[10]

Subordination, the second element, means that the employer directs the activity performed by the individual. This may take various forms, such as, for instance: the imposition of procedures for performance of the work; establishment of working hours; designation of the tasks to be performed; the place in which these tasks will be performed, etc. Officers of limited liability partnerships (*sociedades limitades*) are not deemed to be employees unless there is evidence of

9. Regional Labour Court (TRT), 1st Circuit, 3rd Panel, Ordinary Appeal No. 16963/96, Reporting Judge Nídia Aguiar (published in the Rio de Janeiro State Court Gazette on 12 Jan. 1999, 96) (Labour Law Review (RDT)) 2/99, 65).
10. Note that the courts have taken a very lax view of this provision. Courts often disregard the existence of the corporate veil of the company to find that in fact there is an employment relationship in place.

subordination. If, before having been appointed as a director, the worker already provided services to the company as an employee, his or her employment contract is not terminated, but rather suspended,[11] which means that during the relevant period the employment contract will not produce effects and employee's rights will not apply.

The requirement that the work be performed on a regular basis means that, those who provide services on a sporadic basis are not deemed to be employees, as opposed to those who provide services on an ongoing and recurrent basis.

For an employment contract to exist, it is equally necessary that the worker perform his or her activity in order to receive remuneration, which is generally his or her salary. Charitable and goodwill work or work provided to assist a needy person, will not be deemed to be an employment contract.

Finally, the existence of an employment contract further presupposes that the service provider (who, as stated above, must be an individual) cannot be replaced by another person in the performance of his or her duties – the work must be of a *personal nature*. The employee is hired because of his personal status; therefore, this relationship does not allow for change in the service provider.

The existence (or not) of the five elements mentioned above is determined by taking into account not the formal aspect of the contract entered into between the parties, but rather the actual relationship between the parties (the facts prevail over the contractual terms, however solemn and formal they may be). This is a mere result of the principle of prevalence of reality, which states that what occurs in practice matters more than what the parties have agreed to in documents.[12]

Accordingly, hiring a professional to be responsible for technical responsibilities essential to the company's core business, despite the fact that the employee is the controlling shareholder of the legal entity, does not exclude the existence of an employment relationship if all five elements are present.[13] Registration of an employee as a legal entity or single person enterprise does not invalidate the employment relationship, which must be reviewed by combining the guiding principles of labour relationships.[14]

---

11. Case Law Abstract 269 'The employee elected to hold the position of officer will have his employment contract suspended, and length of service will not be computed during such period, unless the subordination inherent to an employment relationship persists.'
12. See, for instance, TRT, 1st Circuit, 7th Panel, Ordinary Appeal No. 10535/92, Reporting Judge Ricardo A. Oberlaender, published in the Rio de Janeiro State Court Gazette on 5 Jul. 1995, 230. See also TRT, 11th Circuit, Decision No. 206/96, Reporting Judge R. Alencar Albuquerque, published in the Amazonas State Court Gazette on 8 Feb. 1996, 11, and TRT, 2nd Circuit, Decision No. 20020308285, Reporting Judge Ricardo Verta Luduvice, issued on 7 May 2002, published in the São Paulo State Official Gazette, PJ, TRT, 2nd Circuit on 17 May 2002.
13. This stand relies on Art. 9 of the CLT, which defines as 'void by operation of law the acts performed with the purpose of sidestepping, impeding or defrauding application of the precepts set out in these consolidated laws'.
14. TRT, 15th Circuit, 1st Panel, Decision No. 40865/98, Reporting Judge Luiz Antônio Lazarim, published in the São Paulo State Court Gazette on 23 Nov. 1998, 81. See also TRT, 10th Circuit, 2nd Panel, Decision No. 2162/94, Reporting Judge Silva de Aquino, published in the Federal District Court Gazette on 20 Jan. 1995, 382.

Employment contracts may be ordinary or special. Ordinary employment contracts are adopted for activities or workers to which no specific rules apply. Special employment contracts, on the other hand, involve specific rules, applicable only in certain conditions, or to certain activities or employees, such as, for instance, part-time work, contracts with bank employees, railway employees and teachers, in addition to the contracts set out in the aforementioned special laws.

Another important difference involves fixed-term employment contracts and employment contracts for an indefinite term. Under Brazilian law, the general rule is that contracts are to operate indefinitely. However, employees may be hired for a fixed term in three specific events, namely: (a) when the service has a temporary nature or character that justifies the agreed term; (b) when temporary business activities are involved; or (c) when a probation contract is in place. Any contracts containing terms other than those in accordance with these rules will be deemed void.

C. The Employer

The employer may be either an individual who hires employees or a legal entity. This does not change the employee's rights.[15]

Under Articles 10 and 448 of the CLT, changes in the company's legal structure do not affect the employee's vested rights or even existing employment contracts. Transfer of company ownership does not lead to termination of employment contracts. Therefore, when a company is sold, the purchaser must observe the employees' rights, even those created before the sale. Likewise, the party succeeding a given employer in the development of the activity becomes responsible for the labour obligations of the previous employer.

When the company is part of an economic group, all related companies are jointly and severally liable for the obligations to employees. In this case, the actual employer is the group itself and not the specific company that hired the employee. This fact has important consequences. Firstly, even if the employee provides services to two or more companies of the group, there will be only one single employment contract.[16] Secondly, the employee may claim rights from any of the companies that make up the group, including from those to which he or she did not provide services. Thirdly, the employee may be transferred from one company to another within the group without termination of his or her employment contract. Fourthly, determination of the employee's length of service takes into account the period worked for the entire group.

For a group of companies to be considered an economic group, three elements must be present: (a) each company must have its own legal identity, (b) the companies must engage in activities in pursuit of profit; and (c) there must be a uniform

15. There is less red tape for companies with lower turnovers (the so-called small businesses or microenterprises), pursuant to Law 9,841/1999. The employees' rights are the same.
16. Case Law Abstract 129 of the Superior Labour Court.

direction, control or management among them. It is not necessary, however, to formalise the group by means of documents or other registrations.

If the company delegates to another company the performance of a certain non-core activity (outsourcing), such as cleaning or security, it will be secondarily liable for the labour obligations of the outsourced company. This means that the company that takes the services may be sued by the employee if the company that hired him is unable to satisfy its respective labour obligations.[17] Outsourcing of the company's core activity to a third party is not permitted. This gives rise to joint and several liabilities for both the party that conducts the activity and the party that receives services.

D. The Employee

Brazilian labour law deals very little with the non-economic rights of employees. However, with the coming into force of the Federal Constitution of 1988, which emphasised the dignity of the human being and the Civil Code of 2002, which dedicated an entire chapter to personal rights, employers were given further responsibilities vis-à-vis their employees.

Nowadays, the employer must take all the necessary steps within its reach to avoid the occurrence of accidents during performance of the work.[18] Omission may give rise to an obligation to pay damages, which encompasses actual property damages as well as moral damages (pain and suffering). Many suits have been filed seeking moral damages in events of occupational accidents and occupational diseases.

Article 18 of the Civil Code provides that the employer can only use the employee's name with the latter's consent. The same applies to the use of images, vocal recordings, pseudonyms and so on.

Brazilian law protects the privacy of individuals and this protection extends to employees. In light of the subordination inherent to employment contracts, the employer is entitled to monitor the activities performed by the employee. Thus, harmonisation of the employee's right to privacy with the employer's right to monitor the activity performed is a delicate task. The CLT merely prohibits the intimate body search of women. General body searches of employees are allowed if carried out within reasonable limits and for justified reasons (in view of the activity performed).[19] Control of e-mails sent and received

17. Case Law Abstract 331, Item IV of the Superior Labour Court.
18. In view of the protection granted to life and to the physical integrity of persons in general (Arts 13 through 15 of the Civil Code), as well as the usual civil liability rules (Arts 186 and 927 of the Civil Code).
19. In this sense, please refer to the following decisions: TRT – 3rd Circuit, 2nd Panel, Reporting Judge Alice Monteiro de Barros, judged on 30 Oct. 2001, Ordinary Appeal No. 13.305/2001, published in the Minas Gerais State Court Gazette (DJMG) on 14 Nov. 2001, 21; TRT – 3rd Circuit, 2nd Panel, Ordinary Appeal No. 14.596/2001, Reporting Judge Ricardo Marcelo Silva, judged on 4 Dec. 2001, published in DJMG on 12 Dec. 2001, 21; and TRT – 3rd Circuit, 5th

at work[20] and the installation of closed-circuit cameras[21] are also allowed, provided that the employee is previously informed of the practice.

Protection of privacy also involves protection of the employee from specific questioning by the employer, whether during the hiring process or the employment contract. Certain questions, such as those relating to political convictions, religious beliefs and sexual orientation, among others, cannot be asked of the employee. Some questions are lawful if they concern the services to be performed. Use of the information obtained by the employer is restricted. The law does not allow the employer to impart such information to third parties without the prior consent of the employee, except in justified cases, such as an order from the public authorities or a in the case of a disease subject to compulsory notification.

E. Work Hours

Under Brazilian law, work hours, in general, comprise the period during which the employee is at the disposal of the employer, performing the orders given by the employer or simply awaiting instructions. As a rule, work hours do not include breaks and the time spent commuting to and from the workplace. This system applies to practically all cases, with very few exceptions.

When there is no other limit set by law, the maximum number of working hours in a day is eight and the maximum in a work week is forty-four. Working hours are shorter for certain activities. Ordinary bank employees and elevator operators, to mention only two examples from among the many provided for by law, have a six-hour workday. Back-to-back rotating shifts are also limited to six hours.

Work hours may be exceeded in five main situations. Firstly, unless there is a specific legal prohibition such as that set out in part-time employment contracts, it is possible to agree by contract or collective bargaining an agreement with the provision of up to two extra work hours per day. Secondly, it is possible to extend the workday by up to two hours, offsetting the extra work hours against hours worked in other days when the worker will work fewer hours. Thirdly, the workday may be extended, without a pre-established maximum limit, in the event of force majeure.[22] Fourthly, the workday may be extended to allow for the completion of works that cannot be postponed, provided that the total workday does not exceed

---

Panel, Ordinary Appeal No. 8932/97, Reporting Judge Fernando Antônio Ferreira, published in the Minas Gerais Court Gazette on 30 May 1998, 15.

20. Superior Labour Court (TST) – 1st Panel, Motion to Review No. 613/2000-013-10-00, Reporting Justice João Oreste Dalazen, judged on 18 May 2005, published in the Federal Court Gazette on 10 Jun. 2005.
21. TRT – 3rd Circuit, 2nd Panel, Ordinary Appeal No. 4.165/03, Reporting Judge José Maria Caldeira, judged on 29 Apr. 2003, published in the Minas Gerais Court Gazette on 7 May 2003.
22. Force majeure is defined in Art. 501 of the CLT as 'any inevitable event as far as the employer's will is concerned, to which the employer has not contributed, either directly or indirectly.

twelve hours.[23] Finally, it is possible to extend the workday by two hours during forty-five days, to make up for the period of time in which there was 'interruption of the work because of accidental causes'.[24] In the first two cases, extension of the workday must be set out by agreement. In the other three cases, it does not. Refusal to work by the employee constitutes, in fact, improper behaviour, which may lead, in theory, to a termination of employment for good cause. To prevent abusive conduct on the part of the employer, the law imposes, in any of the last three scenarios, that an extension of the workday be reported to the labour oversight administrative bodies. In the fifth event, in which work hours are offset, prior authorisation of the labour oversight administrative bodies is most important.

Work performed beyond the maximum work hours constitutes extraordinary service or overtime, and the employee is entitled to receive one and one-half times his or her regular rate of pay – unless a higher rate is provided for in a special law,[25] in an agreement with the employee or in a collective bargaining agreement. No overtime rates are payable, however, in the second case mentioned in the preceding paragraph in the event of offsetting of work hours there is no increase in the total number of hours worked, merely a spreading of the same workload over several days.

Two categories of employees are exempt from the maximum workday and maximum workweek limits: (a) those who carry out outside activities; and (b) those who hold management positions. For the former, the reason is that outside services do not allow for control of the duration of the work, thus rendering it impossible to limit work hours. Precisely because of this, if there is any type of control by means of reports, electronic tracking systems, telephone contacts or other similar mechanisms, the rules on maximum daily work hours and overtime will still apply.[26] For the latter, the underlying principle behind the law is that holding a position of trust is incompatible with a strictly time-limited workday. When assessing whether a person is in a position of trust, what matters are the actual events, not the mere name given to the position. It is required, however, that the employee have decision-making power and a salary higher than that of other employees that perform comparable tasks.

F. Night Work

Night work is defined as the work performed between 10:00 p.m. of a day and 5:00 a.m. of the following day. Special rules set out different criteria for other employees, such as lawyers and rural employees.

---

23. At 61, main section and para. 2 of the CLT.
24. At 61, para. 3 of the CLT.
25. For lawyers, who are entitled to a 100% premium pay, please refer to Art. 20, para. 2 of Law 8,906/1994.
26. See TRT – 4th Circuit, Ordinary Appeal No. 96.004864-2/1996, Reporting Judge Paulo Caruso.

Night work gives rise to two consequences: the time worked is computed differently: 52 minutes and 30 seconds are deemed to be one hour of actual work and the employee is entitled to hourly rates at 20% above his or her hourly rate for day work.

G. Breaks

Employers must offer employees breaks for rest, according to the respective work hours. Employees working from four to six hours per day are entitled to a fifteen-minute break. If the workday exceeds six hours, the break will be at least one hour and at most two hours. If the workday does not exceed four hours, the employer is not required to offer a break. As explained above, the break is not regarded for the purposes of calculating the workday. As a result, the employee hired to work eight hours per day may provide services from 10:00 a.m. to 7:00 p.m., with a one-hour break from noon to 1:00 p.m. If breaks other than statutory breaks are offered, the respective time is computed as work-time.[27] In the example provided above, if the employer gives another thirty-minute break between 4:00 p.m. and 4:30 p.m., the workday must still end at 7:00 p.m. If the employee works until 7:30 p.m., he or she will be entitled to overtime pay.

There must be an interval of at least eleven hours between one workday and another. Therefore, if on one day the workday ends at 10:00 p.m., the employee can only work again the next day after 9:00 a.m. If he or she starts working at 7:00 a.m., he or she will be entitled to two hours of overtime pay, even if he or she does not work more than eight hours on such day.

H. Weekly Day of Rest

Employees are entitled to one day of rest per week. This right is regulated by Law 605/1949.

The general rule is that the day of rest must fall on a Sunday, when work is prohibited except in specific cases, such as: when it is technically impossible to interrupt the activity, when the activity involves public interest; in case of force majeure; when services cannot be postponed; and in retail businesses in general. There must be a twenty-four-hour rest period, with due regard for the eleven-hour interval between workdays.

If the employee was not absent or tardy in the week proceeding the day of rest, he or she will be entitled to receive, for his or her day of rest, the same compensation paid to him or her on a normal workday. Such compensation will include overtime pay for extra hours worked on a regular basis (i.e., if the employee regularly does overtime, then those hours will be taken into account as if they

27. Case Law Abstract 118 of the Superior Labour Court.

were part of the employee's regular working hours).[28] If the employee was absent or tardy, he or she will lose the right to compensation but not the right to the day of rest. Most federal holidays, in addition to state and municipal holidays, are afforded the same treatment given to the weekly day of rest.

If the employee is required to work on a day of rest, for any reason whatsoever, the employer must either give him or her another day of the week for rest or pay him or her twice the regular workday pay.[29]

I. Vacation

The employee's right to vacation is established in Article 129 through 153 of the CLT. In 1999, however, Brazil ratified Convention No. 132 of the International Labour Organization (ILO), which also deals with the subject, setting out rules partially different from those adopted by the CLT. This has led to some uncertainty as to the rules in force.

Under the CLT, the employee is entitled to vacation after a twelve-month period of service. The duration of the vacation will depend on the number of absences of the employee during a twelve-month period, in accordance with the following ratio: thirty days of vacation, if he or she was not absent more than five times; twenty-four days, if he or she was absent from 6 to 14 days; 18 days, if he or she was absent from 15 to 23 days; and 12 days if he or she was absent from 24 to 32 days. If the employee was absent more than 32 days, he or she will not be entitled to vacation time. Justified absences, such as those of maternity leave, occupational accidents, occupational diseases and others, do not affect the duration of vacations. For part-time employees, the ratio is different and takes the workweek into account: 18 days of vacation for a workweek ranging from 22 hours to 25 hours; 16 days for a workweek ranging from 20 hours to 22 hours; 14 days for a workweek ranging from 15 hours to 20 hours; 12 days for a workweek ranging from 10 hours to 15 hours; 10 days for a workweek ranging from 5 hours to 10 hours; and 8 days, for a workweek equal to or under 5 hours.

Once the vacation entitlement accrues, the employer has twelve months to determine when the employee may take his or her vacation. The employer may set the date at its discretion, except for employees who are also students, who are entitled to take their vacations during school breaks, and employees who are members of the same family and work at the same company, who are entitled to take their vacations together, provided that this does not affect the operation of the company. The employer must inform the employee of his or her vacation period in writing at least thirty days in advance, and the vacation must be enjoyed in one single period – the general rule is that fractioning of vacation time is not permissible.

---

28. Case Law Abstract 172 of the Superior Labour Court.
29. Case Law Abstract 146 of the Superior Labour Court.

During his or her vacation, the employee will receive his or her regular compensation plus a bonus equal to 1/3 of the monthly compensation. This payment has to be made at least two days before commencement of the vacation period. The payment of overtime worked on a regular basis is included in the amount payable.

Although this occurs in practice, conversion of full vacation time into cash is prohibited. Again, the principle that labour rights cannot be waived or changed by contract comes into play. The law allows for conversion of only 1/3 of vacation time into cash. If, for instance, the employee is entitled to a thirty-day vacation, he or she may elect to rest for twenty days and be paid in cash the amount corresponding to the remaining ten days. This is called 'vacation trading' (*abono de férias*). The employee is entitled to decide whether or not to convert part of his or her vacation time into cash – the employer cannot impose or prevent this conversion, if the employee chooses to adopt it.

If an employment contract is terminated without the employee having taken his or her vacation, the amount corresponding to such vacation time must be paid in cash, as compensation for a vested right not exercised. When the employment contract has been in force for at least twelve months and the right to vacation has been vested in the employee, compensation will always be due, even if the contract was terminated by breach by the employee (with good cause). If the twelve-month period has not elapsed, the employee will be entitled to proportionate vacation pay, unless he or she was dismissed for good cause.[30] This ratio corresponds to 1/12 of the regular vacation pay, plus a 1/3 bonus on such amount, for a period equal to or in excess of fifteen days. Therefore, if the employee worked for six months and eighteen days and then quits, he will be entitled to receive 7/12, plus 1/3, of the amount otherwise payable if he had earned his or her vacation entitlement.

It is also important to mention the concept of collective vacation, which is subject to slightly different specific rules, such as the possibility of fractioning the rest period and of giving employees a shorter vacation notice and is intended to enable the employer to go through temporary changes in production levels or demand slowdowns.

J. Payment of Employees

Brazilian law sets forth two basic concepts when it comes to employee payments. The first, which is the broader of the two, refers to compensation. The second, narrower, refers to salary. *Compensation* encompasses all the advantages enjoyed by an employee under his or her employment contract, including amounts offered by third parties, even without the knowledge or agreement of the employer, such as tips. *Salary*, in turn, covers only the economic advantages received directly by the employee from the employer. It is important to make this distinction because

30. Case Law Abstract 171 of the Superior Labour Court.

certain rights, such as vacation pay, are determined by taking into account the employee's entire compensation, whereas other rights, such as a weekly day of rest, are determined on the basis of the employee's salary rate.[31]

Fringe benefits offered by the employer to the employee, such as rent-free accommodation, air tickets for leisure purposes etc., are considered 'salary-in-kind' (*salário in natura*) and are included in the salary when determining other entitlements, taking into account their actual economic value.[32] Thus, if the employee receives a monthly salary of BRL 3,000 and lives rent-free at a property provided by the employer, the use of which corresponds to the amount of BRL 1,000, then his or her salary, for labour law purposes, will be BRL 4,000. Some fringe benefits, however, are not included in the employee's salary by force of express legal provisions, such as equipment required to carry out the job (vehicle used on company business, uniforms, etc.), education expenses, medical, hospital and dental care, life insurance, and private pension plans.

Article 7, XI of the Constitution excludes amounts paid by the employer as profit sharing from the employee's salary. Therefore, such amounts are not taken into account when determining other employment entitlements. However, strict limits have been imposed on profit sharing payments in order to curb fraudulent practices. Such payments can only be made at intervals not shorter than six months (no advances being permissible), and must be previously agreed by negotiation with the employees' union or committee. If these limits are not observed, profit sharing payments will be treated as part of the employee's salary.

Salary rates may be freely determined by the parties, subject to the minimum rate provided by law (minimum wage rate). There are also higher minimum rates established by agreements with unions, i.e., salary floors (*salário normativo*) that must be observed for employees pertaining to the professional category represented by these unions. Finally, for certain professions, there are specific legal provisions that provide their own professional salary floor (*salário profissional*).[33]

Salaries may be agreed upon based on time unit (i.e., per hour, per day, per week or per month) or by piecework (i.e., a certain payment per piece of work completed). In any event, payment must be made by the fifth business day after the reference month.

K. Additional Pay

In addition to salary, other amounts may be owed to employees, some of them as a result of specific working conditions.

Employees working under hazardous occupational conditions, as defined by the administrative authorities (such as high noise levels, excessive heat and

31. Case Law Abstract 354 of the Superior Labour Court.
32. Case Law Abstract 258 of the Superior Labour Court.
33. For instance, as in the case of radiology technicians, whose salary floor is twice that of regular employees pursuant to Art. 16 of Law 7,394/1985).

suspended particles in the workplace), are entitled to a health hazard allowance (*adicional de insalubridade*). The employer is required to adopt the steps necessary to avoid or mitigate these nuisances by offering individual protective equipment to employees or adopting new working methods. Any omission that causes injury to the employee may give rise to an obligation to redress. The health hazard allowance may be set at 10%, 20% or 40%, depending on hazard levels. This percentage is calculated based on the minimum wage rate or, when applicable, on the professional salary floor or the salary floor established by union/employer agreements,[34] irrespective of the actual salary rate of the employee. The health hazard allowance is included in the employee's earnings and is computed when determining his or her rights such as vacation pay. Once the hazardous occupational condition is removed, be it by adopting new working methods, by relocating the employee from one place to another, or by offering employees individual protective equipment, the employee is no longer entitled to the health hazard allowance, even if it has been receiving it for a long period of time.[35]

Payment of risk premium (*adicional de periculosidade*) is mandatory when the employee works in contact with flammable substances, explosives or high voltage systems and is exposed to the risk of death. The risk premium corresponds to 30% of the salary rate paid the employee, not the minimum wage rate. Payment of risk premium is mandatory even when risk exposure is not permanent, for as long as it is recurrent. The payment will not be mandatory, however, if contact occurs only on an accidental basis.[36] Like the health hazard allowance, once exposure to risk ceases, for any reason, the employer is no longer required to pay the risk premium.

The thirteenth salary or Christmas bonus (*décimo-terceiro salário*) is a mandatory benefit payable to all employees. This bonus corresponds to the compensation paid in the month of December and includes tips and other additional premiums such as overtime pay, night pay and health hazard allowance. The thirteenth salary must be paid in two instalments. The first instalment, equal to one half of the amount owed, must be paid by the end of November. The second instalment must be paid by 20 December. If the employee did not work the entire year, his or her thirteenth salary will be computed proportionally to the time worked (1/12 per month worked, with a fraction equal to or above fifteen days being computed as one month). For instance, the employee hired on 7 August will be entitled to 5/12 of his or her December compensation as the thirteenth salary.

L. Equal Pay

The Brazilian Constitution expressly prohibits salary discrimination on the basis of 'gender, age, colour or marital status'. The Constitution does not list, however, all

34. Case Law Abstract 17 of the Superior Labour Court.
35. Case Law Abstract 80 of the Superior Labour Court.
36. Case Law Abstract 364 of the Superior Labour Court.

discrimination criteria. The Constitution prohibits all arbitrary discrimination based on unlawful criteria, as would also be the case, among others, of discrimination based on the employee's religion, sexual orientation, nationality or political convictions.

Whenever the work performed by two employees who carry out the same function for the same employer at the same location has identical value, the salary rate paid for such work must be the same. Equal work is defined as the work performed, with equal productivity and the same technical skill, by persons whose difference in length of service does not exceed two years. Same location is defined, as a rule, as the same municipality.[37]

The bidden is o the employer to show that the payment of different salaries to employees carrying out the same work is justified. The employer may establish, for instance, that the work performed by one of them is more productive than that performed by the other. If the employer fails to produce such evidence, the employee with a lower salary will be entitled to receive the existing salary difference in relation to the other employee.

M. Protection of Salary Rights

As a rule, the employee's salary is deemed to be the consideration required to enable the worker to meet his or her essential needs. Therefore, salary credit is the subject matter of several measures intended to ensure its proper payment. These measures protect the employee's salary against the employer, the employer's creditors, and creditors of the employee himself or herself.

The first salary protection measure, which refers to employers, has already been mentioned: the compulsory payment of salaries up to the fifth business day after the reference month. The second protection measure consists of the requirement that the salary be paid directly to the employee himself, against a receipt signed by him or her, or by deposit in a bank account. Salaries must be paid in local currency. Salary payments in foreign currency, even if this is for the employee's advantage, are deemed not paid. Salary cannot even be agreed upon in foreign currency: the agreed sum must be calculated into local currency as of the contract execution date.[38] Salary deductions are also prohibited, except in extraordinary cases expressly provided for by law, such as advances, taxes owed by the employee, and loans taken out by the employee under Law 10,820/2003 (loan repayment through payroll deduction). If the employer suffers damages as a consequence of the employee's wilful misconduct or even mere fault, provided that this measure has been provided for in the employment contract, a deduction will also be allowed. Payroll deduction of payments made to medical care plans,

---

37. Case Law Abstract 6, Item X of the Superior Labour Court.
38. Superior Labour Court, SBDI II, Ordinary Appeal in Suit on the Judgment No. 301409, Decision No. 301409, Reporting Justice Carlos Alberto Reis de Paula, published in the Federal Court Gazette on 11 Dec. 1998, 43.

recreation clubs, life insurance, etc., which are always voluntary, depends on the prior written authorisation of the employee.[39] Salary rates cannot be reduced unless there is an agreement with the trade union (collective bargaining agreement or collective labour convention). In the event of termination of the employment contract, the salary and other amounts owed to the employee must be paid within a short period (from one to ten days, depending on the circumstances). If the employer fails to observe this time frame, a fine equal to a one-month salary will apply. It is also mandatory to itemise the amounts paid on the salary payment slip. Different salary items cannot be paid as a single, indiscriminate whole. If, for instance, the employee works in contact with flammable substances and is exposed to risk of death, he or she will be entitled to a risk premium in addition to his or her regular salary pay. The payment slip must list the amounts relating to salary and to the risk premium separately. If payment is made only as salary, without indicating the risk premium amount, the latter will be deemed unpaid.[40]

Salary protection against the employer's creditors involves giving salary credit priority ranking in the event of liquidation. Under Article 83, I of Law 11,101/2005, salaries and other credits arising under labour legislation, up to the limit of 150 minimum wages per employee, must be paid first. The portion in excess of 150 minimum wages is not afforded special ranking and will rank unsecured creditors pari passu.

Finally, the protection granted against the employee's creditors consists of the impossibility of attaching/garnisheeing any part of employment compensation. This guarantee is not subject to any ceiling no matter how high the employee's salary is. The entire salary amount is protected against attachment/garnisheeing.

N. Change in Working Conditions

Changes in working conditions are subject to more stringent rules than changes in civil and commercial agreements. The governing rule on this matter is Article 468 of the CLT, which states that: 'In individual employment contracts, only mutually agreed amendments are deemed to be lawful, and even so, provided that they do not, directly or indirectly, adversely affect the employee, with any clause to the contrary being deemed null and void.' Thus, in principle, the employment contract can only be amended when two conditions are concurrently satisfied: (a) both employee and employer have agreed to the amendment; and (b) the amendment translates into a working condition that is more favourable to the employee. There are certain exceptions to this rule, particularly when changing the employee's role and workplace. In these specific cases, the employer is entitled to change the employment contract (*jus variandi*).

An employee's role may be changed, even without the employee's consent and to his or her detriment, when the employee is ordered to return to his or her

39. Case Law Abstract 342 of the Superior Labour Court.
40. Case Law Abstract 91 of the Superior Labour Court.

actual position after having held, on a temporary basis, a position of trust. Unless payment has been made for at least ten years, this change will entail loss of the right to additional pay for exercise of a position of trust.[41] These changes may also apply to an employee who, because of an occupational accident, is no longer able to carry out his or her former activity.

The workplace may be changed, even without the employee's consent, in five different situations. The first refers to a relocation that does not entail a change in the employee's domicile. For instance, transfer of the company from one district to another within the same city is legitimate. The second situation involves employees who hold a position of trust, who may be transferred by the employer's unilateral decision. In this case, however, the employer must show an actual need to transfer the employee, or else the employer's actions will be deemed to be abusive.[42] Transfer is also permissible, provided again that it is necessary, when there is a contractual clause to such effect.[43] The fourth situation is when the employee is transferred due to a shutdown of the establishment. The last situation involves a transitory need of service and presumes a temporary relocation. Only in this latter event is the employer required to pay a 25% premium, called the relocation allowance, on the salary rate. In all of these situations, the employer is responsible for any moving expenses incurred by the employee, including new commuting expenses.[44]

O. Unemployment Compensation Fund (*Fundo De Garantia Do Tempo De Serviço*)

The FGTS was created by Law 5,107/1966. The 1988 Constitution gave it a broader scope. Today, FGTS is regulated by Law 8,036/1990. Under FGTS's rules, all employers are required to deposit in a special bank account opened in the name of the employee at an official federal public bank 8% of their employees' monthly compensation. This deposit must also be made in the case of fixed-term contracts and for farm employees.[45] This deposit is optional for domestic workers only. When determining the amount to be deposited, the employer must compute the employee's entire salary plus other payments such as thirteenth salary, overtime pay,[46] night pay, risk premium and relocation allowance, as well as tips.

The FGTS funds are managed by a joint committee (oversight board) comprised of representatives of the federal government, of employees and of employers. FGTS funds accrue interest at 3% per year plus monetary adjustment. Funds

41. Case Law Abstract 372, item I of the Superior Labour Court.
42. Case Law Abstract 43 of the Superior Labour Court.
43. This may be either express or implied, as when the employee is hired to work in a circus that travels through different towns.
44. Case Law Abstract 29 of the Superior Labour Court.
45. Law 5,889/1973.
46. Case Law Abstract 63 of the Superior Labour Court.

deposited in FGTS accounts cannot be withdrawn freely. Withdrawal is authorised in very specific cases only, such as unfair dismissal (or dismissal without good cause) of the employee, termination of the company, retirement or death of the employee, purchase by the employee of his or her own home and expiration of a fixed-term contract. Withdrawals are also allowed when the employee or his or her dependents suffer from a serious illness, such as cancer or AIDS.

P. Termination of Employment Contract

The employment contract may be terminated for various reasons. Sometimes, termination results from the occurrence of a single event, such as the employee's death. Sometimes, it results from the end of the term in a fixed-term contract. Retirement, which was already deemed to terminate an employment contract,[47] is no longer a reason for termination, as decided by the Federal Supreme Court.[48]

When the contract is terminated on the initiative of the employer, there is a dismissal, which may be with or without good cause (also known as fair or unfair dismissal). When the contract is terminated on the initiative of the employee, resignation is held to occur. If the employee decides to terminate the contract for a cause which is attributed to the employer, constructive termination or constructive dismissal occurs.

As a rule, dismissal is always possible under Brazilian law. Only when the employee is protected by job tenure will dismissal be forbidden. However, the general rule is that there is no job tenure: the employment-at-will doctrine prevails. Only in exceptional cases will the employer be prevented from dismissing the employee.

In the event of dismissal of the employee without cause, the employer must: (a) inform the employee in advance by means of a termination notice; and (b) pay compensation to the employee. This compensation consists of a fine equal to 40% of the balance existing in the employee's FGTS blocked account at the time of dismissal. Only where an event of force majeure is involved, pursuant to Article 501 of the CLT, will the fine be reduced to half of the actual amount (20% of the balance in the employee's FGTS blocked account.

When dismissal occurs by virtue of the employee's breach of his or her obligations, there is a dismissal with good cause. In this case, the employee is not entitled to receive any compensation nor is he or she entitled to withdraw the amounts deposited in his FGTS blocked account.[49]

The fixed-term employment contract may be terminated by either the employer or the employee before its expiration date. If it is terminated without

47. Abstract 295 of the Superior Labour Court.
48. Decision handed down on the Direct Suit for Unconstitutionality No. 1721 – 3, Reporting Justice Carlos Britto, published in the Federal Court Gazette of 20 Oct. 2006.
49. Such amounts will only be withdrawn in specific circumstances.

good cause by the employer, the latter must pay the employee half the salary due up to expiration of the contract, as well as the fine equal to 40% of the amount deposited in the employee's FGTS account.[50] If the employment contract is terminated by the employee, also without good cause, the employer will be entitled to receive a compensation for the losses it has suffered, up to the limit otherwise payable to the employee had the employment contract been terminated by the employer.

Q. Termination Notice

Termination notice is required in two circumstances: (a) when the employment contract is entered into for an indefinite term; and (b) when the employment contract is terminated without cause (unfair dismissal). There is no termination notice in a fixed-term contract, as it is already known in advance (since the hiring date) when the employment relationship will end. On the other hand, when there is a good cause, no termination notice is required.

Article 7, XXI of the Constitution provides that the termination notice period should be 'proportionate to the length of service' observing the minimum period of thirty days. This proportionate period has not been regulated thus far. Therefore, the minimum period of thirty days prevails. In certain specific cases there are agreements with labour unions (collective bargaining agreement or collective labour convention) providing for a longer termination notice period for long-serving employees and employees over a certain age.

Termination notice need not be necessarily given in writing, but written notice would be advisable as a means of proof. Once termination notice is received by the person to whom it is addressed, no unilateral revocation is permitted. Revocation depends on the consent of the person who received it. Since termination notice is given when there is no good cause for termination, the party giving termination notice need not and should not state the reasons for the decision taken.

If termination notice is given by the employer, during the respective period of thirty days the employee is entitled to reduce his workday by two hours, without prejudice to his or her normal pay. Instead of reducing his or her workday, the employee is legally entitled to be released from work for seven consecutive days, without prejudice to his or her compensation.

If the employer fails to give termination notice, the employee will be entitled to (a) compensation equal to his or her salary for the period; and (b) inclusion of the termination notice period in the actual length of service, for all legal purposes. If the employee does not give termination notice, the employer may deduct the salary for the period from other amounts due (such as unused vacation pay or the salary for the days worked).

50. Abstract 125 of the Superior Labour Court.

R. Good Cause (*Justa Causa*)

Good cause means a sufficiently material reason for termination of the employment contract. Both the employee and the employer may give rise to good cause. The employee may be dismissed for good cause, as set out in Articles 158 and 482 of the CLT, in the following events: (a) dishonest act; (b) misconduct or lack of rectitude; (c) regular activities on his or her own account or for the account of a third party without the employer's permission when such activity competes with the employer's business or is detrimental to the employee's work; (d) criminal conviction of the employee under a final judgment, when enforcement of the sentence has not been suspended; (e) dereliction in the performance of his or her duties; (f) intoxication on an usual basis or during working hours; (g) violation of a trade secret; (h) act of indiscipline or insubordination; (i) abandonment of job; (j) act injurious to the honour or reputation of, or physical assault against, any person at the workplace, except for his or her own or a third-party's legitimate defence; (k) an act injurious to the honour or reputation of, or physical assault against, the employer and hierarchical superiors, unless in case of his or her own or a third-party's legitimate defence; (l) constant gambling; (m) act contrary to national security, as duly proved in an administrative inquiry; and (n) failure to observe an occupational safety rule or to use individual protective equipment. Some of these events have been deemed to be overridden by court decisions. Alcohol intoxication, for instance, is usually viewed as a disease rather than as an undue act of the employee – which means that even if the employee is usually drunk, it is unlikely that the employer will be able to dismiss him or her for good cause.[51] Acts contrary to national security constitute an overridden and currently unjustifiable vestige of the authoritarian regime instituted with the military coup in 1964. There are also events of good cause that apply only to certain employees, such as continuous non-payment by a banking employee of a legally enforceable debt.

Pursuant to Article 483 of the CLT, the following acts constitute grounds for termination of the employment contract for good cause by the employee: (a) the employer demands services beyond the employee's capabilities, against the law and good morals, or outside the scope of the employment contract; (b) the employee is treated too strictly; (c) the employee is exposed to evident risk of considerable danger; (d) the employer fails to comply with its contractual obligations; (e) the employer or its representatives perform acts prejudicial to the employee's or his family's honour or reputation; (f) the employer or its representatives offend the employee, except in their own or a third-party's defence; (g) the employer reduces the employee's work in a manner that considerably affects his or her salary.

---

51. TRT – 2nd Circuit, 10th Panel, Ordinary Appeal No. 00928-2002-019-02-00, Reporting Justice Vera Marta Publio Dias, Decision No. 20060006190, judged on 17 Jan. 2006, published in the São Paulo State Official Gazette, PJ, of 7 Feb. 2006.

The events of termination with good cause by the employee or the employer involve legal concepts that are still unsettled, allowing for inclusion of behaviours not expressly prescribed by law. Brazilian courts have already ruled that good cause is attributable to the employee who: (a) sexually abuses a child with the assistance of the employer;[52] (b) performs lascivious acts during working hours;[53] (c) drives a vehicle recklessly and dangerously, exposing others to risks;[54] and (d) forges a medical certificate.[55] Good cause is imputable to the employer that: (a) obligates the employee, who was hired as laboratory technician, to work as receptionist;[56] (b) leaves the employee without any work during an indefinite period, without a material reason;[57] and (c) delays consistently payment of salaries[58] or fails to deposit the FGTS amounts.[59]

In order to invoke good cause as grounds for termination of the employment contract, in addition to the acts set out above, the following conditions must be observed: (a) the act should be, taking into account the specific conditions of the employment contract, sufficiently serious; (b) the act must have been performed recently; and (c) no other punishment must have been imposed on account of the act. Evaluation of the specific conditions of the employment contract is important: for instance, use of coarse language in an environment where good manners prevail and where both men and women or minors work together constitutes good cause,[60] but the same does not occur in a place where use of such a language is commonplace and viewed as a normal behaviour, such as at the docks. If the undue act has not been performed recently, without prompt termination of the employment contract, the act is deemed to have been pardoned (implied pardon).[61] One may not invoke, for instance, reckless and dangerous driving of a vehicle in 2004 to dismiss the driver only in 2006. By the same token, delay in the payment of the

52. TRT – 1st Circuit, 4th Panel, Ordinary Appeal No. 3935/2000, Reporting Justice Luiz Alfredo M. Lino, published in the Rio de Janeiro State Court Gazette of 14 Mar. 2001, 134.
53. TRT – 3rd Circuit, 4th Panel, Ordinary Appeal No. 19722/98, Reporting Justice Sebastião G. Oliveira, published in the Minas Gerais State Court Gazette of 28 Aug. 1999, 10.
54. TRT – 15th Circuit, 1st Panel, Decision No. 45870/98, Reporting Justice José Otávio Bigatto, published in the São Paulo State Court Gazette of 12 Jan. 1999, 6.
55. TRT – 1st Circuit, 2nd Panel, Ordinary Appeal No. 16253/98, Reporting Justice Amélia V. Lopes, published in the Rio de Janeiro State Court Gazette of 22 Jan. 2000, 142.
56. TST – 1st Panel, Decision No. 2194/95, Reporting Justice Ursulino Santos, published in the Federal Court Gazette of 9 Jun. 1995, 17485.
57. TRT – 1st Circuit, 1st Panel, Ordinary Appeal No. 23101, Reporting Justice C. Teixeira, published in the Rio de Janeiro State Court Gazette of 14 Jan. 1997, 68; TRT – 10th Circuit, 1st Panel, Ordinary Appeal No. 5039/97, Reporting Justice André R. P.V. Damasceno, published in the Court Gazette of 15 Sep. 2000, 7.
58. TRT – 12th Circuit, 2nd Panel, Decision No. 522/95, Reporting Justice Godoy Ilha, published in the Santa Catarina State Court Gazette of 15 Mar. 1995, 119.
59. TRT– 12th Circuit, 3rd Panel, Decision No. 6917/94, Reporting Justice José E. Manzi, published in the Santa Catarina State Court Gazette of 11 Apr. 1996, 53.
60. TRT – 12th Circuit, 1st Panel, Decision No. 3576/98, Reporting Justice Licélia Ribeiro, published in the Santa Catarina State Court Gazette of 19 Aug. 1998, 180.
61. TRT – 24th Circuit, Decision No. 4425/95, Reporting Justice Geralda Pedroso, published in the Mato Grosso do Sul State Court Gazette of 18 Oct. 1995, 55.

January salary, which must occur in February, cannot authorise termination for good cause of the employment contract in November. Finally, if the employee has performed an undue act and has been punished by means of a warning or unremunerated absence, termination for good cause does not apply. A punishment shall not be inflicted twice for one same undue act (*non bis in idem*).

The employee who gives grounds to termination for good cause is not entitled to receive payment related to the termination notice period, the thirteenth salary or the vacations he or she has not yet been entitled to. Likewise, he or she is not eligible to receive the FGTS 40% fine and to withdraw the amounts deposited in the FGTS account, as these amounts can only be withdrawn in the cases prescribed by law. If good cause is attributable to the employer, the employee may deem the employment contract terminated (constructive termination) and claim all amounts otherwise payable to him or her had he or she been unfairly dismissed by the employer, including the FGTS 40% fine and the payment in lieu of termination notice.

Good cause for termination of an employment contract does not depend on prior court recognition, since under Brazilian law job tenure is the exception rather than the rule. As a consequence, the party concerned (employee or employer) that believes an undue act was performed by the other takes the initiative to terminate the contract. Should there be excesses or abuse, the aggrieved party may seek damages in court. Accordingly, if the employer dismisses the employee for good cause on the grounds of an undue act that is not sufficiently serious or that has already been punished by way of a warning, the employee may pursue in court the compensation otherwise payable to him or her had he not been unfairly dismissed.

S. Job Tenure

Job tenure is an exceptional guarantee under Brazilian law that prevents the employer from unfairly terminating the employment contract. The following employees, among others, have job tenure: (a) the union leader, effective from his or her candidacy for the position up to one year after expiration of his or her term of office, if elected; (b) pregnant women, effective from confirmation of pregnancy up to five months after childbirth; (c) the employee who suffers an occupational accident or develops an occupational disease, for a period of twelve months after returning to work at the end of the medical leave granted by the National Social Security Institute; and (d) the employees' representative at the in-house job accident prevention commission, which is mandatory in companies having over a certain number of employees. There are other less important cases of job tenure under Brazilian law. Often times, the agreements entered into with labour unions (collective bargaining agreement or collective labour convention) provide for other events of job tenure, such as for employees near the retirement age or for members of a workers' commission (*comissão de fábrica*). Job tenure can also be provided for in a clause of the employment contract, but this practice is seldom adopted.

When an employee has job tenure, the employer cannot dismiss him or her without good cause. Should there be a good cause, sometimes it is necessary to obtain prior court approval for termination of the contract, as in the case of a union leader. In other circumstances, such as in the case of a pregnant woman, the employer may dismiss the employee without prior court approval. Nonetheless, the aggrieved employee can challenge in court the sufficiency of the reason invoked for dismissal. If the court finds for insufficiency of the reason invoked, the employer must reinstate the employee and pay all salaries and other labour amounts, such as thirteenth salary, related to the absence period. If in the court dispute the court finds it would not be advisable to reinstate the employee, the court has the power to convert reinstatement into compensation and, consequently, order that the employment contract be terminated.

T. Non-competition Obligation

Brazilian law does not expressly provide for the possibility of making a non-competition agreement between the employee and the employer to prevent the employee from competing with the employer after termination of the employment relationship. It only provides that, if the employee competes with the employer during the term of the employment contract, this will constitute grounds for termination with good cause. Although Brazilian law is silent about the non-competition obligation, this obligation can be established by the parties concerned, as advocated by some authors and courts.[62] The freedom to work, as prescribed by the Constitution, is not, like freedom in general, an absolute right or free from limitations.

In order for the non-competition agreement to be valid, it is necessary: (a) to impose restrictions on the employee's freedom of work in view of the activity he or she performs and the company's legitimate interests; (b) to limit and specify the activities the employee is forbidden to perform; (c) to define territorial limits; and (d) to define time limits for the non-competition obligation. To deprive the employee from performing his or her work at all is unlawful and so is to prevent him or her from working for an excessively long period or elsewhere in the world, when it is otherwise sufficient to prohibit his or her working in a certain city or region to protect the company's business interests. Despite there being no provision under Brazilian law for validity of the non-competition obligation, it is also necessary to establish payment of compensation to the employee. This compensation must be proportionate to the obligation imposed on the employee.

---

62. TRT – 2nd Circuit, 7th Panel, Case No. 02870094455, Decision No. 02880177116, Reporting Justice Wilma Nogueira de Araujo Vaz da Silva, judged on 29 Aug. 1988, published in the Court Gazette of 16 Sep. 1988.

When the non-competition obligation is too stringent with respect to time and geographical scope and other aspects, it may be amended by court order, pursuant to Article 184 of the Brazilian Civil Code.

Whoever intends to hire an employee is legally entitled to ask the candidate whether he or she is bound by a non-competition agreement. The employee himself has the duty, guided by the principle of good faith contemplated by Article 422 of the Civil Code, to advise the employer about the existence of a non-competition obligation. If the employee enters into an employment contract with a third party, violating the non-competition obligation and failing to mention its existence, the third party will not be held liable as the non-competition obligation is unknown to it (*res inter alios acta, allis nec prodest nec nocet*). If the third party is informed of the non-competition obligation, but maintains the employment contract, the third party becomes liable.

III. WORKERS AND EMPLOYERS' ORGANISATIONS

A. Establishment of Workers' and Employers' Organisations

Workers' and employers' organisations in Brazil, even after the 1988 Constitution, still maintain the characteristics of the authoritarian model adopted by previous constitutions and laws. Freedom of association, as defined in Convention No. 87 of the ILO, is not absolute. This convention still has not been ratified by Brazil.

Workers' and employers' organisations must be established by categories, as following specific criteria set out in Article 511 of the CLT and the 1988 Constitution. It is not possible to form workers' and employers' organisations according to other criteria, such as by company, by political identity of their members or by location. The term *category* is defined by law and means a community of interests that justify the establishment of organisations composed of members engaging in the same economic activity (economic categories) or of members working in the same field of activity (professional categories). The members of the economic categories form employers' organisations, while the members of the professional categories form workers' organisations. There are specific organisations for certain professions, such as drivers, telephone operators and secretaries, i.e., the so-called differentiated professional categories, which have an exceptional character.

Another important restriction on freedom of association is set out in Article 8, II of the Constitution: the rule of one organisation per category (*unicidade sindical*): 'It is forbidden to create more than one workers' or employers' organisation, at any level, representing a professional or economic category, within one territory, which shall be defined by the interested workers or employers and which shall not be smaller than the area of a municipality.' Therefore, there will be only one bank employees' organisation in the City of Rio de Janeiro, for example. By the same token, there will be only one chemical industry organisation in the City of São Paulo. For this reason, since there was already an airplane pilot organisation in

Brazil, the creation of the civil aviation airplane pilot organisation to represent the same category was deemed to be illegal.[63]

The decision whether or not to join a workers' or employers' organisation is guaranteed by the Constitution. Therefore, no one is obligated to join an organisation or prevented from leaving the organisation of which one is a member. According to some surveys, in 2002, only 17% of workers were members of workers' organisations. In any event, the workers' organisation or the employers' organisation represents parties who would be entitled to become members of a union, whether or not they are actual members.

The 1988 Constitution banned any interference or intervention in the workers' or employers' organisation by the Executive Branch. Only pursuant to a court decision, with due regard being taken of applicable procedural guarantees, may a workers' or employers' organisation be dissolved or have its activities suspended.

B. Structure and Revenue of Workers' and Employers' Organisations

With respect to their internal structure, workers' and employers' organisations are comprised of three different bodies: (a) the general assembly; (b) the executive board; and (c) the audit committee. The general assembly, predominantly a decision-making body composed of the organisation's members, elects the executive board and the audit committee members and sets the general guidelines for the activities of workers' and employers' organisations. The executive board is the administrative body in charge of the routine activities of the organisation and represents it before third parties and authorities. In workers' organisations, the executive board members have job tenure. The audit committee is in charge of inspecting the organisation's finances.

The external structure of the workers' and employers' organisations is split into three different levels. At the bottom are the organisations themselves, which are generally entities of a more restricted territorial reach, comprised of few municipalities. Groups of at least five organisations with identical or similar activities may form federations, which are generally entities formed at state or regional level. The union at least three federations forms confederations, which necessarily have nationwide reach. Curiously, the so-called 'federations', with intense activities, such as the *Central Única de Trabalhadores* (CUT) and the *Força Sindical*, are not actual unionised entities but rather mere civil associations under Brazilian law. Therefore, they do not enjoy the prerogatives of the workers' organisations, cannot legally represent employees or employers, and their leaders do not have job tenure.

As a means to compensate for the complete absence of freedom of association and for the prohibition against performance of economic activities, lawmakers

63. Federal Supreme Court, Appeal in a Motion for Writ of Mandamus No. 21305, Reporting Justice Marco Aurélio, judged on 17 Oct. 1991, published in the Federal Court Gazette of 29 Nov. 1991, 17326.

have created several sources of revenues for these organisations. While the 1988 Constitution eliminated some of the restrictions on freedom of association, it maintained others. Nonetheless, the sources of revenues for workers' and employers' organisations have not been reduced. On the contrary, they have even been increased.

The supposed predominant source of revenue is the monthly contribution paid by workers or employers to the organisation to which they belong. In Brazil, this revenue is contemplated by Article 548(b) of the CLT and is designated membership dues (*contribuição dos associados*). However, in practice, the most important revenue for the organisations, is received pursuant to the contribution provided by Article 548(a) and Article 578 et seq. of the CLT. This contribution must be paid by all members of the professional or economic category (workers and employers) and even by non-members. Payment of this contribution cannot be opposed or denied. For the employees, this contribution corresponds to the amount of one day's salary, to be deducted by the employer annually, in March. For the employers, this contribution corresponds to a percentage calculated on the company's capital.

Another contribution, payable only by employees, is usually provided collective for in bargaining agreements or collective labour conventions. This contribution is called 'solidarity fee' (*contribuição assistencial*) and is based on the assumption that employees must give a contribution in return for the benefit obtained by the labour union for carrying out collective bargaining. Its amount is not set by law, but rather in the agreement itself. The employee is allowed to oppose the deduction, however.[64]

Finally, the Constitution created a contribution called a 'confederation fee' (*contribuição confederativa*). The better view is that the confederation fee is not compulsory for non-member employees.[65]

C. Collective Bargaining

Collective bargaining is a negotiation aimed at reaching an agreement on working conditions. Only workers' organisations have the right to negotiate as a group on behalf of the employees. The employees' representative, as defined in Article 11 of the Constitution and mandatory in companies with more than 200 employees, is only responsible for promoting direct discussions with the employer, but not for negotiating as a group the working conditions.

There are two types of agreements that can be executed with the workers' organisations. Those entered into between workers' organisations and employers'

64. Normative Precedent No. 119 and Case Law Statement No. 17, SDC, of the Superior Labour Court.
65. TST – 3rd Panel, Interlocutory Appeal in Motion to Review No. 784/2003-057-02-40, Reporting Justice Luiz Ronan Neves Koury, judged on 29 Nov. 2006, published in the Federal Court Gazette of 19 Dec. 2006.

organisations are called *collective labour conventions*. Those agreements entered into between workers' organisations and one or more companies are called *collective bargaining agreements*. This distinction is important: while collective labour conventions apply to all employees who provide services to companies whose employers' organisations have participated in the negotiation, collective bargaining agreements apply only to employees of the companies that have signed it.

Collective bargaining agreements and collective labour conventions must be in writing, and have a maximum term of two years. A shorter term is usually adopted, most frequently of one year. There is no provision on early termination of either type of agreement. Nothing prevents renegotiation of new working conditions, provided that there is mutual consent to this effect. Only if the original conditions of either the agreement or the convention are substantially changed to the point of imposing undue hardship for performance thereof the aggrieved party will be entitled to claim judicial revision in view of the need to maintain a contractual balance (*rebus sic stantibus*).

After expiration of the collective bargaining agreement or of the collective labour convention the agreed conditions will no longer apply as they are not considered to be permanent amendments to employment contracts.[66] These conditions may be renegotiated, in which case a new agreement will have to be made. Consequently, if a collective bargaining agreement effective until 31 January provides for payment of overtime at 100% above the regular rate of pay, any work performed beyond normal working hours as from February shall be paid pursuant to law, i.e., 50% above the regular rate of pay.

As a rule, collective bargaining agreements and the collective labour convention can only establish working conditions more favourable than those prescribed by law. They cannot remove rights conferred on employees pursuant to law. A collective bargaining agreement cannot, for instance, reduce the vacation period, exclude payment of the thirteenth salary, or release the employer from its obligation to make the FGTS monthly contributions. Only exceptionally is an unfavourable change (*ajuste in pejus*) allowed, such as for salary reductions.

D. Right to Strike

The right to strike is guaranteed by the Federal Constitution and is regulated by Law 7,783/1989.

The general rule is that all employees are entitled to go on strike. However, it is necessary to adhere to the applicable legal procedure, which is divided into different stages. First, a strike is an extreme measure within the scope of activities

---

66. Federal Supreme Court, 1st Panel, Special Appeal under Specific Court Regulations in Interlocutory Appeal No. 150,475/RJ, Reporting Justice Ilmar Galvão, judged on 12 Sep. 1995, published in the Federal Court Gazette of 27 Oct. 1995, 36337 and Abstract 277 of the Superior Labour Court.

of workers' organisations (*ultima ratio*). Therefore, a strike is to occur only if collective bargaining is thwarted. A strike must be approved at the meeting of the workers' organisation or of the interested workers (Article 4). After being approved, the workers' organisation must inform the interested employer(s) of the strike at least forty-eight hours in advance. Whenever the strike affects essential services or activities, seventy-two hours' termination notice must be given to service users as well (13). During the strike, third-parties' fundamental rights must be respected and no damage or threat to property or person is permitted (Article 6, paragraphs 1 and 3). Employees who elect not to join the strike are not to be prevented from working. The practice of sabotage or other violent acts is absolutely prohibited. Employees must maintain those essential services indispensable to meet the basic needs of society. Among the essential services are: treatment and supply of water; production and distribution of electric power, gas and fuels; medical and hospital care; distribution and sale of medicines and foods; funerals; collective transportation; collection and treatment of sewage and garbage; telecommunications; safekeeping, use and control of radioactive substances, nuclear materials and equipment; data processing related to essential services; control of air traffic; and bank clearance. Moreover, employees shall continue to perform those activities which, albeit not essential, when interrupted might cause irreparable damage that is difficult to repair.

Employees on strike cannot be dismissed. Strikers are entitled to seek funds to support the strike and to persuade their peers to join it. The employer is forbidden to prevent or hinder disclosure of the strike or to coerce employees to work, or even to hire replacement workers, except in the case that essential services or activities are interrupted as mentioned above.

There is no legal limit for the duration of the strike. Since the 2004 constitutional amendment, the courts have been forbidden to interfere in the solving conflicts and their role has been limited to curbing abuses and preventing illegal acts.

IV. RESOLUTION OF LABOUR DISPUTES

A. Labour Courts

Disputes between the employee and the employer, when of an individual character, are settled in court. Other dispute resolution mechanisms used in other fields of the law have proved to be unfeasible in labour disputes.

Direct settlement, even by mediation, is not a useful mechanism for the employer. This is because direct settlement reached between the employee and its employer, even if after termination of the employment contract, does not prevent a subsequent court dispute in view of the impossibility of relinquishing labour rights. The release given directly by the employee produces little effect, as opposed to the effect produced in civil and commercial law. Take, for instance, a scenario in which the employee who believes he has a credit equal to 100 hours of overtime, not recognised by the employer, accepts to receive an amount equal to fifty hours of overtime and gives the employer release in connection with such payment: despite having received payment, the employee may claim in court the other fifty hours of overtime not paid.[67] Therefore, the employer has no security whatsoever by reaching a direct settlement with the employee.

Arbitration is not a proper mechanism to settle individual labour disputes (i.e., involving an employee and his employer). Under Brazilian law, arbitration requires that the right in controversy to be disposable,[68] i.e., the holder of the right must be capable of relinquishing it. The impossibility of relinquishing a labour right renders it non-disposable by implication.[69]

The scenario is completely different in relation to collective disputes, i.e., disputes between the employer and undetermined groups or categories of workers, such as between airlines and airplane pilots, in which the latter seek a salary increase for the professional category. In this case, direct settlement is perfectly feasible through execution of collective bargaining agreements or collective labour conventions. In such cases, arbitration can also be resorted to, as expressly set out in the Federal Constitution, despite not yet being frequently adopted.

B. Hierarchy of Labour Courts

In Brazil, there is a judicial court hierarchy specialised in resolving labour disputes. The Labour Courts are structured in three different levels of jurisdiction.

In the first level of jurisdiction are the Lower Labour Courts (*Varas do Trabalho*). There are approximately 1,300 Lower Labour Courts in Brazil, which are as a general rule, the first to entertain a labour claim. Each Lower Labour Court has a labour judge.

In the second level of jurisdiction are the Regional Labour Courts (*Tribunal Regional do Trabalho*), which generally operate as appellate courts. There are twenty-four Regional Labour Courts, one in each Brazilian state, except for the State of São Paulo, which has two Regional Labour Courts (2nd Circuit and 15th Circuit), and for the States of Acre, Amapá, Roraima and Tocantins, where there is no such court, in which case the Regional Labour Courts in the nearest states act as the former states' Regional Labour Courts. The number of judges in each Regional

67. Abstract 330 of the Superior Labour Court.
68. Article 1 of Law 9,307/1996.
69. The following court rulings deny the possibility of resolution of an individual dispute between the employee and the employer by arbitration: TRT – 2nd Circuit, 6th Panel, Case No. 02128200437102000, Reporting Justice Adalberto Martins, Decision published in the State Official Gazette of 26 Aug. 2005; and TRT – 2nd Circuit, 4th Panel, Case No. 02632200205702008, Reporting Justice Odette Silveira Moraes, Decision No. 20060119564, published in the State Official Gazette of 17 Mar. 2006.

Labour Court varies from eight judges, in the smallest courts, to sixty-four judges in the 2nd Circuit Court in São Paulo, the largest in Brazil.

Finally, the foremost body of the hierarchy of the Labour Courts, located in Brasília, is the Superior Court of Labour (*Tribunal Superior do Trabalho*), with jurisdiction over the entire Brazilian territory. The Superior Court of Labour is responsible for settling unsettled case law in labour matters and ensuring compliance with federal legislation by the other bodies of the Labour Court structure. It is comprised of twenty-seven judges.

C. Labour Court Procedure

The procedure for labour dispute resolution is regulated by Article 763 through 901 of the CLT. There are also other separate specific laws dealing with this matter. In cases where the CLT or such other laws are silent, the civil procedure rules, particularly those set out in the Code of Civil Procedure, will apply for as long as they are compatible with labour procedure.

As a rule, labour procedure is simpler, more informal, speedier and more streamlined than civil procedure. Unlike what usually occurs in civil procedure, in labour procedure both the employee and the employer may act on their own behalf, without the need for a lawyer. Various procedural steps may be made orally, unlike general civil procedure which requires almost all steps to be taken in writing. Both complaint/statement of claim may and the defence may be made orally. In theory, the whole procedure (after the filing of the complaint and service of process on the defendant) should be finalised on the same day as when the defence is filed, given that evidence should be tendered at the same time as the defence as well. The judge, then, should render his or her decision and notify the parties. In practice, however, often times this course of action is not followed. Especially in large cities, where the caseload in each Lower Labour Court is heavy, or when an expert must be appointed to provide a report, the hearing is split into several parts which renders the proceedings substantially lengthier.

Mediation and settlement between parties in labour litigation is largely encouraged by law. Settlement may occur at any time in the course of the proceeding The court is bound to attempt a mediation between the litigants in at least two different phases: first, at the beginning of the first hearing, even before filing of the defence by the defendant; and, second, before handing down the judgment of the case.

The decision handed down in the labour case is immediately enforceable. In other words, the appeal that might in theory be filed against the decision (ordinary appeal) does not prevent enforcement of the decision. The term for filing this appeal (eight days) is shorter than that prescribed for appeals in civil procedure (fifteen days). In cases involving a smaller amount (up to two minimum wages), no appeal is possible, unless there is a serious vice in the decision (violation of a constitutional rule), which rarely happens in practice.

Selected Bibliography

In English

E.Amadeo and J.M. Camargo, 'Labour Legislation and Institutional Aspects of the Brazilian Labour Market' (2007) 7 *Labour* 157.
R. Buchanan, 'The Future of the Brazilian Labor Law under the Federal Constitution of 1988' (1989) 10 *Comparative Labor Law and Policy Journal*, 214.
S.A. Gacek, 'Revisiting the Corporatist and Contractualist Models of Labor Law Regimes: A Review of the Brazilian and American Systems' (1994) 16 *Yeshiva University Cardozo Law Review* 21.
G.W. Vause and D. de Holanda Palhano, 'Labor Law in Brazil and the United States – Statism and Classical Liberalism Compared' (1995) 33 *Columbia Journal of Transnational Law* 583.

In Portuguese

E. M. Baracat, *A Boa-fé no Direito Individual do Trabalho* (LTR, São Paulo, 2003).
V. Carrion, *Comentários à Consolidação das Leis do Trabalho* (34th edn, Saraiva, São Paulo, 2009).
A.M. de Barros, *Proteção à Intimidade do Empregado* (LTR, São Paulo, 1997).
M.G. Delgado, *Curso de Direito do Trabalho* (LTR, São Paulo, 2004).
W.D. Giglio, *Justa Causa* (Saraiva, São Paulo, 2000), 342.
O.B. Magano, *Os Grupos de Empresas no Direito do Trabalho* (RT, São Paulo, 1979).
E. Mallet, *Competência Legislativa em Matéria Trabalhista na Constituição,* in *Temas de Direito do Trabalho* (LTR, São Paulo, 1998), 48.
E. Mallet, *Direitos de Personalidade e Direito do Trabalho in Direito, Trabalho e Processo em Transformação* (LTR, São Paulo, 2005), 22
E. Mallet, Trabalho gratuito in Direito, Trabalho e Processo em transformação (LTR, São Paulo, 2005), 42.
A.M. Nascimento, *Compêndio de Direito Sindical* (LTR, São Paulo, 2000).
A.M. Nascimento, *Direito do Trabalho na Constituição de 1988* (2nd edn, Saraiva, São Paulo, 1991).
E.G. Saad, *Consolidação das Leis do Trabalho: Comentada* (41st edn, LTR, São Paulo, 2008).
A.G. Peres, *Contrato Internacional de Trabalho* (LTR, São Paulo, 2004).

Chapter 11

Civil Procedure and Arbitration

*Welber Barral & Rafael Bicca Machado**

I. CIVIL PROCEDURE IN BRAZIL AND THE FEDERAL CONSTITUTION OF 1988

Although the vast majority of rules of civil procedure in Brazil are contained in the Code of Civil procedure (*Código de Processo Civil*, 'CPC'), the Brazilian Constitution of 1988 also presents some important principles, as guidelines for the Brazilian judicial system.

The main principles in the Brazilian Constitution on this subject are: (a) the need to respect the due process of law;[1] (b) a full right of defence;[2] and (c) the requirement that any judicial decision be justified and made upon request.[3] These constitutional articles are fundamental, and any legal process which overlooks them can be regarded as void.

The Brazilian Constitution also establishes the organisation of the judicial power.[4] Judicial Power is headed by the Federal Supreme Court (*Supremo Tribunal*

* Welber Barral, former Secretary of International Trade (Brazil). LLD (USP) LLM (UFSC) LLB (UNIMONTES). Visiting Scholar (Georgetown). Rafael Bicca Machado, MSc (PUC/RS). LLB (PUC/RS). The author would like to thank his friend Rafael Pellegrini Ribeiro for assisting with the translation and adaption of the article.

1. Article 5, LIV of the Brazilian Constitution.
2. Article 5, LV of the Brazilian Constitution.
3. Article 93, IX of the Brazilian Constitution.
4. Set out in Arts 92 to 126 of the Brazilian Constitution.

Fabiano Deffenti & Welber Barral (eds), *Introduction to Brazilian Law*, pp. 183–203.

Federal, 'STF'), which is Brazil's highest court. The STF is composed by eleven justices called *Ministros*, and is based in Brasília. The STF's primary role is to adjudicate over constitutional matters. Also in Brasília is the Superior Court of Justice (*Superior Tribunal de Justiça*, 'STJ'), with thirty-three judges, also called *Ministros*, vested with the power to adjudicate over matters concerning federal law.

In the Brazilian legal system, there are no binding precedents, even when the decisions are handed down by the STJ or the STF. The most analogous principle to binding precedents is a concept created by the 45th Constitutional Amendment in 2004 which are called binding summaries (*súmulas vinculantes*). The *súmulas vinculantes* are summarised statements drawn from repeated decisions made by the STF and may be issued after many decisions made by the STF on a particular topic. When issued, a binding summary must be followed by all other courts and government departments. It is important to note that it is the binding summary that is binding upon other courts, but not the judgment itself. So far, there have been thirty-one *súmulas vinculantes* issued.

In the STJ, the system is different, since there are neither binding decisions nor *súmulas vinculantes*. In this court, the only loose counterparts of binding precedent are the also newly created[5] appeal preventing summaries (*súmulas impeditivas de recurso*). These are also summarised rulings issued by the court; however, their main objective is to restrain the possibility to file an appeal on specific issues. If a certain issue has a *súmula impeditiva de recurso* and the decision taken by the lower court judge was consistent with the *súmula,* then no leave to appeal to the STJ will be granted.

Furthermore, besides the STF and the STJ, two kinds of other higher courts deserve attention. Each State of the Federation has a local appeals court, called Court of Justice (*Tribunal de Justiça*) and for appeals regarding federal matters, there are Regional Federal Courts (*Tribunais Regionais Federais*).

II. THE CODE OF CIVIL PROCEDURE

Federal Law 5,869/73 contains the *Código de Processo Civil.* As a whole, except for some constitutional dispositions and special statutes, all rules regarding civil procedure are set out in the CPC. The CPC contains 1,220 articles and applies uniformly to all Brazilian courts. Only some administrative procedures may vary in accordance to internal regulations of local and appellate courts.

The CPC was strongly influenced in its origins by the Portuguese and the Italian legal systems, mainly by the Italian lawyer Enrico Liebmann. More recently, however, it is possible to notice a weakening of these Italian and Portuguese influences, opening space to new ones, especially from the German and the common law legal traditions.

In the last few years, particularly since 1994, the CPC has suffered successive legislative reforms prompted by studies and by bills drafted with the help of

5. Laws 11,276/2006 and 11,277/2006.

renowned lawyers, judges and professors, with the common objective of assuring faster and more effective judicial proceedings. It appears to be a consensus in the Brazilian legal community that more reforms are still necessary, which hopefully could occur in the next few years.

III. THE THREE MAIN FORMS OF LEGAL PROCEEDINGS: RECOGNITION PROCEEDINGS, ENFORCEMENT PROCEEDINGS AND PREVENTIVE INJUNCTIONS

The CPC is divided into four books: Book I – Recognition Proceedings (*Processo de Conhecimento*); Book II – Enforcement Proceedings (*Processo de Execução*); Book III – Provisional Actions (*Ações Cautelares*); and Book IV – Special Proceedings (*Procedimentos Especiais*). It must be emphasised that these are independent types of legal proceedings and not different phases of a same legal process.

In the sections below, the first three forms of legal processes (recognition proceedings, enforcement proceedings; preventive injunctions) will be addressed. Special Proceedings will be treated separately.

A. Recognition Proceedings

Recognition proceedings are commonly known as ordinary proceedings (*processo ordinário* or *processo comum*). Its name stems from the procedure that is to be used when the other forms of specific procedures cannot be used.

This procedure starts with the plaintiff filing the initial petition, which must be in writing and signed by an attorney duly registered with the Brazilian Bar Association. The initial petition must: (a) contain the name of the judge or court to which it is addressed; (b) the names, surnames, profession, civil status, domicile and residence of the parties; (c) the facts and legal arguments; (d) the prayer for relief; (e) the amount in dispute; (f) list the evidence that the plaintiff intends to tender in order to prove their allegations; and (g) a request for the defendant be served. Furthermore, the plaintiff must attach to the initial petition all documents required to establish the claim.

After filed the initial petition is allocated to a lower court judge. If the judge finds that any formal requirements of the initial petition, then the plaintiff will be notified to amend the initial petition within ten days. If the plaintiff fails to amend the initial petition, then the petition will be rejected and judgment will be entered for the defendant without prejudice. Rejection of the initial petition can be appealed under a *recurso de apelação* (one of the types of available appellate proceedings).

Where the initial petition complies with all formalities, the judge will order that the defendant be summoned to present its defence (*contestação*). The initial summons cannot be served by or on behalf of the plaintiff, since this is an exclusive act of the Judiciary effected by a court employee called *official de justiça*. The notification can be served by mail, personally or by public notice.

The defendant must present the defence in writing, no more than fifteen days after the document that proves that service was effected is attached to the court file.

In the defence, the defendant may put forth any arguments, exposing the facts and law which contradicts the plaintiff's pleadings. The defendant must also specify the evidence that he or she intends to produce. Like the initial petition, the documents that are relevant to the defence must be attached to the written defence.

If the defendant fails to file a defence within the prescribed time, the defendant will be deemed to be in default and regarded as a *revel* (defendant in default). Even where the defendant is a *revel*, there is no certainty that a suit will be decided for the plaintiff, but all matters pleaded in the initial petition are presumed to be true (there is a shift in the onus of proof).

As soon as the defence is filed, the instruction stage (*fase de instrução*) begins. It is in the instruction stage that all evidence must be tendered (other than the evidence already tendered in the initial petition and defence). Documentary evidence is made up of any type of material document, such as contracts, e-mails, companies' books of account, films, tape recordings and the like. Documentary evidence, as a general rule, must be attached to the initial petition by the plaintiff, and in the defence, by the defendant, together with their pleadings. If they do not, documentary evidence will only be allowed to be tendered if the party seeking to tender the evidence can establish that it was absolutely impossible to do so at the proper time.

The pleadings and initial evidence will be analysed by the judge who must hand down a decision called a *despacho saneador*, where preliminary objections are decided and the parties are given notice to tender evidence. The judge may also make a final decision immediately if it is merely a question of law, there is no need for further evidence or no defence was filed. If evidence is required to be adduced, the parties may request the judge to order two other types of evidence: expert and oral evidence.

The parties or the judge may request expert evidence when there is a technical dispute that is beyond the court's expertise. In these cases, the judge himself or herself will appoint an expert who he or she trusts in order to prepare a report with the findings regarding the matter in dispute. As soon as the expert is appointed, the parties have five days to present questions that must be answered by the expert. Within the same five days, the parties may appoint their own technical assistants to supervise the expert's work.

The expert's report is not binding on the court. The trial judge may decide in accordance with other evidence, so although the expert's findings are very important, the final decision may be contrary to the judge's findings.

Oral evidence, on the other hand, is only possible in a formal court hearing, where the judge, by his or her own motion or by the parties' request, interrogates witnesses, informants and parties (see below). When the judge sets the date for the hearing, the parties can file, up to ten days before the hearing, a request for certain witnesses to be heard. Each party can request that the court hear up to ten witnesses only; however the judge must hear only three for each fact that needs to be proved and may choose not to hear the others.

Every person with full capacity may give evidence as a witness (*testemunha*), if there is no impediment (*impedimento*) or suspicion (*suspeição*) regarding his or her relationship to the parties. The insane, those incapable to remember or understand the facts when they occurred, those incapable of communicating his or her perceptions, those aged under 16 years, the blind, the deaf and those whose knowledge of the facts depends on a sense which he or she lacks will not be allowed to testify as witnesses.

Certain persons are only allowed to give evidence as informants (*informante*). An informant is a person who gives unsworn evidence to the court. The evidence given is not regarded as evidence (*prova*), but merely as information (*informação*).

A party's spouse, parents and heirs or any relative up to the third degree, of any of the parties to the proceedings, are not allowed to give evidence as witnesses unless: (a) they are requested to do so by the public power (the State); (b) when the matter is related to the situation of one or more an individuals; (c) there is no other way to provide the evidence to the court; or (d) if the judge finds that is indispensable for the information to be provided so as to reach his or her decision.

The parties to the proceedings also cannot testify – they can only give unsworn statements. The same applies to persons who committed perjury or who customarily should not be relied upon, enemies of the party, intimate friends of the party and persons interested on the final result of the matter.

During the evidence gathering stage, each party must tender the evidence required to prove the facts pleaded by that party. The burden of proof is on the plaintiff, regarding the facts that may establish their rights and on the defendant to show facts that will establish the termination, modification or impediment of the right alleged by the plaintiff. There is no need to present evidence on: (a) facts of public knowledge; (b) facts pleaded by one party and admitted by the other; and (c) facts not in controversy.

Once all evidence is gathered, the judge analyses the court file to make his or her final decision. The judge must accept (completely or partially) or reject the orders sought by the plaintiff. The final decision must contain the findings on the fact (called a *relatório* or 'report'). This report must contain: the name of the parties, a summary of the pleadings and of the important findings made during the proceedings and the judge's reasons for reaching his or her decision.

There are two kinds of final decisions: one which resolves the merits of the dispute and the other which does not resolve the merit of the dispute.

A final decision which does not resolve the merits of the dispute is handed down where: (a) the initial petition is rejected; (b) the proceedings are stopped for more than a year due to the parties' inaction; (c) the plaintiff does not comply with the court's orders or abandons the suit for more than thirty days; (d) formal requirements are not present; (e) the judge accepts a petition for summary dismissal of the proceedings; (f) there is res judicata; (g) there is no legal possibility to enforce the pleadings; (h) there is lack of standing of the parties; (i) there is an arbitral clause; or (j) the plaintiff withdraws from the proceedings.

On the other hand, the final decision which resolves the merits of the case is given where: (a) the judge rejects or accepts the plaintiff's pleadings; (b) the defendant admits all of the plaintiff's pleadings; (c) the parties reach a settlement; (d) the plaintiff's rights have been extinguished (called a *decadência*) or otherwise time-barred (*prescrito*); or (f) the plaintiff expressly renounces the rights claimed in the plantiff's pleadings.

Once the judgment is delivered, the judge of the case cannot make any other decision regarding the matter in dispute, with the exception being corrections to any formal inaccuracy or when accepting the appeal to clarify the decision. The appeal to modify the final decision is the called simply 'appeal' (*apelação*). The appeal must be filed within fifteen days after the initial judgment is handed down.

B. Preventive Injunctions Proceedings (*Processo Cautelar*)

Preventive injunctions (*ações cautelares*) can be filed to resolve urgent disputes which cannot wait until the end of recognition proceedings. Preventive injunctions are accessory to recognition proceedings.

There are several types of preventive injunctions.[6] These can be filed by a party in order to request the judge to grant the petitioner a preliminary order,[7] which must be immediately obeyed by the enjoined party.

Considering its characteristic to serve as a preliminary decision for urgent matters, there are two essential elements for a preventive injunction to be granted: (a) the plausibility of the requested order (*fumaça do bom direito*, from the Latin *fumus boni iuris*); (b) the risk that a delay in not granting the preventive relief may cause an irreversible damage or a damage difficult to be reversed (which in Brazil is summarised in the Latin expression *periculum in mora*).

If the petitioning party is unable to satisfy the court that these two elements have been established, then the preventive injunction will not be issued. Furthermore, the requesting party must file recognition proceedings (the main proceedings of the action) no later than thirty days after the preliminary injunction being granted or else the injunction will automatically become unenforceable.

Article 797 of the CPC provides that preliminary injunctions will only be granted after the respondent is heard, which means that the granting of a preliminary injunction on ex parte proceedings (*inaudita altera parte*) should be an exception. However, the courts' practice is to grant most preliminary decisions without waiting for the respondent to file arguments. This is often explained by the

---

6. There are two forms of Preventive Injunctions in the CPC: The ones which are expressly stated in the CPC, such as the preventive injunctions for seizure (*arresto*) or search and seizure (*busca e apreensão*) and the preventive injunctions that not receive a specific name, called *ações cautelares inominadas*. Those preventive injunctions are made for situation not written into the CPC but that can be judged as urgent.
7. The preventive injunctions can be reversed at any time by the judge who granted it, in accordance with Art. 807 of the CPC.

fact that the urgency of a preliminary order is contradictory with the necessity to hear the respondent.

In Brazil, all preventive injunctions must be filed in writing. The Brazilian procedural civil rules provide that the same elements set in Article 282 of the CPC must be fulfilled.

Whether or not a provisional injunction is issued by the court, the respondent will be notified to present a written reply within five days.[8] If the reply is not filed or if the defendant fails to timely file the reply, the defendant will be considered to be in default and all facts alleged in the initial petition will be presumed true.

As soon as the defendant files the reply to the allegations presented by the plaintiff, the fact-finding stage begins with the presentation of evidence. However, in some cases, the court may enter summary judgment.

As in the recognition proceedings, preventive injunction proceedings end with a final decision, which can be appealed. The filing of an appeal of a final decision on a preventive injunction will generally not prevent the injunction from being enforced.

C. Enforcement Proceedings (*Processo de Execução*)

For many years, enforcement proceedings (*processos de execução*), were the 'weakest link' of Brazilian civil procedure. Enforcement proceedings amounted to a completely autonomous action, with its own notices, appeals, defence, etc., for the enforcement of court decisions. This meant that after the final decision in a recognition proceeding, the winning party had to start a new set of court proceedings to enforce the rights declared as his or hers in the recognition proceedings. In practice, plaintiffs had to endure long delays in enforcing their rights that had already been recognised by the courts.

This situation was changed with Law 11,232/2005, which added Chapter X (titled 'Enforcement of Judgments' or *Do Cumprimento de Sentença*) to Book I, Title VIII the CPC.

Under Brazilian law, the following judicial documents are valid to proceed to enforcement proceedings: (a) a final decision which recognises an obligation to do, not to do, pay or delivery a thing; (b) a final criminal decision; (c) a decision which the court has accepted the party's settlement; (d) an arbitral award; (e) an out of court settlement recognised by the court; (f) a foreign court's decision recognised by the STJ; and (g) a testamentary distribution.

A decision can be enforced in various ways depending on its nature. The final decision, which demands a payment of an exact amount, must be complied with by

8. Article 802 of the CPC. The issue regarding when does the five days term for response depends on the following: When the judge grants the preliminary order, the term starts on the day when the notification of execution of the preliminary order is annexed to the docket; when the preliminary order is not granted, the term of five days starts when the proof of the notification of the defendant is attached to the docket.

the judgment debtor within fifteen days, otherwise the judgment debtor must pay a 10% fine over the total amount of the debt. If the judgment debtor fails to pay the amount, a seizure warrant will be issued.[9] Once the judgment debtor's properties are seized, the judgment debtor will be notified, in person or by notice served on the lawyers, to challenge the seizure order within fifteen days. The challenge can be mounted on the following grounds: (a) lack or nullity of service; (b) if judgment was entered in default; (c) if the document establishing the right was not capable of being claimed; (d) improper seizure of assets; (e) excess on the enforcement of the debt (the asset seized is substantially above the amount of the debt owed); (f) legal incapacity of the parties; and (g) change or termination of the obligation, if occurred after the final decision.

Against the decision regarding the acceptance or the rejection of the defence, the available appeal is the *recurso de agravo*. This appeal does not stay the enforcement of the final decision. The enforcement steps which follow are the valuation of the properties seized and their subsequent auctioning. The result of the auction is used to towards payment of the judgment debt.

When a final decision demands a party to deliver certain property, the debtor will be notified to hand over possession of the property to the court within ten days of being notified. If the debtor fails to do it, the property will be seized by the court. As soon as the property is handed over, the debtor may file a petition called *embargos do devedor* seeking to retake possession over the property. If the *embargos do devedor* are rejected, the property will be handed over to the creditor.

In enforcement proceedings for obligations to do something or not to do something, the judge will have a discretion in relation to the time given to the debtor to comply with them in accordance with the nature of the obligation. If the debtor complies with the order, an official document will be prepared stating that the obligation has been fulfilled and enforcement proceedings come to an end. In case the debtor does not comply with the orders contained in the notification, there are two possible situations: (a) if the obligation can be only fulfilled by the person subject to the order, enforcement proceedings are transformed into a debt collection proceeding to recover damages; or (b) if the obligation can be fulfilled by someone else, the debtor can choose between paying the creditor the debt or by indicating a third party to do so. Every expense will be imputed to the judgment debtor and the creditor can start debt collection proceedings against the judgment

9. Never can be seized the properties which are inalienable (as for example, the property where the debtor resides, unless if this property was used as a guarantee in a lease contract), the properties declared, by a voluntary act, not subject of enforcement proceedings; food and fuel for a month; the weeding ring; family portraits; the wages of the judges; professors; the wages of the public workers, unless for alimonies; military equipment; the books, machines, utensils and instruments necessary to exercise any profession; pensions or benefits received from social security or by a private person with the objective to maintain the debtor or his family; the material necessary for ongoing civil works, if not seized; the life insurance; a rural state, until the limit of one module, and only if this module is the only one in the debtor's name and if it not subject of rural mortgage. Can be seized, if other properties are not found: the interest generated by the inalienable properties, only if it not used for the alimony of incapable person, widow, single female or elderly person; the images and objects used for religious acts, if monetary valuable.

debtor regarding any expenses. In these new collection proceedings, the debtor, after being served with a summons, may file an *embargos do devedor* petition.

Under Brazilian Law, the following documents are valid to commence enforcement proceedings without a prior recognition proceeding include: (a) negotiable instruments; (b) documents registered with a public notary and signed by the debtor; (c) documents signed by the debtor and by two witnesses; (d) a settlement recognised by the public prosecution service, by the public defender or by the attorneys of the parties; (e) mortgage or pledge agreements; (f) life insurance contracts; (g) personal accident insurance contracts, (h) rights arising from rent, fee for alienation; (i) condominium fee; (j) credits of court employees; expert, or translator, where their fees were recognised by a judicial decision; and (k) certified debts with public entities. Note that other laws may provide for certain types of documents to be enforced in enforcements proceedings as well.

In these cases, the creditor can skip recognition proceedings and proceed directly to enforcement proceedings. To start enforcement proceedings, the creditor must file a claim against the debtor attaching the documents that will prove that the debt was incurred and that the defendant's obligations were not fulfilled.

In the cases of an obligation to pay, the debtor will be notified[10] to pay the debt in twenty-four hours or, alternatively, to provide to the court a list of assets that are to be seized by the court.

If the debtor pays the debt, the enforcement action comes to an end, but the debtor will pay also all court costs and the creditor's attorney's fees, usually set between 5% and 10% of the amount of the debt.

If the debtor provides a list with the assets to be seized,[11] the creditor will be notified to advise the court if the creditor agrees or not with the assets contained in the list. If the creditor agrees, a document describing the assets seized will be issued and signed by the debtor. Then the debtor may file an *embargos do devedor* petition in no more than ten days after attachment of the document which describes the assets seized. If the creditor does not agree with the asset listed by the debtor, the judge will either accept the creditor's objection and request that the creditor to list the assets of the debtor that can be seized, or reject the objection and order the seizure of the assets indicated by the debtor.

If the debtor fails to pay or even fails to put forward an asset to be seized within twenty-four hours,[12] the creditor has the right to advise the court of the assets owned by the debtor that are to be seized. As soon as the assets are seized, the judge orders that the document which describes the seized properties to be drafted.

The *embargos do devedor* is the appropriate appeal when the defendant wants to oppose enforcement proceedings. As soon as the *embargos do devedor* petition is filed, enforcement proceedings are automatically stayed.

---

10. Under the terms referred in the recognition proceedings.
11. The defendant has the burden of proof to prove that the property is sufficient to satisfy the credit.
12. If the servant of the judicial power who serves the notification notes that the defendant has property that can be seized, he can at that moment seize those properties and then inform that to the judge.

In enforcement proceedings, there is no limitation on the types of arguments that can be raised in the *embargos do devedor* petition (as it used to be the case in enforcement of a judgment obtained through recognition proceedings). Indeed, the *embargos do devedor* will follow the same procedures as recognition proceedings, allowing the tendering of evidence, oral arguments, etc., and will be judged with a final decision, which can be appealed via an appeal (*apelação*). However, unlike the position in recognition proceedings, appeals from trial court decisions relating to *embargos do devedor* will not stay enforcement proceedings.

As soon as there is a decision on the *embargos do devedor*, the enforcement proceedings recommence. If the *embargos do devedor* is rejected, the judge will order that the debt be brought up to date (recalculated) and that the seized assets be auctioned. If the *embargos do devedor* is accepted in full by the judge, enforcement proceedings end immediately. If the *embargos do devedor* is accepted partially, enforcement proceedings continue under the terms of the decision regarding the *embargos do devedor.*

In the cases of an obligation to deliver an asset, proceedings are similar; the only difference is that the time for handing over possession is ten days, not twenty-four hours. If the debtor fails to hand over possession, the asset will be seized by the court. If the asset is deposited into court as ordered, the debtor will have the opportunity to file the *embargos do devedor* and if they are rejected the property will not be auctioned but delivered to the creditor.

In enforcement proceedings over obligations to do or not to do (*obrigações de fazer ou não fazer*), the debtor is notified to do or not to do something in a period of time set by the judge depending on the nature of the obligation. If the debtor complies with the court order, a court document is prepared stating that the debtor has done so, and the enforcement proceedings come to an end. If the debtor does not comply with the order, there are two possible courses of action: (a) if the order can be only be complied with by the person served, the enforcement proceedings are transformed into debt collection proceedings, seeking compensation; (ii) if another person could comply with the order, the debtor can choose between paying damages to the creditor or selecting a third party to do so. Every expense will be paid by the debtor and the creditor can start a debt collection suit against the debtor for any expenses. In this type of proceeding, the debtor, after being served, may file an *embargos do devedor*, as mentioned above. The difference, here, is that there is no need for any assets to be seized for the defendant to be allowed to file *embargos do devedor*.

IV. SPECIAL PROCEEDINGS

Book IV of the CPC deals with special proceedings, which can be divided by the nature of their jurisdiction: contentious or spontaneous. A series of actions is listed in Book IV, each having their own different types of procedures.

Among the special proceedings of contentious jurisdiction, we have the payment in consignment proceedings (*ação de consignação em pagamento*, when the debtor wants to pay but the creditor refuses to receive); the action of detinue (*ação de depósito*, to retake possession of a deposited good); proceedings for rendering of accounts (*ação de prestação de contas*, to order a person to render accounts); repossession proceedings (*ações possessórias*, to take possession of certain property); adverse possession proceedings (*ação de usucapião*, to declare the property of a place under the possession of a person for a set period of time); probate proceedings (*ação de inventário e partilha*, to divide the property of a deceased person); and the *ação monitória* (to collect debts using only certain documentary evidence which does not strictly comply with the formalities for filing enforcement proceedings), among others.

The *voluntary* special proceedings are, among others: court conveyance (*alienações judiciais*, to sell a good deposited into court), non-litigious divorce (*separação consensual*, when husband and wife decide to end their marriage) and guardianship proceedings (*curatela*, to determine the need for a legal guardian for a person).

V. THE BRAZILIAN APPELLATE SYSTEM

The Brazilian appellate system is an issue frequently discussed and the object of many recent legislative reforms. In practice, appeals are used too often – the vast majority of decisions made by lower courts' judges are appealed.

This high number of appeals could be explained by various factors, such as: (a) provisions in the CPC for different and successive appeals; (b) the non-existence of binding precedents, which leads to a disagreement between the decisions made by the lower court judges and the local appeal courts, and these with decisions handed down by the STJ and the STF; and (c) low cost of filing appeals in Brazil and the lack of strong penalties for appeals filed merely for the purposes of delaying a final resolution of the dispute.

A. General Appellate Principles

Apart from the legal provisions in the CPC, the appellate system is also based on general principles or maxims, which are very often applied by courts.

Among the main general principles, we will focus on: (a) the guarantee of a two-step jurisdiction (although there is no constitutional provision and that there are decisions by the STF affirming the inexistence of such principle under Brazilian law; this principle is well recognised in lower courts and opens the way to an appeal to a higher court of every decision); (b) the prohibition of *reformation in pejus* (this principle establishes that the decision made after an appeal cannot worsen the situation of the appellant);[13] (c) singularity and adjustment of the

13. In case, both parties appeal from the decision it may occur that one of the parties will have its situation aggravated. However, this will occur only in the case when one party's appeal is considered and the other party's appeal is rejected.

appeal (a party cannot file two appeals against the same decision,[14] which follows the rule that there exists one kind of appeal for each kind of decision,[15] being the obligation of the party to file the adequate appeal, invalidating all forms of appeals which are not prescribed by law); (d) fungibility of appeals (which applies in those cases where there is a reasonable doubt on what form of appeal is best suited for the circumstances of the case, the court must hear the appeal even if it is not the correct procedure for the situation); (e) motivation (all appeals must contain the reasons for the eventual reversal of a judgment; the court will dismiss any appeal which fails to explain why the party is requesting a reversal of the lower court decision); and (f) fulfilment and preclusion (the law establishes how and when the appeal may be filed and, after having been filed, it cannot be modified, and if a party misses the prescribed time limitation, it loses the right to appeal on that matter).

B. Types of Appeals

1. Appeal on the Merits (*recurso de apelação*)

The appeal on the merits (*recurso de apelação*, which means simply 'appeal'), is the appropriate appeal for final judgments of lower court judges and must be filed no later than fifteen days after the notification of the decision.

The Appeal must be filed in writing, addressed to the judge who handed down the original judgment and must contain: (a) the name and details about the parties; (b) the grounds based on facts and on law for requesting the reversal of the judgment; and (c) an express request for reversal of the lower court's decision. New evidence can only be introduced if the appellant could not tender it before the trial court due to force majeure.[16]

When filing the *apelação*, the plaintiff must pay court costs (*preparo*). If the payment is not made, the *apelação* will not be heard by the court, unless the plaintiff proves that the plaintiff was unable to make the payment for an acceptable reason, in which case the court will set a new time for payment to be effected.[17]

---

14. This principle requires a special attention since in same cases, as for example, the appeals to the STJ (*Recurso Especial*) and to STF (*Recurso Extraordinário*) are normally filed at the same time. In this event, however, there is no offence to the principle since a judgment may have multiple decisions and each one of these decisions may be appealed with correct the kind of appeal.
15. A fungible principle may attenuate this rule. In some cases, it might not be clear which is the correct appeal, considering the conflicting precedents and the complexity of the legal system. Therefore, if the party files an appeal which is not correct but the error is judged reasonable due to the difficulty of choosing a correct appeal this appeal may be accepted under this fungible principle. Since different kinds of appeal have different terms for filing, it is recommended that in doubt of which appeal might be the correct one, the appeal should be filed as to avoid the procedural term.
16. In accordance with the terms set in Art. 517 of the CPC.
17. Nowadays, a legislative reform on this matter is being discussed in the Brazilian Congress. If approved, the new law will establish that the failure to pay the judicial taxes will no more be

The filing of the *apelação* has, as a rule, two effects: the reviewing effect (*efeito devolutivo*) and the staying effect (*efeito suspensivo*). The reviewing effect establishes that the Court to which the appeal was addressed must examine every point argued by the appellant. The staying effect stays enforcement of the appealed decision, which means that once the appeal is filed, the lower court's decision cannot be enforced.

In some cases, however, only the reviewing effect is granted, which means that the filing of the appeal does not stop the other party from enforcing the judgment. There is no staying effect in the cases of: (a) division or demarcation of lands; (b) granting of alimony; (c) preliminary injunctions; (d) summary rejection of the defence in a debt collection suit; (e) an order for the matter to proceed to arbitration; and (f) confirmation of a preliminary order. In these cases, though, the winning party may proceed with a provisional enforcement of the judgment (*execução provisória*).[18]

The judge who handed down the original judgment must decide the effect under which the appeal is being heard: if under the reviewing effect and in the staying effect or if only under the reviewing effect. If the appellant disagrees with the decision, a *recurso de agravo* is the correct appeal in order to challenge the lower court's decision in this regard.

If the appeal is filed within the term established in the CPC and in accordance with the formalities prescribed, the judge whose decision was appealed must notify the other party to submit a written reply (*contra-razões*) within fifteen days. As soon as the *contra-razões* are filed, the documents of the case are sent to the Court of Appeals which has jurisdiction over the decision of the lower court judge. Several members of the Appeals Court will judge the *apelação* jointly.

Although the rule states that the judgment of an *apelação* must be made by a joint committee, Article 557 of the CPC provides an exception to this rule, in cases in which the *apelação* is judged by a single judge, who is also the reporting judge assigned to that particular Appeal. The decision made by a single judge of the Court of Appeals is called a *decisão monocrática.* The reporting judge will: (a) reject the *apelação* if it inadmissible under procedural law or it is not against, jeopardised by or confronting with, binding precedents (*súmulas*) of the same court, STF or other higher court; or (b) accept the *apelação* if the appealed decision was not in accordance with binding precedents (*súmula*) of the STF or other higher courts.

When the appellant does not agree with a decision made by the single judge in a *decisão monocrática,* the correct appeal is the internal appeal (*agravo interno*). With the *agravo interno* the appellant will request the committee of judges to confirm or reverse the decision made by the reporting judge.

In cases, in which the committee finds that the *agravo interno* was inadmissible or groundless, it will order the appellant to pay a fine for the amount of 1% to

cause of rejection of the appeal, but will be penalised with a fine in the amount of three times the amount of the original taxes.

18. In accordance with the terms set in Art. 587 of the CPC.

10% of the value in dispute, and the party will only be able to appeal again after depositing this amount into court.

In accordance with Article 554 of the CPC, when the *apelação* is judged by the committee of judges, the parties' attorneys may make oral arguments. The judgment starts with the reading of the report by the judge assigned as reporter and then the attorneys are allowed to present their oral arguments up to fifteen minutes.

As soon as the *apelação* decision is handed down (the judgment is called *acórdão*), it will be published. The decision will confirm or reverse the appealed decision (in a whole or in part) or render the lower court's decision null and void if the judgment was inconsistent with the formalities established by law.

2. Appeal of a Decision on a Matter Other Than the Merits of the Case (*recurso de agravo*)

The *recurso de agravo* is an appeal that must be filed within ten days following any ruling by a judge other than on the merits of the case, which can be subject to an *apelação* (as explained further above). Thus, if the judge issues a preliminary ruling, rejects a piece of evidence or the hearing of a witness, etc, the possible appeal in order to reverse this decision is the *recurso de agravo.*

There are two forms of *recurso de agravo*: the *agravo de instrumento* and the *agravo retido.* Historically, the *agravo de instrumento* was the most used and the *agravo retido* was the exception. This situation was changed with the enactment of Law 11,817/2006, which was part of the series CPC changes undertaken in 2006.

The *agravo de instrumento* is addressed to and registered within the Court of Appeals with jurisdiction over the trial judge's decision. It is the obligation of the appellant (called *agravante*), to set out the facts of the case as well as the reasons and arguments seeking the reversal of the decision, to attach the main documents of the lower court file and to prove that court fees (*preparo*) have been paid. Moreover, the appellant must notify the judge whose decision was appealed within three days attaching a copy of the appeal, so the judge may reconsider his or her decision. If the judge reconsiders his or her decision, the *agravo* is automatically ended.

As soon as filed, the appeal is sent to a judge of the Court of Appeals (who is randomly chosen) with jurisdiction over the decisions made by the lower court judge. The Court of Appeals judge will analyse the appeal and adopt one of the following alternatives: (a) immediately reject the appeal on the grounds that the appeal contradicts the Court of Appeals' prevailing precedents; (b) decide if the matter in dispute can be appealed using the *agravo de instrumento* (used for urgent matters) or, if an *agravo retido* is the more suitable appeal, order that the original appeal be transformed into an *agravo retido*; (c) decide if it is the case to grant a staying effect,[19] which stays enforcement of the lower court proceedings and until the appeal is decided.

19. Not in every *agravo de instrumento* there is a request for staying effect, since it is at the discretion of the appellant to request it. However, in the great majority of cases the appellant does request it.

At the end of this stage, the judge will ask for the other party, called *agravada*, to file arguments, so as to enable the suit to proceed to judgment.

The judgment is made in a public session by a panel of three judges, made up of the reporting judge who initially analysed the appeal and two other members of the court. In this type of appeal, the lawyers of the parties are not allowed to make oral arguments and may only be present at the judges' deliberations hearing. The parties must be given notice of the time and date when the judges' deliberations regarding the *agravo de instrumento* will take place. Notice must be given by publication in the Judiciary Gazette at least forty-eight hours prior to the time set for the deliberations. During this time, the parties may file briefs to the judges submitting their main arguments (memorials). As soon as the *agravo de instrumento* decision is handed down, it will be published in the Gazette.

The *agravo retido* is a formal challenge by a party against a ruling, other than the final judgment of the matter. For instance, an *agravo retido* will be the procedural tool used by a party who disagrees with a decision that rejecting evidence. In an *agravo retivo*, the challenge will only be appreciated at the end of the trial court proceedings.

The main characteristic of the *agravo retido* is that the challenge is not judged by the Court of Appeals upon filing like the *agravo de instrumento* – this type of appeal is not capable of reversing a decision while the lower court proceedings are still on foot; it will only be considered after the final judgment of the lower court is handed down and only if the trial judge's final judgment is appealed. The appellant must expressly request that the *agravo retido* be considered on appeal.

Furthermore, in the *agravo retido* the party may also refer to the facts of the case, the decision of the lower court and the arguments for reversing the decision; however, unlike the *agravo de instrumento*, the party does not need to attach the main documents in the court file, nor pay any court costs.

When the *agravo retido* is to be considered by the Court of Appeals, the judgment procedure is identical to the procedure adopted to judge the *agravo de instrumento*. However, the *agravo retido* will be judged as a preliminary issue in the appeal on the merits of the decision of the lower court.

Another important point is that the only possible appeal to decisions made by a judge during hearings is the *agravo retido*, which means that the *agravo de instrumento* cannot be used for decisions made during hearings. The *agravo retido* must be made orally during the actual hearing and not by written petition after the end of the hearing.

3. Appeal Requesting Clarification of the Decision (*Embargos De Declaração*)

The appeal which requests clarification of a decision (*embargos de declaração*) does not aim to reverse a decision, but to clarify it. This type of appeal is used very frequently in Brazilian court proceedings.

Although the CPC states that this form of appeal can only be used against final judgments, precedents from the STJ stand for the proposition that it can be used against any judicial decision, from any court.

The *embargos de declaração* can be used in cases of omission, obscurity or contradiction in the decision. It must be filed within five days from the decision being published in a written petition, addressed to the same judge who rendered the decision. It is this judge who will consider the arguments.

Once filed, the limitation periods for other appeals are automatically tolled, which means that the periods for other forms of appeal start running only after the decision on the *embargos de declaração* is handed down.

When deciding whether the *embargos de declaração* are merely a delaying tactic, the judge can fine the appellant up to 1% of the amount in dispute. If a new appeal is filed, the fine can be of up to 10% of the amount in dispute and the appellant must deposit the amount of the fine into court before filing any other type of appeal.

4. Appeals to the STF and the STJ

The appeals to the highest courts in Brazil, the STF and the STJ, are called exceptional appeals. These appeals may only be filed where all other ordinary appeals have been exhausted. The appeal to the STJ, Brazil's highest court for federal law matters, is called special appeal (*recurso especial*). The appeal to the STF, which is Brazil's constitutional court[20] and the highest court of the Brazilian Judiciary, is called extraordinary appeal (*recurso extraordinário*).

Both the *recurso extraordinário* and the *recurso especial* may be filed to appeal from decisions coming from State Courts (*Tribunais de Justiça*) or the Federal Courts and must be filed in the same Court which handed down the decision no later than fifteen days after the parties are given notice of the decision.

These appeals and its proceedings are not found in the CPC, but in the Brazilian Constitution. Some rules regarding procedures for the appeals to the STJ and STF can also be found in the internal rules of these courts.

The *recurso especial* aims to assure uniformity in the application of federal law throughout the country. In accordance to Article 105, III of the Brazilian Constitution a *recurso especial* can be filed where the lower court's decision: (a) was contrary to federal law or an international treaty provision; (b) validates an act of a State government in contradiction to federal law; or (c) makes a different interpretation of a federal law which was already interpreted by another court.

The *recurso extraordinário* is used for matters which involve interpretation of the Federal Constitution. In accordance to Article 102, III of the Brazilian Constitution the *recurso extraordinário* can be filed where the lower court's decision: (a) is inconsistent with the Constitution; (b) invalidates a federal law or a treaty

20. Unlike other countries, the Brazilian higher courts have huge workloads. As an example, between 1989 and 2003 the STJ judged 1,357,565 cases and the STF judged, only in 2005, 103,700 cases. This data can be found at the website <www.stf.gov.br/bndpj>.

based as being against the constitution; (c) validates an act of a State government in contradiction to the Constitution; or (d) validates a State law not in accordance with federal law.[21]

As a general rule, neither the *recurso extraordinário* nor the *recurso especial* has provides staying effect, which means that when filed they do not prevent enforcement of the judgment handed down by the lower courts. However, under extreme circumstances, the party may request staying effect to be granted,[22] if there is risk of irreparable damage if the original judgment is enforced and on its face the appeal to the STJ or STF is likely to succeed.

In the STF, as well as in the STJ, an appeal may only be heard if the appealed decision violated a provision in a law or a constitutional provision, which must be specifically pleaded in the appeal brief. If the appellant fails to prove this, the Court will automatically reject the appeal. This requisite is called *prequestionamento.*

Furthermore, the appeals to the STJ and STF can only contain arguments regarding points of law, not facts.[23] This rule has been interpreted broadly, to the extent that these courts will not consider even interpretation of contractual terms.

VI. SPECIAL STATUTES REGULATING CIVIL PROCEDURE

Beyond the rules contained in the CPC, there are many other statutes which regulate specific situations.

The Law of the Writ of Mandamus[24] (*Mandado de Segurança*), covers only the Brazilian equivalent of Writs of Mandamus. The *Mandado de Segurança* Can be filed when a certain and definite right of a party is infringed by a court decision or by the abuse (or threat of abuse) of power by a public authority. This writ is commonly used, for example, in cases of cargo retention in customs in export or import procedures and in matters related to tax law. There are no recognition or instruction stages in *Mandado de Segurança* proceedings. All evidence must be tendered with the pleadings.

Law 9,099/1999 created the Special Courts (*Juizados Especiais*), which may have jurisdiction over disputes over low amounts (fewer than forty minimum wages) and of little complexity. The procedure in those courts is simplified and conducted more orally and informally than in other proceedings. Companies, with the exception of very small companies (known as *microempresas* or 'microcompanies'), cannot file proceedings in these courts, yet they can be sued in them.

---

21. However, Federal Law is involved, the jurisdiction in these cases is vested in the STF, as established in the Brazilian Constitution.
22. The request for staying effect is requested more often in the STJ than in the STF. In cases of urgency, the request for staying effect will be made to the President of the Court, which decided the appealed judgment.
23. The higher courts only accept a discussion regarding the legal analyses made on evidences by a lower court.
24. Law 1,533/1951.

Consumer class actions and public civil actions are the two types of class actions in Brazil. The public civil actions, provided for in Law 7,347/1975, can be used in many areas of law (environment, consumer, diffuse and collective rights, etc). This kind of action can be filed by any individual, yet they are commonly used by the *Ministério Público*.[25] Consumer class actions, on the other hand, are governed by Law 8,078/1990 (the Consumer Defence Code). It can also be filed by Civil Associations, registered at least for one year and with the goal of promoting the protection of consumers, or by the *Ministério Público*.

Finally, the Federal, State or Municipal Tax departments may file tax enforcement suits against taxpayers. This procedure is not the governed under the CPC, but by the tax enforcement (*execução fiscal*) procedural rules set out in Law 6,830/1980.

VII. ARBITRATION

A. Introduction

The approval the Arbitration Law[26] in 1996 brought joy for the Brazilian advocates of arbitration.[27] Many of the criticisms found in the former legal framework had been addressed by the new law, which encompassed the modern international doctrine on the subject. The most optimistic authors foresaw that, in a few years, Brazil would become a world centre for arbitration.

These jubilant words did not materialise and the initial enthusiasm was reduced by unforeseen barriers, such as the large ignorance of arbitration by Brazilian jurists and the persistence of the formalist tradition.[28] Nevertheless, arbitration is progressing in Brazil, and even impressively in some industries, albeit much more belatedly than previewed when the law was passed. The many hindrances of the Brazilian judiciary, aggravated by the formalist procedural system, have been the main reason for the recent recourse to arbitration.

B. Changes Brought about by the Arbitration Law

One of the main legislative innovations brought by the Arbitration Law is the binding effect of the arbitral clause. The law refers to 'arbitration conventions', which refers both to the obligation to arbitrate (*cláusula compromissória*) and the

25. The *Ministério Público* is the Brazilian equivalent to the Attorney General, yet with much broader powers.
26. Law 9,307/1996.
27. Law 9.307, reprinted in 186 Diário Oficial da União (1996). A version in English may be found at I.L.M. (1997).
28. Restating these problems, see Martins, *Arbitration in Brazil: A Look at Recent Developments* (2003) 58 APR Disp. Resol. J. 68.

resolution of actual disputes (*compromisso*).[29] The new law adopted a liberal language to describe the effects of the arbitration convention, asserting that the arbitrator is 'a judge by law and by fact'[30] and that the arbitral award is not subject to review by the Judiciary, except if it violates principles of public policy or in one of the cases of nullity that basically repeats the New York Convention.

Foreign arbitral awards, defined as the awards issued abroad, have to be recognised before enforcement in Brazil, according to the applicable international conventions. Such recognition was subject to the jurisdiction of the STF until 2004, when a constitutional amendment transferred the jurisdiction to the STJ.[31]

Federal law has also more generally accepted the inclusion of arbitration as a proper forum in particular regulations. Thus, amendments to the Law of Corporations provide that shareholders of a company may use arbitration to resolve disputes arising between them and the company or between controlling shareholders and minority shareholders. The same trend may be identified in other recent enactments.[32]

The landmark case for arbitration in Brazil was undoubtedly *Resil v. MBV*,[33] a case related to the recognition of a foreign award issued against a Brazilian company. It was the first case brought before the STF after the Arbitration Law came into effect and its importance derives the particular interpretation that Justice Sepúlveda Pertence brought to the Court. In his opinion, Justice Pertence declared in obiter dicta the unconstitutional aspect of one of the innovations of the Arbitration Law, which guaranteed the validity of the arbitral award even if one of the parties refused to sign the *compromisso*. Such interpretation would have weakened the scope of the arbitral clause and created substantial legal uncertainty. A bitter five-year debate followed that opinion, and the majority of the Court finally asserted, in December 2001, that the Arbitration Law was constitutional in every aspect.

This trend in favour of arbitration has been confirmed by lower courts in Brazil as well as the STJ. In terms of domestic arbitration, the most important case was decided in 2003, when the STJ gave a broad interpretation for the arbitral clauses, in order to assert the arbitral tribunal's jurisdiction over all the contractual relationships between the parties in dispute.[34]

Other decisions from Brazilian courts have been generally supportive of the recognition of foreign awards. In *SEC 5573-France*,[35] the STF ordered the applicant to prove the existence only of the arbitration clause (a requirement set out in the Arbitration Law), in order to proceed with the recognition of the foreign

29. Article 4 of the Arbitration Law.
30. Article 18 of the Arbitration Law.
31. Constitutional Amendment 45/2004.
32. Public Services Concession Act (Law 8,987/95), Telecommunications Act (Law 9,472/97), Oil Act (Law 9,478/1997), Transportation Act (Law 10,233/2001), and the Public-Private Partnership Act (Law 11,079/2004).
33. STF, Appeal 5206-Spain (*MBV v. Resil*).
34. STJ, Resp. 450881 (*Compushopping Informatica Ltd v. Americel S.A.*). 26 May 2005.
35. Supremo Tribunal Federal, *Appeal 5.573-FR*, per Celso de Mello J.

arbitration award. In December 1999, Justice Maurício Corrêa pointed out expressly in a request of for recognition case that, under the terms of the Arbitration Act, a foreign award can be recognised without having been recognised by the courts of the country where the award was rendered (a very problematic procedure which was required by the previous provisions governing arbitration in Brazil).[36]

The STF has also repeatedly stated that only formal requirements are to be analysed in order to recognise a foreign arbitral award.[37] Thus, in *SEC 5573-France* the Court warned that '[if] the complaining party intends to review the material part of the arbitral award, [such] request [will not be] allowed by the [current] Brazilian legal system'.[38]

Another interesting innovation of the Arbitration Law was positively considered by the STF. Under the old system, a Brazilian party needed to be served by a rogatory letter for the award to be recognised later. The Arbitration Law expressly changed so that service by regular mail is now considered effective. Thus, in *SEC 5.847-United Kingdom,* the Court decided that if the party had rebutted the claim before an arbitral tribunal, the service had been proper, in spite of the absence of an executed letter rogatory.[39]

Soon after the STJ became the proper forum for the recognition of foreign arbitral awards, the court handed down its decision in *SEC 856* (*Textil Uniao S.A. v. L'Aiglon S.A*). In this case, a Brazilian company contested the recognition of an award from the Liverpool Cotton Association, arguing that it had not expressly agreed with the arbitral clause. The Court, however, found that a defence had been filed, by mail, to the arbitral tribunal and that act legitimated the arbitral jurisdiction. As a consequence, the STJ recognised the award, quoting the obligations assumed by Brazil under the New York Convention.[40] This decision indicates a liberal tendency in the STJ, an important trend when one considers the impact of its decisions for the harmonisation of Federal laws and its new jurisdiction to recognise foreign arbitral awards.

---

36. Supremo Tribunal Federal, *Appeal* 5.847-RU, per Mauricio Correa J, 1 Dec. 1999.
37. 'The Court does not, whenever recognizing a foreign judgment, evaluate the merits of the factual allegations, for these allegations were considered by the competent judge whose judgment we are recognising'. Supremo Tribunal Federal. *SEC 3.897-GB*. Per Neri da Silveira J, 9 Mar. 1995.
38. STF, *SEC 5.573-France*.
39. STF, *SEC 5.847-United Kingdom*, per Mauricio Correa J, 12 Dec. 1999. However, such understanding is limited to the service for arbitral tribunals. In the case of foreign judicial decisions, the rogatory letter still is a required element. See Supremo Tribunal Federal, *HSE 5.778-United States*.
40. STJ, *SEC 856* (*Têxtil União S.A. v. L'Aiglon S.A*), 18 May 2005. Previously, in *Elkem Chatering S/A v. Conan-Cia de Navegação do Norte*, the Federal Supreme Court had held that mail service to the Brazilian party was a valid means of commencing an arbitration. STF, *SEC 5.828-7-Norway*, 6 Dec. 2000. For the recent increase in arbitration cases in Brazil, see Gabbay et. al., Arbitragem e Poder Judiciário (2010).

Selected Bibliography

In English

J.C. Barbosa, 'Arbitration Law in Brazil: An Inevitable Reality' (2002/2003) 9 *Journal of Law and Trade in the Americas* 131.
W. Barral and F.P. Cardoso, 'Arbitration in Brazil: The 1996 Act', (1998) 13 no. 8*Mealey's International Arbitration Report* 16.
H.D.B. de Pinho, 'Class Actions in Brazilian Law: General Aspects, Evolution and Some Controversies' (2004) 20 *Connecticut Journal of International* 185.
J.T. de Paiva Muniz and A.T.P. Basílio, *Arbitration Law of Brazil: Practice and Procedure* (Juris Publishing Inc., 2006).
M.A.J. de Santa Cruz Oliveira, 'Reforming the Brazilian Supreme Federal Court: A Comparative Approach' (2006) 5 *Washington University Global Studies Law Review* 99.
J. Dolinger and C. Tiburcio, 'The Forum Law Rule in International Litigation – Which Procedural Law Governs Proceedings to be Performed in Foreign Jurisdictions: *Lex Fori* or *Lex Diligentiae*?' (1998) 33 *International Law Journal* 425.
A. Gidi, 'Class Actions in Brazil – A Model for Civil Law Countries' (Spring 2003) 51 *The American Journal of Comparative Law.*
L.K. McAllister, 'Judging GMOs: Judicial Application of the Precautionary Principle in Brazil' (2004) 32 *Ecology Law Quarterly* 149.
C.S. Romano, 'The 1996 Brazilian Commercial Arbitration Law' (Spring 1999) 5 *Annual Survey of International & Comparative Law Golden Gate University School of Law* 27.
K.S. Roseenn, 'Civil Procedure in Brazil' (Summer 1986) 34, no. 3 *The American Journal of Comparative Law* 487–525.
G.S. Valverde, 'Potential Advantages and Disadvantages of Arbitration v. Litigation in Brazil: Costs and Duration of the Procedures' (2006) 12 *Law and Business Review of the Americas* 515.

In Portuguese

C.A. Carmona, *Arbitragem e Processo: Um comentário à Lei 9,307/06* (Malheiros, São Paulo, 1998).
D. Gabbay et. al. (eds) *Arbitragem e Poder Judiciário* (Fundação Getúlio Vargas, São Paulo, 2010).
H. Theodoro Júnior, *Curso de Direito Processual Civil* (41th edn, Forense, Rio de Janeiro, 2004).
L.R. Wambier, F.R.C. de Almeida and E. Talamini, *Curso Avançado de Processo Civil* (4th edn, Revista dos Tribunais, São Paulo, 2002).
O.A.B. da Silva, *Curso de Processo Civil* (4th edn, Forense, Rio de Janeiro, 2007).

Chapter 12
Criminal Law and Procedure

*Antônio Sérgio Altieri de Moraes Pitombo**

I. BASIC PRINCIPLES OF BRAZILIAN CRIMINAL LAW

Brazilian Criminal Law is based on certain fundamental principles inherent in the Rule of Law, including the legality of crimes and punishment.

Among the fundamental guarantees and rights inserted in Article 5 of the Federal Constitution of 1988, the emphasis is on sub-paragraph XXXIX which provides that 'there is no crime without a previous law defining it, and there is no punishment without a previous law imposing a sentence on it'.

To specify the content of the said constitutional provision, the Federal Constitution prescribes other guarantees that are very important in criminal law. These include the principle of criminal liability;[1] human dignity (Article 1, III); personality (Article 5, XLV); criminal sanctions (Article 5, XLVI) and humanity (Article 5, XLI, XLVII, and XLIX), among others.

A. Principle of Legality

The principle of legality (*princípio da legalidade*) aims to guarantee the freedom of the citizen and to avoid arbitrary state intervention. In this regard, the terms of

* LLD, LLM, LLB (USP).

1. Article 1, III; Art. 4, II; Art. 5, Preamble; Art. 5, XLVI.

Fabiano Deffenti & Welber Barral (eds), *Introduction to Brazilian Law*, pp. 205–225.

Article 5, XXXIX of the Brazilian Constitution, provide that only written law can be the source of crimes, punishments, aggravating circumstances, and the incarceration of the criminally insane to a mental institution.

In addition to the principle of legality, the principle of non-retroactivity of the law is significant, whereby criminal law is not to have a retroactive effect, unless it is for the benefit of the accused.[2]

B. Principle of Criminal Liability

In the Brazilian legal system, an individual's criminal liability is also limited by the overriding principle that there is no punishment without criminal liability (*nulla poena sine culpa*). This is called the principle of criminal liability (*princípio da culpabilidade*) and it is implied in the Federal Constitution.[3]

The level of a criminal offence is measured by the legal consequence of a certain conduct and the seriousness of that particular offence, provided that there is intent (*dolo*) or fault (*culpa*). Therefore, there is no strict liability on the accused in Brazilian Criminal Law.

C. Principle of Human Dignity

The principle of human dignity (*princípio da dignidade humana*) was recognised in the Federal Constitution of 1988. The principle stands for the proposition that human dignity is an essential value of the system of fundamental rights (Article 1, III of the Federal Constitution of 1988).

Under this principle, any violation of criminal law principles is, ultimately, a violation of human dignity.

For instance, the Federal Constitution of 1988 has some provisions which aim to ensure human dignity. These include 'the law may punish any discrimination in violation of fundamental rights and liberties' (Article 5, XLI) and 'prison inmates are ensured respect for their physical and moral integrity' (Article 5, XLIX of the Federal Constitution of 1988).

D. Principle of Criminal Sanctions

The principle of criminal sanctions provides that judges must observe the applicable legal provision, type and length of sentence. The Federal Constitution provides that 'the law must establish criminal sanctions and may adopt, among others, the following sentences: a) imprisonment or restriction of liberty; b) forfeiture of

---

2. Article 5, XL, Federal Constitution; Art. 2 of the Criminal Code.
3. Especially in Art. 1, III (human dignity); Art. 5, preamble (constitutional guarantee of the right to freedom) and Art. 5, XLVI (criminal sanctions).

property; c) fine; d) community service; e) suspension or restriction of rights' (Article 5, XLVI of the Federal Constitution of 1988).

One of the tenets of the principle of criminal sanctions is *personality*. To this end, the Federal Constitution of 1988 provides that the liability of the convicted individual cannot be passed on to his or her successors to the extent that it goes beyond that person's estate (Article 5, XLV of the Federal Constitution of 1988).

Therefore, the sentence imposed on the accused must be proportional and adequate in relation to the criminal offence and must take into account the personal circumstances of the individual.

E. Principle of Minimum Punishment

The principle of minimum punishment (*princípio da intervenção mínima*) provides that only conduct that is very harmful to others may be punished by law.

From a Brazilian Criminal Law perspective, only those injuries deemed to be socially intolerable may be punished by law. Therefore, criminal law seeks selective protection of legal interests, limiting punishment to extremely serious conduct of the accused.

The reasoning behind this principle is that the excessive use of criminal punishment to protect legal interests would weaken criminal law and relegate it to a merely symbolical function.

F. Principle of Exclusive Protection of Legal Interests

The main purpose of Brazilian Criminal Law is to protect the legal interests that are relevant for the human being and for the peaceful coexistence of people in society. This purpose is epitomised in the principle of exclusive protection of legal rights (*princípio da exclusive proteção dos bens jurídicos*).

To define the legal right that must be protected, lawmakers must always enforce the general principles imposed by the Federal Constitution of 1988 in light of the restrictive character of criminal law. The legal interest in criminal law serves in the following ways: to restrict the *jus puniendi* (right to punish) of the State, to help interpret the definitions of crimes, to set the criteria to determine the appropriate sentence and to classify the crimes in the Special Part of the Criminal Code (discussed below).

There is no crime in the absence of injury or threat of injury to a legal right. There must be causation and some proof that the defendant's conduct caused harm to a victim.

G. Principle of Proportionality and the *De Minimis* Doctrine

The principle of proportionality (*princípio da proporcionalidade*) is considered a basic tenet of Brazilian Criminal Law. The punishment prescribed by law must be proportionate to the crimes and to the injury of the legal right protected.

The criminal sanction imposed by the State must be an instrument capable of accomplishing the purpose sought by the legislator. The principle of proportionality requires an actual and adequate link between the offensive conduct and the respective punishment. Under Brazilian law, the de minimis doctrine provides that an immaterial injury to a legal right does not justify the imposition of a sentence involving incarceration – that is, criminal actions that only minimally harm the legal right of another must be deemed to be non-criminal.

II. BRIEF COMMENTS ABOUT BRAZILIAN CRIMINAL LAW

Based on the principal that criminal laws cannot apply to past events and to preserve predictability in the Brazilian legal system, the conflict of law is governed by the constitutional principle of non-retroactivity,[4] with the application of the law in force at the moment the crime is committed, unless the accused would benefit from the new law. Also, with respect to the timing of the crime, the Brazilian legal system provides that 'the crime is deemed committed at the time of the act or omission, even if the result occurs at a different time'.[5]

Another relevant aspect relates to the spatial scope of criminal law. Brazilian Criminal Law adopts the principle of territoriality (*princípio da territorialidade*), which provides that Brazilian Criminal Law will only apply to crimes committed in Brazil, irrespective of the nationality of the accused, of the victim, or of the legal right protected.[6]

There are exceptions to the principle of territoriality. In this regard, the situations when the extraterritoriality principle applies are found in Article 7 of the Criminal Code, which is divided into: (a) *unconditional extraterritoriality*, whereby Brazilian law applies regardless of where the crime takes place, even if the individual was tried abroad, on the grounds of the principles of national interests and universality (Article 7, I, a, b, c, of the Criminal Code); and (b) *conditional extraterritoriality*, whereby Brazilian law applies in the presence of certain connecting elements of legal personality, flag and defence (Article 7, II, a, b, c of the Criminal Code).[7]

Apparent conflict of criminal laws occurs when many laws apply to the facts, but only one law can be applied. There are three principles used to settle the conflict: the specialty principle, whereby the special law repeals the general

4. Article 5, sub-para. XL of the Federal Constitution of 1988. It states: 'Criminal law has no retroactive effect, unless to benefit the accused.'
5. Article 4 of the Criminal Code.
6. Article 5, Preamble of the Criminal Code states: 'Brazilian law applies to the crimes committed within Brazilian territory, without prejudice to conventions, treaties and rules of international law.'
7. Article 7 of the Criminal Code.

law; the lower law principle, whereby one law applies when another cannot be applied, whether it is expressly provided or otherwise by logical interpretation; and the merger doctrine, whereby the crime committed is the means to commit another crime and the lesser offence will ordinarily merge into a conviction for a greater offence.

III. ELEMENTS OF THE OFFENCES (*TIPICIDADE PENAL*) AND UNLAWFULNESS

Tipicidade penal is the matching of a certain type of conduct to the statutory definition of the crime.

The definition of the crime (*tipo penal*) is an abstract description of a fact prohibited by law, characterising a conceptual idea of the forbidden act. Firstly, the conduct of the accused will be matched against the *tipicidade* provided by the law. Then, the conduct of the accused will be analysed so as to ascertain whether it is unlawful and to verify if the conduct in question had any justification and culpability.

In this regard, there are two important elements: one is the *tipicidade* of the conduct and the other is the unlawfulness of the act or omission.

A. The 'Tipicidade Penal' and the Subjective Element of the Conduct

Unless expressly provided otherwise, the intent of the accused is the essence of the subjective element, which means that the accused, under the definition of the relevant crime, must act with the purpose of bringing about harm to another.

With regards to direct intent, the Brazilian legal system adopted the 'theory of will' (also known as the 'guilty mind') which provides that the accused must act voluntarily with the knowledge that harm will occur as a result of his or her action (Article 18, I, of the Criminal Code). In addition, Brazilian Criminal Law is interpreted in light of the 'theory of consent' (also known as the 'assumption of risk theory'), which provides that the accused must be aware that committing the crime as defined in the law is possible, but accepts such possibility and proceeds with carried out the act. In this case, he or she assumes the risk of producing a criminal result (Article 18, I of the Criminal Code).

Crimes where intent is not an element are only those expressly established by law. In the absence of an unequivocal statutory provision, there is no criminal act without intent. According to Article 18 of the Criminal Code: 'Unless otherwise expressly established by law, nobody may be punished by a fact defined as a crime, unless it is committed intentionally.'

Fault, which is described as the violation of the duty of care, is the normative element of an intentional crime. To this end, Article 18 of the Criminal Code describes the general types of fault: recklessness, negligence and lack of skill.

Recklessness (*imprudência*) is a positive act characterised by a certain conduct without due care (i.e., acting with awareness that one's conduct is creating a risk of harm); negligence (*negligência*) is inaction, whereby the accused could have avoided the crime if he or she had acted carefully; incompetence (*imperícia*) is characterised by the lack of skills to engage in a certain activity.

There is another kind of fault known as conscious fault (*dolo eventual*). Under the theory of conscious fault (a concept created by scholars), the accused sees the possibility that a certain result may occur but hopes that it will not occur. The accused's denial of the possible risk of harm is the tenuous line between the theories of conscious fault and assumption of risk explained above.

B. Unlawfulness and the Reasons for Its Exclusion

As mentioned further above, the existence of a defence makes a certain act or omission, which was defined as a crime, to be considered lawful. In this regard, Article 23 of the Criminal Code states: 'There is no crime when the accused committed the act: I – in necessity; II – in self-defence; III – in strict compliance with a legal duty or while exercising a right.'

The legal rule of necessity (*estado de necessidade*) is set forth in Article 24 of the Criminal Code. The article provides that a person will be considered to be acting in the State of necessity when the person acted reasonably to prevent actual danger that could not otherwise be avoided and that did not came about due to that person's acts. Also, the right protected must be one which justifies the person's actions. This rule cannot be used by the person that had the legal duty to face the danger (Article 24, Paragraph 1, of the Criminal Code), such as a fire fighter or a police officer.

Also considered as a defence, self-defence (*legítima defesa*) is the prevention of an unlawful act of aggression. Self-defence is defined as the use of necessary force to avoid aggression or harm if the threat of aggression is imminent. Self-defence will apply both to situations where the accused is defending his or her rights, as well as when defending the rights of another.

To establish self-defence, one must use only the necessary force to repel the aggression, taking into account the surrounding circumstances. Where excessive force is used, the defence will not apply; the acts of the accused will be deemed unlawful and consequently the accused will be committing a crime.

The two remaining provisions concerning defence (Article 23, paragraph III of the Criminal Code) are: strict compliance with a legal duty (*estrito cumprimento de dever legal*) and regular exercise of a right (*exercício regular de direito*).

Strict compliance with a legal duty occurs when the accused acts in strict compliance with the rules of law and therefore his or her conduct is deemed to be lawful, while the regular exercise of a right applies to those who use a certain discretion permitted by law. The latter defence is justified because no punishment must apply to conduct which is permitted by law, provided that it is performed in a regular and non-abusive manner. An example of a regular exercise of a right would occur when a person is injured during the consensual practice of sports.

C. Merger of Crimes

In the Brazilian legal system, there is a merger (*concurso*) of crimes when the accused, by acting or omitting to act, commits two or more crimes. In this case, there are three types of merger of crimes adopted by Brazilian Criminal Law: a substantive merger (*concurso material*), a formal merger (*concurso formal*) and a continuous crime (*crime continuado*).

There is a *concurso material* when the accused, by acting or omitting to act, commits two or more crimes (whether identical or not). A *concurso material* is said to be homogeneous (*homogêneo*) when the crimes are of the same nature (Article 69 of the Criminal Code). An example would be when an individual robs a victim and then injures the victim. A *concurso material* is established where the prison terms are imposed on the accused cumulatively: the total length of imprisonment must be added together.

A concurso formal occurs when the accused, by a single act or omission, performs two or more crimes, identical or not (Article 70 of the Criminal Code). An example of a *concurso formal* would be where a person runs a red traffic light, crashes his car and kills three people.

Finally, the last kind of merger of crimes is the *crime continuado* (Article 71 of the Criminal Code) which is intended, in some cases, to avoid the application of a *concurso material*. The *crime continuado* occurs when the accused, by acting or omitting to act, commits two or more crimes of the same kind and under certain given circumstances (including time, place and manner of carrying out the crime), the subsequent crimes are deemed to be the continuation of the first crime. In the event of a *crime continuado*, the sentence of only one crime is imposed if the first and subsequent crimes are identical. If the first and subsequent crimes are different, a harsher sentence is imposed.

D. Criminal Sanctions in the Brazilian Legal System

According to the nature of the crime committed, Brazilian Criminal Law system adopts the following kinds of sentences: imprisonment (*penas privativas de liberdade* or 'punishment restricting freedom'), restraint of rights (*restrição de direitos*) and fines (*multas*).

Imprisonment is divided into incarceration (*reclusão*) and detention (*detenção*). The difference between them is restricted to the regime used for serving the sentence. In incarceration, the sentence is served in the closed (*fechado*), semi-open (*semi-aberto*) or open (*aberto*) regime, while detention is served only in the semi-open or open regimes (Article 33, preamble of the Criminal Code). No prison term can exceed thirty years (Article 75 of the Criminal Code).

Restraints of rights are not imposed in addition to other punishments – they are autonomous. Brazil has adopted the system of alternative sentences in order to replace prison terms when certain conditions are met (Article 44 of the Criminal Code).

The types of restraints of rights implemented by the Criminal Code are: fines, forfeiture of property, community service, temporary restriction of rights and weekend incarceration.

According to Article 49 of the Criminal Code, a fine is defined as the payment of a pecuniary sum fixed in the final judgment and calculated daily. The fine is payable to the penitentiary fund (*fundo penitenciário*).

Brazilian Criminal Law adopts a three-stage method of calculating the length of sentences. First, the judge must determine the basic and appropriate sentence by analysing the circumstances and possible aggravating circumstances; secondly, the judge must consider the mitigating circumstances, and, finally, the judge must consider the general and special circumstances for increasing or decreasing the length of the sentence.

The accused may also benefit from two other less harsh sanctions: suspended sentence (*suspenção de pena*) and parole (*livramento condicional*).

Under Brazilian Criminal Law, *suspenção de pena* is a partial suspension of short-term imprisonment for a definite time after certain conditions are met and according to objective and subjective elements set out in Article 77 of the Criminal Code.

In turn, *livramento condicional* is the release of the prisoner after a portion of the sentence is completed, only if the requirements for granting the release are met and are in compliance with the conditions previously set by the judge (Article 83 of the Criminal Code). These conditions may be revoked in the event of a breach.

Finally, where a person is declared by the court as legally insane, he or she must serve his or her sentence at a psychiatric hospital or institution for the criminally insane. In sentencing the person, the judge will be guided by reason of special deterrence, which takes into account the danger posed by the accused and his or her potential to commit other crimes.

E. Causes of Termination of Sanctions

In Brazilian Criminal law, after a crime takes place there is the possibility that a certain event could stop the enforcement of the corresponding sentence.

The causes that terminate sanctions are waivers issued by the State, resulting in the non-imposition of the sentence, or a release from enforcing the sentence imposed. The requirements for termination of sanctions (*extinção da punibilidade*) are listed in Article 107 of the Criminal Code.

Expiration of time limits (*prescrição*) is the loss of the right to punish because of the inertia of the State. It occurs when the State fails to carry out the right to punish within the period of time set by law. There are two kinds of limitations: the limitation of the punitive claim (*prescrição antes de transitar em julgado a sentença condenatória*) which occurs before the judgment becomes final and appeals are no longer available and the limitation of the enforcement (*prescrição depois de transitar em julgado a sentença condenatória*) which occurs after the judgment becomes final and appeals are no longer available.

Another kind of important limitation is the subsequent limitation (*prescrição da pretensão punitiva*) which is not governed by the maximum open prison term but by the sentence imposed in the final judgment.

Finally, retroactive limitation (*prescrição retroativa*) is also considered to be a ground for termination of a sanction. The principal term is regulated by the actual sentence but the sentence is counted retroactively, if the State's lack of action was one of the causes of interruption of time limit.

IV. CONSTITUTIONAL GUARANTEES RELATED TO CRIMINAL PROCEDURE

It was not until 1988 that due process of law became a right expressly guaranteed in a Brazilian Constitution. Article 5, LIV of the Federal Constitution of 1988 establishes that 'no one shall be deprived of freedom or of his assets without due process of law'.

Other sub-paragraphs in Article 5 establish guarantees that expand the due process protection contained in Article 5, LIV. They include: the guarantee that no court or tribunal of exception may be set up (Article 5, XXXVII and LIII); that trials must be in accordance with the right to challenge evidence and reply to arguments (the adversary system) and the guarantee for a full defence (Article 5, LV); the public availability and the provision of written reasons of all court decisions (Article 5, LX and Article 93, IX); the inadmissibility of evidence obtained through unlawful means (Article 5, paragraph LVI); the presumption of innocence (Article 5, paragraph LVII); the right to compensation for wrongful convictions (Article 5, LXXV); the prohibition of arrest except when caught during the act or as a consequence of a judicial decision (Article 5, LXI); the release on recognisance (Article 5, LXVI); prohibition of incommunicability of the convicted, the right to a lawyer and the right to remain silent (Article 5, XII); and the right to a court hearing within a reasonable time after being detained (Article 5, paragraph LXXVIII),[8] among others.

The following constitutional principles are the basis for understanding the Brazilian criminal procedure system:

---

8. Although the reasonable duration of the procedure was already granted through Art. 8, para. 1 of the San José of Costa Rica Treaty, such was listed in the list of individual rights and guarantees as per Constitutional Amendment 45/2004.

In the area of unlawful evidence, it is also important to mention that the Federal Constitution of 1998 created an exception to the protection of the right to privacy by allowing wiretapping in cases expressly authorised by law.[9]

F. Presumption of Innocence

The Federal Constitution of 1988 (Article 5, paragraph LVII) establishes that 'no one will be considered guilty until a final decision is made and there is no constitutional right to appeal his or her convictions'. This establishes the principle of presumption of innocence (*presunção de inocência*).[10] When observed from the individual's perspective, the presumption of innocence principle requires the State to treat the person investigated or accused as innocent until a final decision is reached as well as other rights for appealing convictions.

As such, the freedom of the person investigated or the accused is the general rule applicable during the entire criminal prosecution process. Their freedom can only be limited in exceptional cases that follow specific criteria and the proportionality of freedom restriction is fully demonstrated to judicial authorities.

The criteria for taking an individual's freedom away must be recognised by reasoned written decisions issued by competent judicial bodies (except in cases of lawful arrest when the person is caught while committing the crime), which should be submitted to the adversary system and allow for a full defence. The presumption of innocence produces special effects related to the burden of proof in the criminal proceeding. If the defence established that the accused is not guilty, the accused will not have to prove his or her innocence. The prosecution, however, is required to prove that the crime took place.

In the case of doubt (i.e., if the prosecution cannot exhaustively prove a fact necessary to establish the existence of a crime), the presumption of innocence will lead to a favourable decision for the accused. This is due to the application of the *in dubio pro reo* rule.

G. Written Reasons and Publicity of All Court Decisions

The Federal Constitution of 1988 (Article 93, paragraph IX) establishes that 'all judgments of the bodies of the Judicial Power shall be public and all decisions shall be reasoned, under penalty of nullity, and the law may, if the public interest so requires, limit attendance in given acts to the interested parties and their lawyers, or

---

9. The matter is regulated through Law 9,296/1996 which establishes the following authorised questionings: (a) existence of any reasonable elements of the authorship in the participation of a crime; (b) the impossibility of collecting evidence by any other means; (c) characterisation of a crime that is subject to an imprisonment penalty.
10. The São José of Costa Rica Treaty, in Art. 8, para. 2, establishes that 'every person accused of a crime have the right to be presumed innocent until considered guilty by a court judgment'. From such text, one can extract the principle of 'presumption of innocence'.

only to the latter in cases in which the preservation of the right to privacy of the interested party does not prejudice the public interest to information'.[11]

No publicity limitation can be extended to the person investigated or the accused and his or her defence lawyer.[12]

V. CRIMINAL INVESTIGATION

In Brazil, the police forces of the States and of the Union[13] are in charge of criminal investigation under the State Public Attorney and the Federal Public Attorney's Offices' control, respectively (Article 144, paragraph IV of the Federal Constitution of 1988).

The criminal investigation carried out by the police follows a procedure called police inquiry (*inquérito policial*), which is traditionally defined as an administrative investigation procedure for determining the offence and its authorship to be used in future prosecutions. The *inquérito policial* can be initiated as a result of an order by police authorities, if they become aware of any offence or at the victim's request. Moreover, a police inquiry may be ordered at the request of the members of the State Public Attorney or the Federal Public Attorney's Office (depending on whether it is a State or Federal matter) or by judges. The police inquiry procedure is not defined by law. It consists of all necessary acts to elucidate the facts, at the discretion of the police authority.

The victim, as well as the person investigated, is assured certain rights, such as the right to request any investigations that may be necessary to elucidate the facts (Article 14 of the Code of Criminal Procedure) and to request preventive seizure of the accused's assets (Article 125 and following of the Criminal Code of Procedure) in order to assure the payment of any damages resulting from the criminal offence.

It is important to mention that notwithstanding the fact that police authorities have powers to investigate and find offenders, these powers are not unlimited, in accordance with the rules implemented by the Federal Constitution of 1988. Firstly, in order to avoid unlawfulness and abusive acts, police activities are subject to the control of the State Public Attorney or the Federal Public Attorney's Office (depending on whether it is a State or Federal matter) and the courts. Accordingly, during criminal investigations, only judges are empowered to order any measures that impose any restrictions on individual rights and guarantees of the person investigated or of third parties, as well as to order seizure of assets.

After completion of all necessary investigations to elucidate the facts, the police authorities must prepare a report (*inquérito*) on the facts found, which,

11. See also Art. 5, LX of the Federal Constitution of 1988.
12. Article 20 of the Code of Criminal Procedure establishes that in the police investigation phase, the public authority may assure the confidentiality that may be deemed necessary to elucidate facts or that may be necessary for the public interest. With the Federal Constitution of 1988, such legal text began to be interpreted strictly.
13. Except for specific military crimes, whereas investigation is carried out by the Military Police.

together with the police investigation records, will be submitted to a member of the police forces whose role loosely resembles that of a sheriff and crown prosecutor (called a *delegado*). It is the *delegado* who will be responsible management of the *inquérito* and decide whether to proceed with charges against the person under investigation.

In light of the conclusions of the investigation set out in the report, a representative from the State Public Attorney or the Federal Public Attorney's Office or the victim may initiate criminal proceedings against the suspects of the crime and may request further investigations.

The file may be requested if it is shown that the findings do not constitute a criminal offence, the statute of limitations has expired, the perpetrator has not been found or the criminal offence have not been proved. In the latter case, the file of the investigative proceeding may be opened provided that new evidence was obtained.

Over recent years, there have been discussions regarding the possibility of the State Public Attorney or the Federal Public Attorney's Office conducting parallel criminal investigations. This discussion is in light of a constitutional provision that grants these bodies the power to issue notices and to request information and documents to support the administrative proceedings under their responsibility. Many scholars argue that the investigative activities should be exclusively conducted by the police forces and that the performance of such activities by those responsible for initiating criminal proceedings might compromise an impartial investigation. Although scholarly writings and case law still do not have a settled view on the matter,[14] it is clear that investigations conducted directly by the members of the State Public Attorney or the Federal Public Attorney's Office with no participation from the police forces have occurred.

Also, inquiries conducted by the Parliamentary Investigation Committee of the House of Representatives and Senate are often used as grounds to initiate criminal proceedings. Parliamentary investigations are regarded as a proper way to conduct criminal investigations, although they do not have that as their original purpose in the Federal Constitution of 1988.

VI. FREEDOM AND IMPRISONMENT

Under Brazilian law, the right to freedom is a constitutionally guaranteed presumption. For that reason, prima facie prison should only be the result of a final judgment where a prison sentence is handed down.

Despite this rule, there are exceptions authorising the imprisonment of the accused prior to a final criminal sentencing. In this case, preventive imprisonment (*prisão preventiva*) is not regarded as a sanction but a measure to protect criminal investigations and the possible application of criminal laws.

14. The legality of this kind of investigation is currently being analysed by the Federal Supreme Court.

Imprisonment prior to a sentence which is no longer subject to a possible appeal is only justified where: (a) if there is sufficient circumstantial evidence that the accused committed the crime (*fumus comissi delicti*); and (b) if there is evidence that the accused could prevent the authorities from preparing the case to prove the crime or could have avoided the enforcement (*periculum libertatis*).

The Brazilian legal system has five different types of preventive imprisonment: (a) *in flagrante delicto* (where the defendant is caught committing the crime) (Articles 301 to 310 of the Code of Criminal Procedure); (b) preventive imprisonment (Articles 311 to 316 of the Code of Criminal Procedure); (c) imprisonment resulting from the indictment (Article 408, paragraph 1 of Code of Criminal Procedure); (d) imprisonment resulting from an appellate conviction (Articles 393 and 594 of the Code of Criminal Procedure); and (e) temporary imprisonment (*prisão temporária*) (implemented by Law 7,960/1989).

Of those, only arrest *in flagrante delicto* is not subject to a prior court order, being permitted as a result of a lawful arrest. Due to the fact that it is not subject to a court order, this type of imprisonment is conditioned to the strict compliance of certain formal requirements listed in the Code of Criminal Procedure. Anyone is entitled to carry out an arrest *in flagrante delicto* (whether or not the person is a member of the police forces) yet he or she must promptly notify the authorities who are responsible for confirming its illegality.

As for the others types, only a court can order preventive imprisonment. Such imprisonment can be induced during any investigative or procedural stage if it is related to criminal offences punishable by imprisonment. Preventive imprisonment requires evidence that links the suspect to the crime and the necessity of a measure that guarantees public order, economic order, proper criminal proceedings and enforcement of the criminal laws. The court's order may be revoked at any time, whenever the reasons given to grant a preventive measure are no longer present.

Preventive imprisonment cannot be for an undetermined period of time. Case law has fixed a maximum term of preventive imprisonment of up to eighty-one days corresponding to the sum of the timeframes applicable to all applicable criminal acts.

Apart from preventive imprisonment, the Code of Criminal Procedure (Article 408) sets out the possibility of imprisonment resulting from the indictment. After the Federal Constitution of 1988, it became necessary to demonstrate the presence of *periculum libertatis* (necessity of this exceptional measure) through a court order defining the basis for its decision to order the accused's arrest. The same applies to imprisonment resulting from a final decision where the defendant still has the right to appeal – even if the trial court has already found the accused guilty and handed down the sentence.

Law 7,960/1989 introduced to the Criminal Procedure system the concept of temporary imprisonment (*prisão temporária*) which is applicable to crimes of greater severity. In accordance with the criteria established by this law, an order for temporary imprisonment depends on the prosecution establishing certain factors which relate the conduct the criminal investigation relating to the crimes. One example is a case where the suspect does not have a permanent address or does not give sufficient elements for his or her identification. This type of imprisonment can only last for five days (which can be extended for another five days) or, if the crime under investigation is classified as a heinous crime,[15] thirty days (which can be extended for the same period of time).

In line with preventive imprisonment, the Federal Constitution of 1988 (Article 5, paragraph LXVI) established the release on recognisance within the list of individual guarantees, when providing that nobody will be taken to prison or will be kept in prison when the law admits release on recognisance, with or without bail bonds.

The Code of Criminal Procedure establishes the cases in which bail bonds may be granted (Article 321 and following articles), as well as the cases in which release on one's recognisance is admissible without bail: (a) if the act is carried out under any lawful excluding clause set out in Article 23 of the Criminal Code (see further above); or (b) if none of the requirements of preventive imprisonment are shown. The Federal Constitution of 1988 establishes that crimes of a racist nature are not subject to bail bonds (Article 5, paragraph XLII), as well as crimes related to torture, drug dealing, terrorism and heinous crimes (Article 5, paragraph XLIII).

VII. CLASSIFICATION OF CRIMINAL PROCEEDINGS

In accordance with the system introduced by the Federal Constitution of 1988, criminal proceedings may be classified as public or private. In general, standing to file such criminal proceedings varies according to the charges laid against the accused. In the majority of cases, it is the Public Attorney's Office which has standing to initiate criminal proceedings. In crimes that relate to individual matters, it is the victim who has standing to file criminal proceedings. Private criminal proceedings are secondary to public criminal proceedings and may apply when the Public Attorney's Office does not initiate action.

Public criminal actions may be conditional or unconditional. In certain situations, public criminal proceedings can only be initiated by the Public Attorney's Office upon prior authorisation from the Ministry of Justice, the victim (or the victim's representative or successor). In most cases, however, the criminal proceedings are unconditional, and can be initiated through a complaint from the representative of the Public Attorney's Office.

---

15. The 'heinous' crimes are defined in Law 8,072/1990. Under Art. 1 of this law provides that heinous crimes are the following: (a) homicide, when carried out as a killing gang, even where it has been carried out by a single member, and qualified homicide; (b) robbery leading to murder; (c) extortion causing death; (d) extortion by kidnapping and rape; (e) rape; (f) obscenity; (g) epidemic causing death; (h) forgery, corruption, adulteration or change of therapeutic or medical product; and (i) genocide. Terrorism and drug trafficking are also considered heinous crimes.

Although procedural criminal law grants the victim standing to occasionally file criminal proceedings, the victim always has the right to intervene in public criminal proceedings acting as the prosecutor's assistant.

A. Criminal Proceedings: Obligations and Consensual Justice

Historically, in Brazil the Public Attorney's Office had the obligation to initiate criminal proceedings before the courts. The Federal Constitution of 1988 (Article 98, paragraph I), however, created the possibility for the Congress to set up special courts at the Union, State, Federal District and the Territories' level to decide over misdemeanours.

In 1995, Law 9,099/1995 set up the concept of 'special criminal courts' in the States. This law, which defines misdemeanours, introduced consensual justice into Criminal Procedure and set up summary proceedings for criminal trials in the special criminal courts. Under the terms of Law 9,099/1995, offences that have a maximum penalty of imprisonment of one-year or less are classified as misdemeanours. The concept of misdemeanours was later revised by Law 10,259/2001, which established that offences of such a nature are those with a maximum penalty of imprisonment of two years or less. Law 9,099/1995 also introduced the conditional stay of the proceedings which applies to all misdemeanours that have minimum imprisonment penalties of a one-year period or less.

B. General Characteristics and Types of Proceedings

The Code of Criminal Procedure is wide in scope. In addition to the Code of Criminal Procedure, there are sparse criminal procedural laws for the judgment of a myriad of offences. In general terms, Brazilian Criminal Procedure follows three major stages: (a) offering and receiving the accusation, (b) procedural discovery and defence; and (c) judgment.

The Code of Criminal Procedure establishes the following types of proceedings: (a) common proceedings (*processo comum*); (b) proceedings for crimes subject to jury trial (*processo dos crimes da competência do júri*); (c) proceedings for crimes committed by civil servants (*processo dos crimes de responsabilidade dos funcionários públicos*); (d) proceedings for crimes against one's honour (*processo dos crimes contra honra*); (e) proceedings for crimes against intangible assets (*processo dos crimes contra a propriedade imaterial*); and (f) summary proceedings (*processo sumário*). Law 9,099/1995 also introduced special proceedings (*processo sumariíssimo*) that are not contemplated in the special criminal procedural laws.

The common proceeding, which is applicable in the judgment of the great majority of criminal offences, begins with the filing of a written complaint that may be accepted or denied by the judge. If the written complaint is accepted, witnesses of the accused and the defence are heard. Once evidence is produced, prosecution and defence have twenty-four hours to request additional diligence should new facts or circumstances come to their knowledge. Once such diligence is carried out or if there is nothing to request, the parties present final written arguments and the court hands down its decision.

The summary and the special summary proceedings are a variation of the common proceedings and characterised as procedures in which there are fewer procedural acts due to the fact that less complex offences are being dealt with by the court.

Finally, there are those crimes subject to jury trial. These are the crimes which only relate to wilful crimes against one's life. The jury proceeding is comprised of: (a) 'the creation of a guilt stage' (*sentença de pronúncia*) carried out before a single judge; and (b) a plenary session before a jury.

The first stage of the jury proceeding is very similar to the common proceeding. It begins with the acceptance of the complaint, followed by questioning of the accused, witness examination, written allegations and final judgment; which can be an argument, summary dismissal or disqualification.

If oral argument takes place and the trial judge understands that there is sufficient evidence to conclude that the accused has carried out a wilful crime against one's life, the judge may require the accused to be submitted to judgment in plenary session of the court. If, however, the accused is subject to summary dismissal, the judge may decide that he or she is convinced of the existence of any of the causes of extinguishment of punishment.[16] Finally, where a decision is rendered disqualifying the crime, the judge recognises the crime but understands that the case should not go before the jury. Thus, the judge will determine that criminal proceedings must be carried out by a single judge.

The second phase of the jury trial proceeding begins with the filing of a new accusation document called the prosecutor's opening statement. In the case that the opening statement is accepted, a timeframe in which the accused can offer his or her arguments begins. The discovery phase is repeated in plenary session, oral arguments are presented and the judgment is entered. Judgment is decided by the sentencing council, formed by jurors.

VIII. APPEALS AND OTHER MEANS OF CHALLENGING DECISIONS RELATED TO CRIMINAL MATTERS

Criminal appeals in Brazilian law are as follows: appeals (*apelações*), appeal in a strict sense (*recurso em sentido estrito*), witness letters (*carta testemunhável*), request for rehearing en banc (*embargos infringentes*), request for amendment of judgment (*embargos de declaração*), partial correction (*correição parcial*) and bills of review (*agravo de instrumento*), as well as special and extraordinary appeals (*recursos especiais e extraordinários*), which are requested before higher

16. Articles 20 to 23 of the Criminal Code – see further above.

courts. Criminal review, habeas corpus and writ of mandamus are considered autonomous challenging actions.

Apelações are available when challenging final decisions. *Recursos em sentido estrito* and *agravos de instrumento* are applicable when challenging interlocutory decisions issued in criminal proceedings or in the enforcement of penalties.

All interlocutory decisions issued in criminal proceedings are subject to appeals. The appeal in a strict sense is only applicable in specific cases set out in Article 581 of the Code of Criminal Procedure. That is why many decisions that are not listed in the Code can only be subject to challenges through writs of habeas corpus or *mandamus*.

The witness letter is an appeal applicable to decisions that do not allow criminal appeals. The requests for *embargos infringentes* are applicable only by the defence against decisions issued by a panel in which one of the judges has a dissenting opinion. The petition for *embargos de declaração* is a mechanism by which the written reasons contain any omission, contradiction or ambiguity need to be clarified. Finally, *correição parcial* is applicable when challenging decisions that cause disturbance to proceedings.[17]

The *recursos especiais* and *recursos extraordiários* are sought before the Superior Court of Justice and to the Federal Supreme Court, respectively. They are commonly used in civil proceedings and can also be used in criminal proceedings. Different to the appeals mentioned above, special and extraordinary appeals do not allow arguments over any factual matters. They are appeals that relate only to the review of questions regarding rights and that seek the correct and due application of the relevant Federal Law and the Federal Constitution in each of the States.

In Brazilian Criminal Procedure, the writs of habeas corpus and *mandamus* also have different purposes. The writ of habeas corpus, following the Anglo-Saxon tradition, can be used to avoid any illegal restrictions imposed on an individual's freedom of movement and can be filed by any individual through his or her lawyer or otherwise. On the other hand, the writ of mandamus is applicable against illegal acts or acts carried out with abuse of power by any authority, provided that such acts cause harm to any unquestionable rights, other than the right of movement. Since the writs of habeas corpus and *mandamus* can be used in many ways and in any phase of the criminal proceedings, they can also be considered appeals, when used in a criminal investigation or during the stages of a criminal action.

Finally, the Code of Criminal Procedure introduced a special action to terminate the res judicata effect of final judgments (Article 621). A final decision may be reviewed where: (a) a final judgment is opposite to the text established in criminal

17. The partial correction, different from the *error in procedendo* and the *error in judicando*, was introduced to Brazilian law not as a type of appeal, but as a remedy. However, prevailing case law has not only granted it the nature of an appeal, but in certain cases it has been recognised in law (such as in the State of São Paulo).